GW00372272

Ethnologia Europaea

Journal of European Ethnology

Volume 46:2
2016

Silence in Cultural Practices

Edited by Elo-Hanna Seljamaa and Pihla Maria Siim

MUSEUM TUSCULANUM PRESS · UNIVERSITY OF COPENHAGEN

Copyright © 2016	Ethnologia Europaea, Copenhagen
Printed	in Sweden by Exakta, Malmö 2016
Cover and layout	Pernille Sys Hansen, Damp Design
Cover photo	Liina Siib, *A Woman Takes Little Space*, 2009
	ISBN 978 87 635 4544 0
	ISSN 0425 4597

This journal is published with the support of the Nordic Board for Periodicals in the Humanities and Social Sciences.

Ethnologia Europaea is an official journal of Société Internationale d'Ethnologie et de Folklore (SIEF).

sief

Museum Tusculanum Press
University of Copenhagen
Birketinget 6
DK-2300 Copenhagen S
Denmark
www.mtp.dk

CONTENTS

WHERE SILENCE TAKES US, IF WE LISTEN TO IT

Elo-Hanna Seljamaa and Pihla Maria Siim, University of Tartu

Careful ethnographic analysis of what goes without saying, or who is being silenced and how, can reveal a great deal about the society, community or situation under study. Yet questions concerning the modes and roles of silence in everyday cultural practices tend to go unasked. As Billy Ehn and Orvar Löfgren write in their book *The Secret World of Doing Nothing*, cultural researchers have been "preoccupied with the explicit, eventful, and dramatic," failing to pay attention to or grasp "mundane activities that are generally considered inconspicuous and unimportant – not worth paying attention to – or pursuits that remain unnoticed by others" (Ehn & Löfgren 2010: 4–5). Furthermore, silence itself is an elusive term. William O. Beeman argues that even if silence were to be defined in "essentialist" terms as "the absence of sound" it would still be a cultural construct since silence can only be "established in contrast to *particular*, culturally designated sound […] and this contrast is likewise a construction" (Beeman 2006: 24, emphasis in the original). Listening to silence means listening to particular categorisations of sound.

Indeed, James Fernandez (2006) reminds us that silence and silencing are ever present in fieldwork, as well as in other parts of the research process, because we privilege, often tacitly, the voices of some interlocutors and pass hasty judgements on the credibility or worth of others. We also tend to prioritise verbalised knowledge and information gathered by means of sight at the expense of messages received by smell, touch, taste or through emotions. Yet vision, too, is always particular and mediated, offering no route to disembodied, objective knowledge (Haraway 1988).

Contributors to this special issue[1] join Ehn and Löfgren in looking for the seemingly insignificant and the overlooked, taking what may be called a back-door approach to the study of cultural practices. We are interested in silence as it occurs in daily life, aiming to keep our senses open, and to listen to where it takes us. We also join Gregory Bateson and scholars inspired by his concept of noncommunication in exploring situations and circumstances where communication is avoided or deemed undesirable because it "would somehow alter the nature of the ideas" (Bateson & Bateson [1987]2005: 80). Withholding information can be a means of acquiring and abusing power, a tool of manipulation (e.g. Vesala et al. 2002: 30–37). Bateson, however, discusses the avoidance of communication as a necessary precondition for maintaining the "sacred", a domain "where angels fear to tread" "for the sake of the whole system." In his words, the damage is done not "due to a local effect of the message alone, but is a result of relationship between the message and the total system that is its overall context" (Batcson & Bateson [1987]2005: 89).

The main themes of this introduction – agency, power and the margins – pinpoint the topics connecting the articles collected here. Yet another recurrent issue is formed by the challenges of doing fieldwork on silence and the wish to increase awareness of the unspoken and the unspeakable as they emerge in fieldwork and the research process (cf. Fernandez 2006; *PoLAR online*). Language is not the only way to grasp people's experiences and to understand cultural practices, nor is it always feasible or even possible to rely on language. However, rather than dichotomising the verbal and the non-verbal, we wish to explore communication as it takes place in many different practices, on many levels and via many channels within a social system (see Vesala & Knuuttila 2012: 5).

Silence, Agency and the Production of Margins

Keeping in mind the concept of noncommunication, on the one hand, and the significance of the obvious and the overlooked, on the other, we aim to investigate various modes of silence and silencing and, in particular, links between silence and agency. Not communicating gains significance under particular circumstances (cf. Ketola et al. 2002). The concept of noncommunication enables us to elucidate the intentionality and purposefulness of silence in cultural practices (cf. Vesala et al. 2002). We analyse noncommunication as a protector, enabler and maintainer of that what matters. Silence emerges from this issue's case studies as a productive and performative force as we trace the roles it plays in "doing family" (Pihla Maria Siim) and "doing old age" (Karoliina Ojanen), achieving control over the surrounding world and personal happiness (Tuija Hovi and Piret Koosa), and sustaining co-existence in societies divided by ethnic or religious lines (Piret Koosa and Elo-Hanna Seljamaa).

Yet systems maintained by means of silence can be fraught with power asymmetry. They can suppress the multiplicity of points of view and inhibit change, while also being safe by virtue of being familiar and predictable, based on a degree of mutual recognition. One can be forced into silence, choose to become or remain silent or appear to be doing so; forced and voluntary silences are not necessarily clearly distinguishable (cf. Thiesmeyer 2003a). These contributions scrutinise how noncommunication is not only (and not necessarily) empowering, how silence can indicate both agency and lack thereof, or serve as a

space where the conditions and limits of action and choice are negotiated, contested and tested. The ability or inability to mute certain aspects of reality or retreat into doing or saying nothing appears to affect the (in)ability to achieve a sense of discreteness, which is why we conceive of silence as an inspiring concept for broadening our thinking about agency (cf. Achino-Loeb 2006b; Hall 2000).

Linked to the topic of agency is another focus of this special issue, namely the production of margins of society and language through cultural practices of silence. Silence and silencing as culturally constructed practices are never merely matters of personal choice, but are also informed by shared evaluations and resources of conduct deemed acceptable or desirable in any given situation (cf. Muñoz 2014: 25). Our case studies suggest that silence can be an attribute of both the centre and those deemed on the margins of society. Moreover, an act of silencing points simultaneously to the centre and the margins, neither of which are fixed.

In cases of (perceived) refusal or failure to be listened to or to speak using one's own terms, silence and silencing serve as means of marginalisation and can be exercises in social control. Self-imposed silence, on the contrary, can be a means of establishing oneself in the dominant society (Pihla Maria Siim and Piret Koosa, this issue) or a form of resistance aimed at sustaining a centre of one's own (Vallikivi 2012). The inability to withdraw into silence may, correspondingly, result in a feeling of being defined from without and pushed to the margins, as in the case of ethnic groups expected to perform or at least engage with outsiders' stereotypes of themselves (Elo-Hanna Seljamaa, this issue).

However, a person can be forced into silence and marginality by the limitations of language: vocabulary, speech genres and conventions tacitly guiding their usage. Believers may be guided to follow conventional speech patterns that predetermine the form and content of their personal religious experiences. While this has the effect of silencing and marginalising alternative interpretations, it can be a precondition for becoming accepted into the core of the congregation (Tuija Hovi and Piret Koosa, this issue).

One Geography of Silence

Our interest in links between silence and agency and the production of margins in everyday life emerges from case studies from Estonia, Finland and the north-western and north-eastern part of European Russia. This focused geographical scope enables us to zoom in on a corner of Europe that has fairly recently experienced drastic cultural, political and economic changes. Post-Soviet societies, which in the past appeared to be rather egalitarian, homogeneous and atheist, have become guided by neoliberal ideals and have diversified, as well as divided along new lines, while older categories, such as ethnicity, have been repositioned. These political and social reconfigurations have also affected Finland, which had a carefully choreographed relationship to the Soviet Union. Since the early 1990s, Finland has received great numbers of immigrants from the former Soviet Union, mostly people with Finnish or Ingrian Finnish backgrounds and their family members.

Experiences of major social and cultural transformations and of relocation require both individuals and groups to selectively silence and reinterpret their past in order to represent it in terms suitable for the altered conditions. Though regime changes occurred over a quarter of a century ago, debates over the meanings and effects of the Soviet period are ongoing and, moreover, fuelled by current tense relations between the Russian Federation and member states of NATO and of the European Union. By taking a back-door approach to societies under scrutiny, we aim to cast light on negotiations over the conditions of belonging to ethnic and religious groups and to national categories as they are experienced and made sense of in the course of daily practices and discourses. The latter can differ markedly from official or public procedures and rhetoric, though the public and private may be tied together intimately behind the scenes (cf. Herzfeld 2005). The contributions collected here demonstrate, furthermore, how established notions of speech and silence play a crucial role in processes of working out new cultural and religious phenomena and negotiating conditions of cultural and societal change.

Silence as an Interdisciplinary Concept

The geographical and thematic foci of this special issue also aim to broaden the scope of scholarly analyses and applications of the concept of silence. Silence first emerged as an interdisciplinary research topic in the 1960s–70s, and its attractiveness to scholars working in the humanities and social sciences appears to have grown steadily since.[2] Ikuko Nakane (2007) links this trend to globalisation, arguing it has created a need for a more comprehensive understanding of silence in intra- and inter-cultural encounters. Among the first authors to connect silence and misunderstandings in intercultural communication was Edward T. Hall (1959) in his book on "silent language" or culturally learned non-verbal behaviour.[3] Keith Basso's (1970) study on the Western Apache was pivotal in that it focused on "situational determinants of silence" and their potential for understanding emic perceptions of social relations and different types of social situations (cf. Kenny 2011: 50–52, 77). Contributions to this special issue (Tuija Hovi and Piret Koosa) attest to the continued relevance of Richard Bauman's ([1983]1998) analysis of the symbolism of silence and speaking among seventeenth-century Quakers.

Linguists and scholars of communication began by conceiving of silence "as a relatively bounded, identifiable phenomenon" (Muñoz 2014: 27; e.g. contributions to Tannen & Saville-Troike 1985; Jaworski 1993) and have since moved gradually towards *silence as metaphor for communication* in order to capture "different instances of 'silence'" in verbal and non-verbal interactions, religion, music and the visual arts (Jaworski 1997b: 3, emphasis in the original; contributions to Jaworski 1997a). This expansion of the concept of silence is also illustrated by lists of different forms and functions of silence presented by Nakane (2007). Such micro-units as pauses can be measured and located precisely within particular conversations, while macro-units – silences that are constitutive of social or religious events and groups or result from acts of suppression – tend to lack a "recognisable 'form'" (ibid.: 5–7). Consequently, the analysis of social and affective functions of silence is necessarily more interpretative than that of cognitive and discursive functions (ibid.: 7–12). Affective functions are linked to emotion management; social functions include means of negotiating and maintaining power and power relationships (ibid.).

Using Nakane's terminology, it could be argued that this special issue is concerned primarily with macro-level silences and silencing that serve affective and social functions, but manifest themselves at the micro-level of interaction and everyday life. Related to these aims are studies that explore interrelationships between silence, concealment and power. Intrigued by tensions between the personally experienced and publicly acknowledged, Eviatar Zerubavel (2006) has analysed "conspiracies of silence": socially patterned collective efforts to deliberately deny the existence or presence of something conspicuous. Melani Schröter (2013), meanwhile, has explored meanings ascribed to silence in public debates on political discourse, asking what happens when politicians do not talk about the things the public expects them to address. Attempting to theorise the relationship of silence and power, Maria-Luisa Achino-Loeb (2006a, 2006b) has drawn attention to the silence inherent in selection and suppression, which are the preconditions for perception and identity construction. In her view, "silence is a vehicle for the exercise of power" because it "allows us to believe that the nonspoken is nonexistent" (2006a: 3, 11), thereby veiling the constructedness of identities and self-interest that motivates ideological programmes (see also Thiesmeyer 2003a: 1–2; contributions to Achino-Loeb 2006c and Thiesmeyer 2003b).

Articles presented in this special issue focus less on revealing ideologies and exposing the covert (re-) creation of unequal relationships and more on silence as a force that is used to both enable and disable agency. Several contributions seek to push the boundaries of silence as an analytical category by testing its applicability to material culture (Karoliina Ojanen), and emotional and embodied manifestations of faith (Piret Koosa), as well as to everyday routines aimed at sustaining urban life partitioned along ethnic lines (Elo-Hanna Seljamaa). At the same time, this journal issue participates in the ongoing folkloristic exploration of the dynamic relationship between the tellable and the untellable: a discussion that is closely tied to silence and silencing, but not yet framed in these terms.

Modes of Silencing

Karoliina Ojanen writes about the "social, cultural and structural invisibility" of old people living in care homes in Finland, arguing that silence constitutes a central element in the cultural narrative of old age in institutional settings. Her careful analysis of mundane interactions between care workers and residents reveals how the attempts of the elderly to construct themselves as coherent subjects of the present tend to fail. This non-recognition, argues Ojanen, is made and remade through different cultural practices – for example, by making private bodily practices public, or silencing the voices and sexuality of the elderly – and even materialised in care units' decor.

We may well ask what makes other kinds of narratives of old age untellable. In the words of Amy Shuman (2005: 19), "we can begin to understand how storytelling is used in negotiations of power by asking what makes one story tellable and another story not tellable in particular historical and social contexts." In her view, personal stories in particular can be untellable because they are about categories that listeners do not recognise or about things that are deemed unacceptable, even unthinkable, and should neither happen nor be talked about (ibid.: 19–23; cf. Zerubavel 2006; La Shawn Pagán's ongoing documentary project *Forced into Silence* on male victims of domestic violence[4]). Some experiences are not shared with others due to a lack of words to verbalise them or because of the emotions these experiences entail (cf. Kaivola-Bregenhøj 2003: 337). Elaine Lawless (2000), analysing battered women's narratives, suggested that women may be unable to find words to re-present violence because narrating re-creates these moments.

Diane Goldstein, analysing rumours and legends that circulated in the aftermath of 9/11, has observed that stories can "become untellable because the space the narratives would normally inhabit is understood somehow unsafe. The risk is not simply a personal discursive risk, but one that may also reflect on the group or community implicated in the narrative events" (Goldstein 2009: 249). In her view, scholars "need to focus more on the process of risk taking and risk making in narrative" (ibid.: 252). Margaret Mills (1991: 20), meanwhile, has distinguished between "the obvious or consensual unsaid" (cf. Ehn & Löfgren 2010), "the unsaid of privileged or private knowledge" and "the unsaid which is omitted because it is not central to the speaker's goals in this particular performance but could be present and foregrounded in other performances of the same story."

The unsaid and untellable are indicative of different modes of silencing at work in everyday communication. Along with risk-taking entailed in narrating, they take us back to the concept of noncommunication and its protective as well as repressive capacities. In the Soviet time, and under Stalinism in particular, non-Russian ethnic origin, religious beliefs and political activities often became family secrets because revealing information on these matters could involve serious consequences for all those who knew. As Pihla Maria Siim (this issue) shows, silencing certain parts of family history has thus been justified by referring to the protective effect of unawareness, and in some cases this pattern of cultural silence may live on after the societal situation changes. This is connected to a more general wish to protect loved ones from negative memories or feelings (cf. Schiffrin 2002: 341).

Absence of narration may thus also function as an enabler of "normal" family life, keeping certain experiences and emotions related to them out of daily routines (cf. Peltonen 1996: 28; Lember 2016). Uku Lember (2016) has found that Soviet-era Estonian-Russian mixed families, in the interests of peaceful family life, avoided the discussion of certain topics. He self-reflectively admits that the question of the repercussions of public conflict in the family was raised during the interviews on his initiative. Lember's findings resonate with Elo-Hanna Seljamaa's observations (this issue) about the means used by Tallinn's Estonian- and Russian-speaking residents

to negotiate, sidestep and neutralise ethnicity and ethnic connotations in ways that bespeak and produce mutual recognition and contribute to quotidian co-existence. Imbued with embodied knowledge of Tallinn's geography, these practices of "silencing ethnicity" contrast rather sharply with Estonia's official approach to multiculturalism, which can be said to amplify ethnicity by means of encouraging staged performances of ethnic particularity.

Piret Koosa's article presents a different case of achieving co-existence by means of silence and accommodation. She analyses how members of an Evangelical congregation in a Komi village in northeastern Russia employ silence and non-verbal expressions of faith to carve out a space for themselves in a pro-Orthodox environment, where Evangelicals are regarded with strong scepticism. Distinctive Evangelical speech practices, such as talking about becoming Christian or testifying to one's conversion, urge believers to declare a dramatic break with the past, whereas local modes of self-expression value continuity. Koosa shows how her interviewees adhered to the latter and combined local ways of speaking with embodied manifestations of faith in an effort to navigate the contradictions of practising Evangelism in contemporary Russia.

The contribution by Tuija Hovi explores silences in another religious community, a Word of Life congregation in Turku, Finland. Hovi revisits fieldwork data from the late 1990s in order to closely examine silences as rhetorical choices meant to keep up the desired order of things. Drawing on Gregory Bateson, Hovi analyses group members' reliance on noncommunication as "a performative practice that supports the Neo-charismatic reality" and distinguishes the saved from the unsaved. Her careful re-reading of interview data reveals how believers shun certain topics in an effort to control both spiritual and material environments, strengthening the feeling of safety, well-being and success in their everyday lives.

By exploring the symbolic meanings of silence (cf. Bauman [1983]1998) and its functions among Evangelicals, the articles by Hovi and Koosa respectively add to the growing body of literature that questions the fundamental role of language in Evangelical Christianity and seeks to broaden perspectives on understanding conversion (e.g. Szuchewycz 1997; Coleman 2007; Luhrmann 2004, 2012; Webster 2013). Not only do Hovi and Koosa demonstrate that noncommunication and non-verbal means of self-expressions are constitutive of Evangelical subjects and communities, but they also make it clear that the uses of silence and silencing by Evangelicals are highly context sensitive and tactical, and grounded in given cultural, social and economic circumstances. Along with standardised, locally conventional ways of talking about conversion and other matters of faith, believers learn from their fellow Evangelicals what is supposed to remain unsaid.

The Challenges of Locating and Understanding Silences

Observations presented by Piret Koosa in particular hark back to issues raised by other scholars working on religious practices of Finno-Ugric peoples, especially those living in the Arctic. When revisiting materials collected by earlier scholars on the religious practices of the Nenets, a nomadic community living in northern Russia and western Siberia, Karina Lukin (2012) found silences, denial and misrepresentation, leading her to question "the possibilities of collecting oral religious data in ethnographic fieldwork" (cf. Vallikivi 2012). The methodological challenges related to studying the unspoken point to fieldwork as an embodied experience (Okely 1992) and to the importance of the sensitivity of the researcher. Studying the un-said involves a strong interweaving of the (fieldwork) method with the role of the researcher and his or her subjective experiences and impressions (see Schmidt-Lauber 2012: 566).

Silences experienced as, for example, soothing, irritating or uncomfortable can be the keys to capturing new knowledge, as illustrated by Karoliina Ojanen's study. The way she experienced silence at care homes as stagnant, as a flow of "non-happenings", led her to pay attention to the significant role silence has in constructing a particular narrative of old age in an institutionalised setting. Elo-Hanna Seljamaa's discussion of "silencing ethnicity" in the

capital of Estonia is similarly guided by the uneasiness she felt when fieldwork prompted her to violate tacit expectations concerning the co-existence of Estonians and Russian-speakers that she had been socialised into while growing up in Tallinn.

Yet fieldwork and interview situations in particular may offer opportunities for negotiations over the (un)tellable and serve as sites for meta-speech on noncommunication. As an outsider, the researcher can "chase after the things that were not expressed explicitly" and people may be ready to share their personal views and experiences they are not willing to discuss with other community members (Tuija Hovi, this issue). Similarly, sharing one's research findings with a faraway audience can be less sensitive and require less self-censorship than presenting them in front of one's compatriots. As Margareta Hydén (2008: 135) points out, sensitivity is not an objective and permanent quality of a topic, but depends on the relationship between the teller and the listener, as well as on cultural, personal and other contextual circumstances of that relationship.

Kristine Muñoz (2014: 20) has emphasised along similar lines that "what counts as silence depends very much on what people expect to happen, and how quickly, in a particular sequence of events." Ethnographic methods are geared towards engaged listening and recording the minute details that make up daily life, at a level of precision that is neither necessary nor sustainable outside of the context of fieldwork. Ethnographers immersed in collecting and analysing data are consequently likely to hear silences or silencing where a bystander would argue there is none.

In order to locate and understand absences, pieces of information or communication left out, we need to study carefully that which has been said (Klein 2006: 21–22; Goldstein 2009: 249). According to Muñoz, the unsaid and unsayable in communication are made possible and can be traced by focusing on those "properties of language use that make it plastic" (2014: 29), flexible and adaptable to given circumstances: polysemy, ambiguity and strategic choice as to what to say or leave unsaid (ibid.: 29–39). In the case of working with large corpora, which is often the case in folkloristic studies focusing on a particular genre, tale type or motif, the unsaid could be traced by means of sifting through seemingly relevant texts and contexts, looking for and comparing recurrent patterns, motifs and textual characteristics (Goldstein 2009: 250).

Whether one is working with large corpora or relying on first-hand ethnographic data, pinpointing the aims and receptions of silences encountered in the field is neither an easy task nor one free of ethical scruples. Spelling out things that "go without saying" can throw light on the production and reproduction of power relations and possibly even contribute to undoing inequalities. However, if silence is used to protect and enable, who are scholars to break the seal of noncommunication? Giving – or receiving – voice is not always empowering (cf. Mills 1991; Strandén-Backa 2013). Moreover, what is at stake for a scholar in interpreting a "sniff" as an expression of silence (Karoliina Ojanen, this issue)? How does one explore rather than assume the meanings of silences (Kingsolver 2015)?

The messiness of the process of analysing culture cannot – and need not – be silenced. As Ehn and Löfgren admit in discussing "doing an ethnography of 'non-events'": "Although our book [Ehn & Löfgren 2010] may give the impression of intentional research, the fact is that many of the choices and decisions determining the final text are concealed even from us" (ibid.: 217). Margaret Mills (1991: 19) has emphasised, along similar lines, that "we must also find ways to include the muddle, that midden of our representation through which later analysts will sift for the objects we could not interpret or did not recognise as artefacts." Including in our research reports that we do not understand could in her view contribute to the openness of scholarly accounts and, ideally, "move our sense of the ambiguities and multiplicities of meaning" closer to those of our fieldwork partners (ibid.: 18).

Conclusions

A lot more remains to be said about silence in cultural practices, including the use of silence in protests and public rituals (e.g. Margry 2011) or the commodification of silence. Silence in its numerous forms appears to be ever-present if we only make an attempt to listen.

None of the case studies presented in this issue were originally about silence. Rather, silence was a feature or analytical tool that emerged in the field and in the process of engaging with fieldwork data. By attempting to listen to silence, authors of this special issue have found it to be filled with intentions, experiences, beliefs and, above all, communication shaped by the particularities of the given context. These "situational determinants of silence" (Basso 1970: 228), however, have histories of their own, prompting scholars to dig deeper into the fabric and flow of daily life as well as into the past. Silence overlaps with the secret and the sacred – too fundamental to be revealed – as well as with things too obvious to be noticed and talked about. From this ambiguous space that is both very personal and collective, silence emerges as an essential constituent of social life and cultural creativity.

Notes

1 This theme issue has its starting point in the "Silence in cultural practices: Agency, power and ideology on the border of language" session of the fifth autumn conference of the Centre of Excellence in Cultural Theory held in Tallinn in 2012. The session was initiated by Laur Vallikivi, who kindly supported our proposal for a special journal issue. Contributions by Piret Koosa, Elo-Hanna Seljamaa and Pihla Maria Siim are based on papers delivered in this panel. Tuija Hovi and Karoliina Ojanen responded to our call for papers for a special issue of *Ethnologia Europaea*. Constructive criticism from Marie Sandberg, Monique Scheer and two anonymous reviewers has been invaluable in honing our diverse takes on silence and tying them together. This special issue was made possible through the generous support of the Estonian Research Council (grant no. 9271 and Institutional Research Project "Tradition, Creativity and Society: Minorities and Alternative Discourses" IUT2-43) and the European Union through the European Regional Development Fund (Centre of Excellence in Cultural Theory).

2 To list just a few titles from the past decade: Ainsworth (2013); Boldt, Federici & Virgulti (2013); Glenn & Ratcliffe (2011); Kenny (2011); Mazzei (2007); Muñoz (2014); Sim (2007); and Weber (2005).

3 The overview provided in Kenny (2011) includes earlier

theoretical approaches, e.g. Max Picard (*Die Welt des Schweigens/The World of Silence* [1948/1952]), Edward T. Hall (*The Silent Language* [1959]) and George Steiner (*Language and Silence* [1967]). See also theoretical overviews by Muñoz (2014: 15–43) and Nakane (2007).

4 Forced into Silence, the documentary. https://lashawn-pagan.com/forced-into-silence-the-documentary/. Accessed June 15, 2016.

References

Achino-Loeb, Maria-Luisa 2006a: Introduction: Silence as the Currency of Power. In: Maria-Luisa Achino-Loeb (ed.), *Silence: The Currency of Power*. New York & Oxford: Berghahn Books, pp. 1–19.

Achino-Loeb, Maria-Luisa 2006b: Silence and the Imperatives of Identity. In: Maria-Luisa Achino-Loeb (ed.), *Silence: The Currency of Power*. New York & Oxford: Berghahn Books, pp. 35–51.

Achino-Loeb, Maria-Luisa (ed.) 2006c: *Silence: The Currency of Power*. New York & Oxford: Berghahn Books.

Ainsworth, Janet 2013: Silence, Speech, and the Paradox of the Right to Remain Silent in American Police Interrogation. In: Michael Freeman & Fiona Smith (eds.), *Law and Language*. Current Legal Issues, Volume 15. Oxford: Oxford University Press, pp. 371–385.

Basso, Keith 1970: "To Give up on Words": Silence in Western Apache Culture. *Southwestern Journal of Anthropology* 26:3, 213–230.

Bateson, Gregory & Mary Catherine Bateson (1987)2005: *Towards an Epistemology of the Sacred*. Cresskill, NJ: Hampton Press.

Bauman, Richard (1983)1998: *Let Your Word Be Few: Symbolism of Speaking and Silence among Seventeenth-Century Quakers*. Quaker Home Service.

Beeman, William O. 2006: Silence in Music. In: Maria-Luisa Achino-Loeb (ed.), *Silence: The Currency of Power*. New York & Oxford: Berghahn Books, pp. 23–34.

Boldt, Leslie, Corrado Federici & Ernesto Virgulti (eds.) 2013: *Silence and the Silenced: Interdisciplinary Perspectives*. Studies on Themes and Motifs in Literature Vol. 119. New York: Peter Lang.

Coleman, Simon 2007: Materializing the Self: Words and Gifts in the Construction of Charismatic Protestant Identity. In: Fenella Cannell (ed.), *The Anthropology of Christianity*. Durham: Duke University Press, pp. 163–184.

Ehn, Billy & Orvar Löfgren 2010: *The Secret World of Doing Nothing*. Berkeley, Los Angeles & London: University of California Press.

Fernandez, James W. 2006: Silences of the Field. In: Maria-Luisa Achino-Loeb (ed.), *Silence: The Currency of Power*. New York & Oxford: Berghahn Books, pp. 158–173.

Glenn, Cheryl & Krista Ratcliffe (eds.) 2011: *Silence and Listening as Rhetorical Arts*. Carbondale, Edwardsville: Southern Illinois University Press.

Goldstein, Diane E. 2009: The Sounds of Silence: Foreknowledge, Miracles, Suppressed Narratives, and Terrorism – What Not Telling Might Tell Us. *Western Folklore* 68:2–3, 9/11 … and After: Folklore in Times of Terror, 235–255.

Hall, Edward T. 1959: *The Silent Language*. Garden City, New York: Doubleday & Company, Inc.

Hall, Stuart 2000: The Multicultural Question. In: Barnor Hesse (ed.), *Un/settled Multiculturalisms: Diasporas, Entanglements, Transruptions*. London: Zed Books, pp. 209–241.

Haraway, Donna 1988: Situated Knowledges: The Science Question in Feminism and the Privilege of Partial Perspective. *Feminist Studies* 14:3, 575–599.

Herzfeld, Michael 2005: *Cultural Intimacy: Social Poetics in the Nation-State*. 2nd ed. New York: Routledge.

Hydén, Margareta 2008: Narrating Sensitive Topics. In: Molly Andrews, Corinne Squire & Maria Tamboukou (eds.), *Doing Narrative Research*. London: Sage, pp. 122–137.

Jaworski, Adam 1993: *The Power of Silence: Social and Pragmatic Perspectives*. Newbury Park, London & New Delhi: SAGE Publications.

Jaworski, Adam 1997a: Introduction: An overview. In: Adam Jaworski (ed.), *Silence: Interdisciplinary Perspectives*. Studies in Anthropological Linguistics 10. Berlin & New York: Mouton de Gruyter, pp. 3–14.

Jaworski, Adam (ed.) 1997b: *Silence: Interdisciplinary Perspectives*. Studies in Anthropological Linguistics 10. Berlin & New York: Mouton de Gruyter.

Kaivola-Bregenhøj, Annikki 2003: The Narrator's Emotions. In: Lotte Tarkka (ed.), *Dynamics of Tradition: Perspectives on Oral Poetry and Folk Belief*. Studia Fennica Folkloristica 13. Helsinki: Suomalaisen Kirjallisuuden Seura, pp. 329–342.

Kenny, Colum 2011: *The Power of Silence: Silent Communication in Daily Life*. London: Karnac Books.

Ketola, Kimmo, Seppo Knuuttila, Antti Mattila & Kari Mikko Vesala 2002: *Puuttuvat viestit: Nonkommunikaatio inhimillisessä vuorovaikutuksessa*. Helsinki: Gaudeamus.

Kingsolver, Ann E. 2015: Representation as an Extractive Economy: Silencing and Multiple Marginalities. *PoLAR Online. Emergent Conversations: Part 2 "Reflecting on Silence and Anthropology"*, March 2015, 3–4, https://politicaland-legalanthroreview.files.wordpress.com/2016/01/emergent-conversation-silence.pdf. Accessed March 27, 2016.

Klein, Barbro 2006: Introduction: Telling, Doing, Experiencing. Folkloristic Perspectives on Narrative Analysis. In: Annikki Kaivola-Bregenhøj, Barbro Klein & Ulf Palmenfelt (eds.), *Narrating, Doing, Experiencing: Nordic Folkloristic Perspectives*. Studia Fennica Folkloristica 16. Helsinki: Finnish Literature Society, pp. 6–28.

Lawless, Elaine 2000: Transformative Re-membering: Describing the Unspeakable in Battered Women's Narratives. *Southern Folklore* 57:1, 65–79.

Lember, Uku 2016: Inter-Generational Transmission of Pasts in Late Soviet Estonia: Oral History Perspective in Inter-

Marriage Setting. In: Raili Nugin, Anu Kannike & Maaris Raudsepp (eds.), *Generations in Estonia: Contemporary Perspectives on Turbulent Times.* Tartu: The University of Tartu Press, pp. 159–187.

Luhrmann, Tanya M. 2004: Metakinesis: How God Becomes Intimate in Contemporary U.S. Christianity. *American Anthropologist* 106:3, 518–528.

Luhrmann, Tanya M. 2012: *When God Talks Back: Understanding the American Evangelical Relationship with God.* New York: Vintage Books.

Lukin, Karina 2012: Talking Religion: Speech about the Non-Reportable. In: Silver Rattasepp (ed.), *Centre of Excellence in Cultural Theory V Autumn Conference "In, Out and In Between: Dynamics of Cultural Borders".* Program and Abstracts. Tallinn, October 18–19, 2012. Tartu: Centre of Excellence in Cultural Theory, University of Tartu, pp. 32.

Margry, Peter-Jan 2011: Civil Religion in Europe: Silent Marches, Pilgrim Treks and Processes of Mediatization. *Ethnologia Europaea* 41:2, 5–23.

Mazzei, Lisa A. 2007: *Inhabited Silence in Qualitative Research: Putting Poststructural Theory to Work.* New York: Peter Lang Publishing.

Mills, Margaret 1991: *Rhetorics and Politics in Afghan Traditional Storytelling.* Philadelphia: University of Pennsylvania Press.

Muñoz, Kristine L. 2014: *Transcribing Silence: Culture, Relationships, and Communication.* Walnut Creek, California: Left Coast Press Inc.

Nakane, Ikuko 2007: *Silence in Intercultural Communication: Perceptions and Performance.* Amsterdam, Philadelphia: John Benjamins Publishing Company.

Okely, Judith 1992: Anthropology and Autobiography: Participatory Experience and Embodied Knowledge. In: Judith Okely & Helen Callaway (eds.), *Anthropology and Autobiography.* London: Routledge, pp. 1–27.

Peltonen, Ulla-Maija 1996: *Punakapinan muistot: Tutkimus työväen muistelukerronnan muotoutumisesta vuoden 1918 jälkeen.* Suomalaisen Kirjallisuuden Seuran toimituksia 657. Helsinki: Suomalaisen Kirjallisuuden Seura.

PoLAR Online. Emergent Conversations: Part 2 "Reflecting on Silence and Anthropology", March 2015. https://politicalandlegalanthroreview.files.wordpress.com/2016/01/emergent-conversation-silence.pdf. Accessed March 27, 2016.

Schiffrin, Deborah 2002: Mother and Friends in a Holocaust Survivor Oral History. *Language in Society* 31:3, 309–354.

Schmidt-Lauber, Brigitta 2012: Seeing, Hearing, Feeling, Writing: Approaches and Methods from the Perspective of Ethnological Analysis of the Present. In: Regina F. Bendix & Galit Hasam-Rokem (eds.), *A Companion to Folklore.* Chichester: Wiley-Blackwell, pp. 559–578.

Schröter, Melani 2013: *Silence and Concealment in Political Discourse.* Amsterdam, Philadelphia: John Benjamins Publishing Company.

Shuman, Amy 2005: *Other People's Stories: Entitlement Claims and the Critique of Empathy.* Urbana: University of Illinois Press.

Sim, Stuart 2007: *Manifesto for Silence: Confronting the Politics and Culture of Noise.* Edinburgh: Edinburgh University Press.

Strandén-Backa, Sofie 2013: Dealing with Emotions. In: Camilla Asplund Ingemark (ed.), *Therapeutic Uses of Storytelling: An Interdisciplinary Approach to Narration as Therapy.* Lund: Nordic Academic Press, pp. 85–100.

Szuchewycz, Bohdan 1997: Silence in Ritual Communication. In: Adam Jaworski (ed.), *Silence: Interdisciplinary Perspectives.* Studies in Anthropological Linguistics 10. Berlin & New York: Mouton de Gruyter, pp. 239–260.

Tannen, Deborah & Muriel Saville-Troike (eds.) 1985: *Perspectives on Silence.* Norwood, NJ: Ablex.

Thiesmeyer, Lynn Janet 2003a: Introduction: Silencing in Discourse. In: Lynn Janet Thiesmeyer (ed.), *Discourse and Silencing: Representation and the Language of Displacement.* Amsterdam, Philadelphia: John Benjamins Publishing Company, pp. 1–33.

Thiesmeyer, Lynn Janet (ed.) 2003b: *Discourse and Silencing: Representation and the Language of Displacement.* Amsterdam, Philadelphia: John Benjamins Publishing Company.

Vallikivi, Laur 2012: The Power of Silence and Words: Language Ideologies in the Missionary Encounter between Russian Baptists and Nenets Reindeer Herders. In: Silver Rattasepp (ed.), *Centre of Excellence in Cultural Theory V Autumn Conference "In, Out and In Between: Dynamics of Cultural Borders".* Program and Abstracts. Tallinn, October 18–19, 2012. Tartu: Centre of Excellence in Cultural Theory, University of Tartu, pp. 33.

Vesala, Kari Mikko, Kimmo Ketola, Seppo Knuuttila & Antti Mattila 2002: Mitä enkelit pelkäävät? In: Kimmo Ketola, Seppo Knuuttila, Antti Mattila & Kari Mikko Vesala, *Puuttuvat viestit: Nonkommunikaatio inhimillisessä vuorovaikutuksessa.* Helsinki: Gaudeamus, pp. 11–41.

Vesala, Kari Mikko & Seppo Knuuttila 2012: Non-Communication as a Perspective on the World of Communication. Elaborating on Bateson. *FF Network* 42, 4–11, http://www.folklorefellows.fi/wp-content/uploads/FFN_42.pdf. Accessed March 24, 2016.

Weber, Myles 2005: *Consuming Silences: How We Read Authors Who Don't Publish.* Athens & London: University of Georgia Press.

Webster, Joseph 2013: *The Anthropology of Protestantism: Faith and Crisis among Scottish Fishermen.* New York: Palgrave MacMillan.

Zerubavel, Eviatar 2006: *Elephant in the Room: Silence and Denial in Everyday Life.* Oxford & New York: Oxford University Press.

SILENCES, OLD AGE AND INSTITUTIONALISED CARE

Karoliina Ojanen, University of Helsinki

The article examines how silence materialises and is performed in residential care homes for the elderly, and how these practices are intertwined with the cultural narrative of old age in Finnish society. The data consisting of ethnographic fieldwork in two care units shows that silence is involved in many aspects of the residents' lives. Though these practices of silence do not mean the absence of the residents' agency, here they both expose and construct stereotypical conceptions regarding old age and concretely narrows the experiences of old people. By considering the décor of care units and interactions, the researcher identifies silence as a central feature of doing old age. It is only partly produced by the elderly themselves, and it carries both negative and positive meanings.

Keywords: old age, narrative, men's studies, institutional care, cultural gerontology

Since antiquity, old age has been connected either to experience and wisdom, or to mental and physical decline, losses and illnesses (de Beauvoir [1970]1992: 34–57; Hazan 2000; Kirk 1995). To stigmatise old age as a negative phase of life has been interpreted as expressing fear of or disgust with growing old in Western culture (Calasanti & Slevin 2006: 3). Old age is seen as a societal problem and health risk (see Ronström 1998: 3). For some time, a cultural discourse of successful ageing has existed. On the one hand, this implies that getting older opens up new possibilities but, on the other hand, it entails expectations and "morally-loaded notions of individual responsibility" (Nikander 2002, as cited in Pietilä & Ojala 2011: 388) that the elderly should remain active in their lives. Usually "successful ageing" refers to the "third age", that is 65+, which has so far usually meant retirement.[1] However, old age is easily defined as an exception from the normal active way of living

(Alftberg 2012: 14; Sandberg 2011: 49). Old people have been characterised as representing the modern "Other" (or one of the "Others") (Lundin 2007: 197).

The Cultural Narrative of Old Age

In this article, I examine how the cultural narrative of old age is constructed in two care units. How are prevailing cultural conceptions of old age exposed and/or challenged in institutionalised care? In particular, I will focus on the theme of silence, which emerged in the field as a crucial constituent of the cultural narrative of old age in institutional settings. I conducted ethnographic fieldwork in two residential care homes during 2011–2013, for 11 months altogether.[2] The care units where I conducted fieldwork are situated in the metropolitan area of Helsinki. Maijala[3] is a "traditional" care home in the sense that residents are expected to spend the rest of their lives there. Approximately 40 residents live in Maija-

Karoliina Ojanen 2016: Silences, Old Age and Institutionalised Care.
Ethnologia Europaea 46:2, 14–26. © Museum Tusculanum Press.

la, most of them women. The inhabitants are offered some activities on a regular basis (singing, physical exercise, reminiscing and outdoor recreation), about once or twice a week. A few residents eat lunch and dinner together every day in the lunch room. The other care home, Kaikula, consists of ten units that each have space for ten–twelve residents. Its aim is to rehabilitate the residents and support them to keep on doing daily chores, maintain their independence as much as possible and, in the best cases, to help residents to return home. Kaikula has more activities, approximately two to four every week. Some of the activities are allocated to a particular group; for example, there is a discussion club for five male residents. Also on hand are physiotherapists, and residents can take part in some kind of physical exercise almost on a daily basis. Despite these differences, both institutions seemed to be operating with similar ideas about old age, which will be discussed in this article.

According to some ethnographic studies on residential care homes or institutional long-term care, the institutional practices of residential care direct, regulate and control the meanings and affect the experiences of old age and the knowledge that is produced about old age (e.g. Ferrer 1981; Lämsä 2013; Magnússon 1996; Townsend 1962). Though I have included the institutional elements in my analysis, I do not assess the characteristics or the circumstances of the nursing sector and its work, although I have, of course, had many discussions with nurses. So even as I analyse how the nurses talk about the death of a resident, I only look at the cultural narrative they reproduce.

Age, like gender, is shaped by cultural norms and ideas of what is considered to be appropriate (Pietilä & Ojala 2011: 381). Both are socially constructed categories that consist of repeated acts, intertwined material and discursive doings (Butler 1993, [1990]1999). In addition to such acts, material objects can also be seen as exposing and constructing our cultural ideas. According to Karen Barad (2007), the material elements of different kinds can be approached as post-human actors or agents that performatively take part in the construction of cultural ideas, discourses and conceptions. This idea is useful for explaining how the material reality is present in the performative construction of old age. Narrative analysis on the other hand adheres to explaining tellability, the presence of small stories, in the construction of old age (see e.g. Shuman 2005; Peltonen 1996).

The perspective of cultural studies on ageing has emphasised the importance of having either the people themselves, or others, analyse how ageing is "done", or how various meanings of age have been constructed in different contexts. Ageing can be, and has been, analysed through the actions, habits and its practical implications (e.g. Alftberg 2010: 43). This article takes as its starting point narrations of old age created by the elderly themselves, in interaction with the researcher. The narrative research tradition generally aims both to create research material through which meanings, identities and world views can be analysed, and to structure awareness of them (Hägg 2010). The narrative research also adheres to performance studies, which have formed a central approach in folklore studies. Applied to narratives, performance studies can be used to explore the interaction of verbal and non-verbal elements of narrating, and the individual and cultural elements of creating a narrative (e.g. Fine & Speer 1992; Honko 2000: 3–13). Here a non-verbal element, silence, constructs a central element of the old age narrative.

In the following, I will analyse some of the social exchanges I recorded in a field diary as "small stories". Small stories are such, either metaphorically or concretely. According to Michael Bamberg and Alexandra Georgakopoulou (2008: 5), small stories refer to tellings of recent and ongoing events, future or hypothetical events, shared events, but also to allusions to tellings, the deferrals of tellings and refusals to tell. By analysing the construction of small stories in ethnographic data, it becomes possible to apply narrative analysis on incidents that may be only loosely connected with the narrative canon (narratives' common structure, rules and standards), that is, to narratives that are small either concretely or metaphorically (ibid.).

Thus, in this article I examine how the cultural narrative of old age is constructed and produced, drawing on my own notes in my field diary and on interview material. The narrative is produced not only in small stories told, but in small stories hidden in silence, perhaps difficult to tell, or which are told only briefly. I also seek to uncover the narrative as it is produced through materiality, for instance in furnishings and decor, but even the silence itself can be approached as an agent that plays a significant part in the construction of this particular narrative of old age. In addition to age, I am interested in what meanings gender entails and how it is produced in this narrative.

First, I analyse the notes of silence that I wrote about in my field diary and came across in interviews. I connect silence to "non-happenings" and a lack of noise. While listening to these silences for eleven months, I began to scrutinise them in relation to the furnishings and, for example, to empty cupboards or photographs that no one recognised. Second, I focus on the interaction between the staff and the residents, and especially on the experiences of the male residents, although some of the social practices in these care units were not dependent on the gender or other social categories of the residents. I did have many conversations with both the residents and the staff during my fieldwork but I did not interview the staff like I interviewed the residents. These interviews and conversations do play part in my interpretations regarding the construction of silences, though in this article I focus more on my field notes.

Old age is a culturally regulated, changing construction with its own culture-specific histories. It is intertwined with material reality and bodily experiences. The observations in the field and my field notes both construct and illuminate the conceptions of old age (Gergen 1999) and the discourse of multidimensional silence: silence that is performed in many different ways and that has various implications and meanings. This does not mean that there are not other narratives about old age in our culture but, in the institutionalised setting, the implications for silence are dominant. Silence becomes an impor-

tant part of the everyday sphere of the institution and, in this sense, it has culturally significant implications. Following Ehn and Löfgren (1982), silence and voice can be interpreted to formulate one basic category of institutional culture and, thus, a category that offers a possibility for cultural analysis.

Everyday Silences

It is very quiet. Everyone is in his/her own room. Some of the residents are sleeping as I walk by the open doors. (FD [Field diary] April 6, 2011)

I go to the lobby again, just for a while. Sakari asks me for a napkin. I bring him two. He sits in his wheelchair, looks straight ahead, putting his head down a bit. It is quiet, stagnant. Nothing happens. I can't hear any voices from the other rooms either, only the occasional clatter of dishes when nurses serve lunch to the residents. (FD May 3, 2011)

When I arrive, Aulis is alone in the lobby, sitting in his wheelchair. He is wearing pink pyjamas. It is quiet, the nurses are having coffee, sitting on the terrace outside, and the sun is shining. (FD June 7, 2011)

The silence, which often materialised as "the flow of non-happenings" and the absence of noise, was a predominant feature of my field notes. Non-happenings refer to situations that I came across in the shared spaces of the institutions: the lobbies, corridors, lunch rooms, living rooms. The concept of "non-happening" is an etic category and refers mainly to "slow situations" of everyday life that had none or only a few participants who were interacting. These non-happenings usually included not talking. These silences in the shared spaces were to some extent connected to the fact that the care homes were institutions: the activities were regulated and daily schedules were quite fixed. The residents were brought together mainly during lunch and dinner, to watch television or to take part in some kind of activity. Otherwise, the residents spent a lot of time in their own rooms or were alone in the shared spaces of the institution, such as the lunch room, corridors or the lobby with the television.

To some extent, the care units appeared to have been maintained as total institutions where it was difficult to deviate from the regulations and schedules. According to Erving Goffman ([1961]1969: 6–7), in a total institution, residents must follow the plan that is defined to execute the official goals of the institution. In care units, especially in Maijala, the multidimensional silence that takes shape, for example in the exiguity of the activities, and how the voice is used throughout the day seem to be unofficial goals of institutions. However, it must be noted that both institutions under study were explicit about the idea of activating residents; for example, they considered it important that they gathered together during lunchtime. According to the staff, this is not practised in every institution. The residents had different views on the issue.

Karoliina: Is there something you would like to change here?
Erkki: No, I am too lazy for that. I just want to be here. Everything is here.
Karoliina: So you would not wish for more exercise or…
Erkki: No, I am too tired for it.
(Erkki, 85, construction worker)

Karoliina: Well, how do you like the activities here?
Seppo: I am not very good at gymnastics. I understand that it must be felt in the body, but it is so repulsive, I would say. Some of us just don't do the moves. You must put your arms here (shows, behind his neck) and swing your arms and so on. You do that for a while and you are dead.
Karoliina: So, you don't like that very much. Are there some activities you like more?
Seppo: Well, bingo. I would like to play bingo. It is nice when you get the answers right.
(Seppo, 76, gardener)

These men were living in Kaikula, which concentrated on rehabilitating the residents and sought to offer more activities. This may have something to do with the fact that the men seemed content, though I also met residents of Kaikula who felt the days were boring (e.g. FD January 25, 2013). It follows from this that stillness, silence or non-happenings had different meanings for different residents. For some of them, to be quiet in one's own peace provided a mode of agency. In this next discussion from my field diary in Maijala, the resident described his situation differently from the excerpts above.

We talk about his week. Timo says that "nothing has happened; I've been nowhere." By nowhere he means that he has not been lifted up from his bed. I ask if there have not been any activities. "Not that I know of," Timo replies. He continues that he would be extremely bored without his television. (FD November 2, 2012)

This excerpt highlights how everyday life with only a few activities may be experienced. Having nothing else to do than to watch television may cause anxiety and feelings of little power over everyday activities. Having nothing to do and being left in bed can be interpreted as a mode of silencing in which silence becomes a restrictive element of everyday life. However, these experiences may not be simply dependent on the actual possibilities of doing something or taking part in activities: in Maijala, different activities were offered almost every week during my field period. According to Aske Juul Lassen (2014) the active ageing has become a central discourse of ageing and is represented as a solution to global ageing. However, this discourse faces challenges in everyday practices. These challenges occur in my study when the aged people do not wish to attend the activities or the staff does not have time to engage them for activities. According to my field work, Maijala and Kaikula offered equally physical group exercises and for instance singing, playing games, and reminiscing that offered a sense of collectiveness. To offer legitimate activities was not restricted only to physical exercise (cf. Lassen 2014).

Furnishing, Paintings, Books and Knick-Knacks

Next, I turn to the material reality of the residential care homes and examine the meanings that the furnishings appear to have and how they can be interpreted as contributing to the constructions of silent old age in institutionalised care. This part of the analysis is based on my observations and interpretations. The furnishings and material objects in the shared spaces of the institution were not discussed in the interviews because they only caught my attention later in the process of reading and re-reading field notes. Moreover, when I was chatting with residents in private rooms, they naturally talked about their lives through the objects they had in their rooms, but there was not a special focus on this theme. In their rooms, most of the residents had only a few objects and photographs of their families and themselves as young, but a couple of rooms of female residents actually seemed like "home" since these had several objects, including furniture, brought from home.

In general, the public spaces of both institutions were furnished in a way that maximised accessibility. All residents used wheelchairs or other equipment in order to move around. Both institutions had two public spaces: a lunch room and a living room with a television and a CD player. The rehabilitative care unit in Kaikula had a device for physical training in the living room on which the residents could exercise. The living rooms had sofas and comfortable armchairs. There were also a few cabinets and cupboards. The lunch rooms had several tables but only a few chairs since most residents used wheelchairs. The lunch rooms in both units had tables intended for the staff; these were marked by chairs surrounding them. In Maijala, there was a piano in the living room. In both institutions there were also more private spaces for the staff, for example a locker room. Both institutions had offices for the staff. In Maijala, these were larger rooms with windows. Residents and staff members could see each other, but one could not hear what the staff were discussing if the door was closed. In Kaikula, these offices were situated in the same space as the living room but the two areas were separated by a door. The nurses in

Kaikula had a laptop so they could do their paperwork anywhere in the care home. Both institutions had paintings or drawings on the walls, which I will discuss later in more detail. The next field note describes one cabinet placed in one of the shared facility rooms, the TV room in Kaikula.

> There are three shelves in the cabinet. The cabinet is quite wide, about two metres. On the other end, there are flowers on the top of it. On the first shelf there is a book, "Eternal Stories", a few magazines, a folder about Kaikula, and nothing else. The second contains porcelain knick-knacks: a bride, an angel, a teddy bear, a swan, a heart-shaped box and a scallop. Nothing more. The third shelf has a book called "The Veterans of Finland", a canister, some papers, lyrics for songs, and then emptiness. The space is used very sparingly. In the other section, there is a glass vitrine that has nothing in it. (FD March 1, 2013)

In the above excerpt, old age is signified through an interesting juxtaposition between the small, cute porcelain figurines and the books telling the stories of Finnish (male) veterans and eternity. The porcelain objects can be described as bland, while the books emphasise other aspects that are considered relevant regarding old people: eternity and the fact that they were the generation who suffered through wars and played a part in building up the welfare state of Finland. On the one hand, the old people were highly acknowledged but, on the other, the knick-knacks produced quite contrary aspects of the cultural narrative of old age.

> In the television lobby, there are two older chests of drawers and a modern one. In the modern one, there are some photo albums, coffee cups, a chess game, some clearly "old stuff", for example an old bottle from a well-known state factory, and some plants. The older chests of drawers are almost empty. Next to the television are two bigger items made of porcelain. They represent an older woman and an older man. The same kind of man and woman are presented in a painting hanging on a

wall in the lunch room. The woman and the man are contextualised in agrarian Finland: they are hard-working, serious people, both wearing heavy clothes; they are round, the woman has a scarf on her head, and the man is wearing a hat. There are also two rocking chairs that the staff sometimes use. Around the corner, there is a "grandfather clock". Next to this is a little shelf with some magazines on it. Another chest of drawers is just beside the office; there are artificial tulips on it, and nothing else. (FD April 19, 2011)

On the wall of the corridor hangs a large handicraft piece that shows an old man and an old woman holding hands and walking together on a green hill in the evening. (FD May 6, 2011)

In both institutions, many cabinets had only a few objects; they were almost or totally empty. In this particular example, the photo albums are an interesting detail since they belonged to a former resident; thus, other residents or members of the staff did not know the motives of the photos. I asked both the residents and the staff about the photos, but their function and origin were unclear. There was also a photo album showing the construction of Maijala, which, of course, was familiar to all.

According to my interpretation, these material objects and furnishings in elderly care units take part in the cultural construction of old age regardless of how they got there or who made the decisions on the decoration. The objects can be understood to have an agency in the construction of cultural understanding and lived realities of old age (Barad 2007). For example, a television seems to represent a post-human agent in this context. It had a crucial role in the organisation of everyday life. Residents often watched television in their own rooms or in the lobby. Residents were brought to watch television in the lobby, but there were occasions when no one watched it; they stared in different directions and were quiet or slept (e.g. FD March 2013). Altogether, the objects had hardly any connection to here and now, implying that the inhabitants had no interest in the present.

Old age does not merely refer to chronological age, but is just as much a matter of social positioning: how one is situated in different networks and positions (Sandberg 2011: 45). In public discussion, the elderly still tend to be lumped into one group, without consideration of the significance of social class, sexuality, ethnic background or family situation on old-age experiences (Calasanti & King 2005, 2011; Holstein 2011; King & Calasanti 2006; Slevin 2006; Slevin & Linneman 2009; Springer & Mouzon 2011). This tendency was also present in the material world of the institutions: the diversity of the lives of the old people was not recognised.

The old people's relationship to children and childhood through the decorations emerges in the next field note.

In the corridor, there are drawings that children have made of old people. In those pictures, there is always a man and a woman together or an old person and a child. In most of the pictures, the sun is shining. The lives of the old are represented in a very consistent way; maybe a teacher in the school has given the children some directions? They do not explicitly describe the children's relationships with their grandparents, though these are probably reflected in the pictures. I don't know what kind of directions they have been given. (FD November 2, 2012)

In the pictures, the couples are depicted as consisting of a male and a female or an old person and a child. The paintings and pictures of the care unit carry special meanings since they are in the particular context of the institutionalised home of old people. The institutionalised care unit can be understood as clearly expressing the cultural understanding of what it means to be old: in a sense also the public spaces of the unit and the corridors where the pictures are located are part of the private home of the residents. According to human geographers in the 1970s and the 1980s, "home" was the most idealised site of human existence, but nowadays there is a stronger argument that home and the domestic sphere are full of contrasting connotations, from safety to exclusion and regulation (Brickell 2011: 225–226).

Presumably, the children had drawn pictures about their grandparents, in some sense. It may be assumed that the residents have grandchildren and that old people, in general, are especially fond of children. It may be interesting to ask why it is considered meaningful for children to describe their ideas of old people and old age and for these ideas to be brought to the residents in the care unit to see. Children and the elderly are both similar to and very different from each other. On a cultural level, children and old people (especially in institutionalised care) share the same characteristics; for different reasons, they both have difficulties in being perceived and treated as autonomous subjects. On the other hand, they represent different phases of life.

The culturally constructed relationship between children and old people includes the idea that old people become children again. The process of infantilisation has been said to commonly occur in institutions. Infantilisation has been conceptualised as the societal approach of old age as a second childhood, with little or no recognition of the lifetime experiences that separate the elderly from children. "Environmental infantilisation" may involve the lack of privacy as well as decor that appears to be in dissonance with the ideas of how adults would furnish their living environments (see Salari 2002: 321–322).

The children's drawings of old people, paintings of the elderly going for evening walks, unknown photographs and half-empty shelves with a few impersonal items imply cultural conceptions of old age that also have material consequences: old people are considered to have lived their lives already. Old people living in institutionalised care units appear as people in a liminal state (see Turner 1974), which is connected with their social, cultural and structural invisibility; this is apparent when examining the modes of silence in institutionalised care. Next, I will illuminate these themes by focusing on interactions between residents and staff, and men's experiences in the care units.

Silence and Agency

In the residential care home, silence is related to the realm of power. In this section, I examine how power is produced by the nursing staff in relation to silence, theirs or the residents'. In addition, I contemplate the sexuality of old men in these institutions and focus on the practices that are applied to silence the gender or sexuality of old people.

I sit with Aulis in the lobby. Aulis ponders why we are not served coffee though we are sitting together in the living room. I reply that lunch is in an hour, and then there will be coffee. Aulis sniffs at me, and says "damn it". Paula comes to sit with us; she has been doing some physical exercises. Aulis asks her: "Did you swing a lot?" Paula sniffs at Aulis. A nurse, Marjaana, comes into the living room, and goes to eat her lunch and have some coffee at the staff table, which is located in this same living room/lunch room combination. The nurse goes to get some water, and Aulis follows her; he steps right in front of her and stares. The nurse does not make any contact with him, but walks away to have her lunch and coffee. Aulis comes back to us, sniffs and says that we should be served coffee or some refreshments. (FD December 10, 2012)

The social exchanges bring out a small story that is shaped by non-reciprocal interaction. Aulis thought we should have coffee, a common habit when socialising. The social norms that he was used to did not apply to us. His words emphasised how he felt that he, or we, were not being treated the way we should be.

In general, the interaction clearly revealed the boundaries between the staff and the inhabitants, which were quite easily discernible. If a nurse was on a break, she did not need to interact with the residents; rather, she could ignore an attempt to make contact and receive a reply. Rather than asking Aulis what he wanted, the nurse totally ignored him. It was not rare for the inhabitants to get drinks or little snacks outside the daily schedule, but it was also quite normal for them to be ignored in this manner.

According to my analysis, this kind of ignoring is a way to silence the inhabitants or to show them when and how they were expected to behave and to what extent the care unit was their home or the staff's workplace. On the basis of daily interaction, fragmentariness, underestimation and silence become predominant features of everyday life in care units.

> When Eero has finished his lunch, he asks for more food. Two female nurses smile and glance at each other, it seems like they are amused by the fact that Eero wants more. One of the nurses says: "Eero is always the first to ask for more food, though he was last to have the meal." A nurse asks another nurse: "Did I give it too little then?" A nurse asks Eero: "Would you like to have ketchup?" Eero replies "yes" and adds that he also wants vegetables; the nurse replies: "Only macaroni casserole then." Eero says: "Also vegetables." There is some food at Seppo's feet; it seems quite difficult for him to eat. He moves his hand slowly and part of the food falls off the spoon before it reaches his mouth. After everyone is finished, there is a little food under the men's table. An assistant nurse says: "Now we should have a dog to eat this food that is thrown here." Two other nurses laugh a little at this comment and reply: "Yes, a dog would be great." Eero comments that a dog would also eat food from the tables. The nurses do not reply. (FD January 25, 2013)

First, I paid attention to the way the staff was amused about Eero asking for more food. Eero had a slight weight problem, and this was emphasised by the staff: in a sense they expressed that it was not suitable for him to ask for more food. Second, the conceptions of old age are illustrated in the way the nurses discussed Eero's amount of food using the pronoun "it" [se] and how they spoke over Eero, not to him. The residents were not seen as subjects and, correspondingly, the excerpt illustrates how old people's (bodily) practices turn from private to public objects that are managed by nurses and institutional practices: Eero should eat less (see Magnússon 1996: 69; cf. Alftberg 2012: 17). This is also interesting in relation to how the assistant nurse who served the food did not hear that Eero also wanted vegetables, not only casserole. This illuminates how the gendered stereotypes work in an institutional setting and how the staff may construct the resident in a way that not only suits their strategies and ideas about him as a resident, but also follows some clearly stereotypical ideas of masculinity and men.

Third, the remark about needing a dog to clean up after the men. The distance that is expressed in this setting is multidimensional: it seems that the staff did not recognise or empathise with the fact that eating was difficult for some residents, and when Eero commented on this condescending remark regarding their eating, none of the nurses replied to him. I interpret Eero's comment in this particular interactional setting as Eero's small story about the situation. Eero tried to challenge the offensive comments by saying that a dog would eat all of the food, but he did not receive a reply and, in a sense, the allusion to his story about the whole situation was cut off (see Georgakopoulou 2006: 127).

According to David Morris (1996: 29), voice is the most precious endowment that suffering may deprive us of. Without a voice it is difficult to be understood by others, and eventually the loss of a voice may constitute or represent a complete shattering of the self, a matter of becoming invisible. In general, the loss of voice may also refer to encounters where a person is not heard even though he or she has a voice.

> Tarmo is sitting in the MOTOmed (a type of exercise equipment). His feet are fastened to the pedals. He is not sitting straight, and he keeps complaining that it hurts. I can see in his eyes that he is suffering... He asks for help from the nurse Kati, who comes by to take him off the MOTOmed.
> Kati: Who put you there then?
> Tarmo: Jaana (another nurse).
> Kati: Well, then, it is Jaana who will take you off.
> Kati walks away. Tarmo glances at me and says:
> Tarmo: Look how we are treated; it is always like this.
> Karoliina: You have to wait.

Jaana comes and takes Tarmo off the MOTOmed. Tarmo complains about his pain to Jaana and wants to lie down in bed.

Jaana: You can go to bed after lunch. Now, watch the telly.

Jaana moves Tarmo right in front of the telly. Jaana goes away and Tarmo repeats: "Look how we patients are treated! I have to languish here and I cannot decide for myself. I should be able to do that, shouldn't I?" (FD February 5, 2013)

The institutionalised setting guided the daily practices of the residents. Tarmo's wishes were not met: he could not get off the MOTOmed and go to bed right away. He explicitly emphasised his lack of autonomy. One crucial issue in elderly care units is how the needs of the residents are met and, for example, how they get assistance and help (see Ojanen 2014). Interpreting Tarmo's comments, it seems that he was dependent on others in a way that caused him frustration. It is noteworthy that Tarmo spoke of himself as a "patient" rather than as a resident or inhabitant. One time I heard a physiotherapist discuss this with a resident who referred to himself as a patient. The physiotherapist emphasised: "You are not a patient: we don't have patients; patients are in the hospital. This is your home; here you are clients or residents." This can be seen as a parallel to the changes in Finnish welfare politics, which has started to strongly emphasise the neo-liberal ideal of active citizens who are primarily responsible for their own welfare (rather than the state) and who as active agents take part in the production, management and evaluation of different services (Palola & Karjalainen 2011; Sihto 2013). The way the two residents referred to themselves as patients reveals that despite the aim of these long-term care units of being "homey" places, the reality appears to be somewhat different. At least some residents felt they were patients, which may imply that they felt that they were strongly dependent upon the staff, but this position also means that they were entitled to demand services. However, not every resident shared these experiences or found living in the care unit difficult.

Jouko is reading a newspaper, and welcomes me as I enter his room. We chat about the daily life in the unit and he says that he really does not want any more of these activities, physical exercise and so on. He says that he is a "static guy" and at this point his life is sort of small; he is "flying low". "I enjoy the way it is, just sitting still. Maybe I am a bit simple man." (FD March 15, 2013)

Jouko had had a career as a lawyer. He had had a stroke but his cognitive ability was still very good; he had a good sense of humour and he seemed to have rather good relations with the staff; also his children often came to see him. There is a distinction between being silenced and being silent. Silence can be a mode of agency: to be quiet does not necessarily mean that one is being silenced. For Jouko, being still and silent in his own peace was a way to experience and perform identity in this social setting. Stillness and silence can be conceptualised as something relaxing, reflective and restful that promotes agency (Fivush 2010: 90). Agency does not refer only to social transformation or resistance. Agency can be small, invisible, changing and unconscious (e.g. Honkasalo 2006; Jyrkämä 2013). However, in the institutional setting, the agency of old people was often challenged. It was hard for them to change the social setting and structures in the care units they were living in. This applies to the wider cultural relationship of the category of old and agency (see Hazan 2000; Salari 2002).

Being silenced is usually conceptualised as negative (Fivush 2010: 91). In the next excerpt, the residents are not directly silenced but they are not really acknowledged or given space either. The impenetrable boundaries between the staff and the residents are striking.

The nurses are thinking about the seating of the residents. Tiina (a nurse) says that there must be room for the memorial table, too. Arja (a nurse) replies: "I removed it; it had been there for several days already! Altti died on Friday!" It's Monday. They continue to talk about the new resident who is moving into Altti's room (whether they've labelled his clothes, where to place him, what his name is, and whether his room is clean). The other residents are already sitting around the tables waiting for lunch. Miina (a resident) looks weary. She is obviously listening to the nurses. After the lunch has been served, all of the inhabitants are quiet. The nurses sit at their own table having their lunch. Arja talks about how she would like to go out and drink beer this Friday; another colleague replies that she is working and cannot join her. Arja goes on to complain about a staff meeting that she does not want to attend. The radio is on. The residents are eating. Miina asks Linnea (a resident) about going to the sauna but the conversation soon dies out. (FD April 15, 2013)

The way death is dealt with in the above excerpt is connected with the stereotypical ideas of being old. In institutional care, old people's bodies turn from private to public, objects that are managed by nurses and institutional practices. Bodily functions become common topics for professional discussion and targets of analysis, as well as signposts for institutionalised care strategies (Magnússon 1996: 69; cf. Alftberg 2012: 17). Here silencing occurs by means of making public something that is usually kept private. Following Foucault's theory of power, the way bodies are controlled represents the way power is performed in a community. Here, the control actualised in the way that nurse Arja talked about the death of one of the residents. She did not seem to realise that some of the inhabitants may find her talk dismissive, too casual and arrogant. Also, in one interview with a resident from this same care home it came up that nurses occasionally would complain in front of the residents about their work, how hard it was and how poorly they were paid, in turn creating an uncomfortable situation for the listening residents.

The residents were silenced in a complex way in this one-way interaction where issues concerning them were talked about in a dismissive manner. According to my observations, the residents were not able to interfere with this practice, partly because of their dependency on the nurses. To approach this on a cultural level, it could be interpreted that it is expected that the old stay quiet, that they do not really understand what is going on and that they do not have the right to get offended when someone evaluates their worth and dignity aloud.

Furthermore, this interaction exposes how the official ideals of residential care units clash with everyday practices. Theoretically, the staff and residents are together, sharing the same space, making the institutional setting as "homey" and equal as possible. Yet, residents do not have the same opportunities to use their voices, to be seen and heard (cf. Ojala 2011 on old women studying at the University of Old Age). The divide between the staff and the residents expresses the cultural ideas and stereotypes about old age: old people are not recognised as autonomous subjects. These stereotypes silence the lived realities of these residents (see Alftberg 2012: 155–157). It appears that in institutionalised care silence becomes, in many different ways, a central aspect of the narrative of being old. This narrative is often connected to the lack of agency and denial of expressing identity.

Horizons of Silence, Emerging Change?

After I had been in the field for a while, I began to feel anxious about silence and non-happenings: how can these field experiences be interpreted as relevant ethnographic data about old age? After "returning home", I started to consider what old age would look like if it was approached by focusing on the materiality of the care units and the particular silence and stillness that were predominant features in the everyday life of these units. The silence was covert in many aspects of the lives of the residents. Though silence does not mean the absence of agency, it seems that in this particular setting of institutionalised care it both exposed and constructed the stereotypical conceptions regarding old age and very concretely narrowed the experiences of the old people.

The environment of the care units was often filled with silence. Silence became one of the voices. Silence was normalised and accepted in the interactions between the staff and the residents. It appeared in the ways nurses used their voices and ignored the residents while they were in the same space, or in the ways they sometimes dismissed a resident's initiative to interact and did not respond to it. In a sense, the furnishings also illustrated the normalisation of silence. The material world constructs the cultural ideas of what it means to be old in our society and these ideas were also present in the everyday interactions between the staff and the residents. The decor constructed a kind of scenery, a staging: some of the closets were empty, the shelves held only a few objects and there were photographs whose purpose was unclear: the photos did not really communicate anything about or to the residents. In addition, the paintings and drawings, for example, referred to (past) sexuality as one central aspect of the old people's lives, while at the same time connecting old people with childhood and children.

Thus, in the care unit, silence was covert in many interwoven ways in constructing the conceptions of old age and gender. It was actualised in practices, interactions, material culture and views that stressed that old people were similar to each other. Though the residents (here the focus has been on men) challenged these practices and sometimes deviated from expectations, this was challenging partly because of the obvious structural power relations in the institutionalised care unit where the residents were highly dependent on the staff. In different ways, silence becomes a central feature of experiencing old age; in many aspects, old people are treated as something other than full subjects or adults with individual wishes and characteristics.

These silences (emptiness, characteristics of material objects, the regulation of voice, non-reciprocal interactions, and a lack of autonomous subjectivity) can be interpreted as representing the cultural stereotypical conception of the category of the old, and how old people are connected to the lack of autonomy, individuality and the opportunity to choose. In addition, these silences illuminate how the old are culturally connected to the past, and thus how these silences and silencing practices have become common and acceptable.

In the context of institutionalised care, silence (in its many aspects) becomes a cultural character of the narrative of old age represented and produced in different practices in residential care homes. However, for the elderly concrete silence and being in one's own peace also had positive meanings and offered a way to construct agency. In the analysis of how small stories construct identity, the emphasis is on variation, inconsistencies, contradictions, moments of tension and the subject's constant navigation between different versions of self-hood in local contexts. Constructions of identities are dialogical and relational (Bamberg & Georgakopoulou 2008: 15–16). The fragments of identities presented in this article are highly subjective: in different contexts, men would tell different stories. In addition, though there are some similarities among men living in these institutions, this analysis shows evidence of variation: the male residents experience and interpret their past and present lives in very different ways. In this article, my focus has been on silence, with its different practices, meanings and implications. The cultural narrative about old age and silence includes conceptions where old people are infantilised and not treated as competent individuals: they can be ignored since they are no longer autonomous; they cannot decide for themselves. In approaching silence as a narrative about old age, it must be emphasised that it is only partly produced by the elderly themselves, and that silence carries both negative and positive meanings. Silence as a narrative about old age is a cultural narrative that is constructed in different cultural practices: from residents' individual views, to practices and behaviour in the nursing sector, to our understanding of what it means to become old and how we assume old people act.

Notes

1 The theory of "third age" was introduced by Peter Laslett in the 1980s. Since then it has been widely criticised; for instance, it does not consider how social differences affect experiences of ageing (see Jyrkämä 2013: 89–114).

2 The article is part of my post-doctoral research ("We're still men anyway or what's left of it: Interpretations of sexuality and gender in the narratives of old men"). The data consists of interviews with 39 men and participant observation. The men's ages range from 71 to 95

years, representing both the "third" and the "fourth" ages (Gilleard & Higgs 2000). All the men who took part in this study are Finnish men with Finnish as their mother tongue. Though they are similar in this sense, their backgrounds vary and their circumstances are different, for instance, in regard to their family situations, social relations, education, sexual orientations, religiousness, economic situations, social class, housing and health. In this article, I concentrate on a very specific part of my data, which is men in elderly care units.

3 Names of the institutions and people are pseudonyms in order to maintain anonymity.

References

Alftberg, Åsa 2010: The Practice of Ageing: The Experience of Being Old and the Significance of Bodies, Things and Places. *Ethnologia Scandinavica* 40, 43–51.

Alftberg, Åsa 2012: *Vad är det att åldras? En etnologisk studie av åldrande, kropp och materialitet.* Lund: Lund University.

Bamberg, Michael & Alexandra Georgakopoulou 2008: Small Stories as a New Perspective in Narrative and Identity Analysis. *Text & Talk* 28:3, 377–396.

Barad, Karen 2007: *Meeting the Universe Halfway: Quantum Physics and the Entanglement of Matter and Meaning.* Durham: Duke University Press.

de Beauvoir, Simone (1970)1992: *Vanhuus.* Helsinki: Gummerus. (First published in France 1970.)

Brickell, Katherine 2011: 'Mapping' and 'Doing' Critical Geographies of Home. *Progress in Human Geography* 36:2, 225–244.

Butler, Judith 1993: *Bodies that Matter: On the Discursive Limits of "Sex".* New York: Routledge.

Butler, Judith (1990)1999: *Gender Trouble: Feminism and the Subversion of Identity.* New York: Routledge.

Calasanti, Toni & Neil King 2005: Firming the Floppy Penis: Age, Class, and Gender Relations in the Lives of Old Men. *Men and Masculinities* 8:1, 3–23.

Calasanti, Toni & Neil King 2011: A Feminist Lens of the Third Age: Refining the Framework. In: Dawn C. Carr & Kathrin Komp (eds.), *Gerontology in the Era of the Third Age.* New York: Springer Publishing Company, pp. 67–85.

Calasanti, Toni & Kathleen Slevin 2006: Introduction. In: Toni Calasanti & Kathleen Slevin (eds.), *Age Matters: Realigning Feminist Thinking.* New York: Routledge, pp. 1–17.

Ehn, Billy & Orvar Löfgren 1982: *Kulturanalys: Ett etnologiskt perspektiv.* Lund: Liber förlag.

Ferrer, Mariné Julio 1981: *I väntan på döden.* Stockholm: Akademilitteratur.

Fine, Elizabeth C. & Jean Haskell Speer (eds.) 1992: *Performance, Culture and Identity.* Westport: Praeger.

Fivush, Robyn 2010: Speaking Silence: The Social Construction of Silence in Autobiographical and Cultural Narratives. *Memory* 18:2, 88–98.

Georgakopoulou, Alexandra 2006: Thinking Big with Small Stories in Narrative and Identity Analysis. *Narrative Inquiry* 16:1, 122–130.

Gergen, Kenneth J. 1999: *An Invitation to Social Construction.* London: Sage Publications.

Gilleard, Chris & Paul Higgs 2000: *Cultures of Ageing: Self, Citizen and the Body.* Essex: Prentice Hall.

Goffman, Erving (1961)1969: *Asylums: Essays on the Social Situation of Mental Patients and Other Inmates.* Chicago: Aldine.

Hägg, Samuli 2010: Narratologisten käsitteiden soveltaminen kulttuurintutkimuksessa. In: Jyrki Pöysä, Helmi Järviluoma & Sinikka Vakimo (eds.), *Vaeltavat metodit.* Joensuu: Suomen Kansantietouden Tutkijain Seura, pp. 117–137.

Hazan, Haim 2000: The Cultural Trap: The Language of Images. In: Jaber F. Gubrium & James A. Holstein (eds.), *Aging and Everyday Life.* Oxford: Blackwell Publishing, pp. 15–18.

Holstein, Martha 2011: Cultural Ideas, Ethics, and Agelessness: A Critical Perspective on the Third Age. In: Dawn C. Carr & Kathrin Komp (eds.), *Gerontology in the Era of the Third Age.* New York: Springer Publishing Company, pp. 225–243.

Honkasalo, Marja-Leena 2006: "Aika aikaa kutakin". Naisnäkökulmia toistoon ja toimijuuteen. In: Tarja Kupiainen & Sinikka Vakimo (eds.), *Välimatkoilla: Kirjoituksia etnisyydestä, kulttuurista ja sukupuolesta.* Joensuu: Suomen Kansantietouden Tutkijain Seura, pp. 103–121.

Honko, Lauri 2000: Thick Corpus and Organic Variation. In: Lauri Honko (ed.), *Thick Corpus, Organic Variation and Textuality in Oral Tradition.* Studia Fennica Folkloristica 7. Helsinki: Suomalaisen Kirjallisuuden Seura, pp. 3–28.

Jyrkämä, Jyrki 2013: Kolmas ikä, sukupuoli ja toimijuus. In: Hanna Ojala & Ilkka Pietilä (eds.), *Miehistä puhetta: Miehet, ikääntyminen ja vanhenemisen kulttuuriset mallit.* Tampere: Tampere University Press, pp. 89–114.

King, Neil & Toni Calasanti 2006: Empowering the Old: Critical Gerontology and Anti-Aging in a Global Context. In: Jan Baars, Dale Dannefer, Chris Phillipson & Alan Walker (eds.), *Aging, Globalization and Inequality: The New Critical Gerontology.* New York: Baywood Publishing Company, pp. 139–157.

Kirk, Henning 1995: *Da aldermen blev en diagnose: Konstruktionen af kategorien "alderdom" i 1800-tals lægelitteratur: En medicinsk-idehistorisk analyse.* Copenhagen: Munksgaard.

Lämsä, Riikka 2013: *Potilaskertomus – Etnografia potiluudesta sairaalaosaston käytännöissä.* Helsinki: National Institute for Health and Welfare.

Lassen, Aske Juul 2014: Biilliards, Rhythms, Collectives: Billiards at a Danish Activity Center as a Culturally Specific Form of Active Ageing. *Ethnologia Europaea: Journal of European Ethnology* 44:1, 57–74.

Lundin, Susanne 2007: Gamla kroppar och nya tekniker. In: Lars-Eric Jönsson & Susanne Lundin (eds.), *Åldrandets betydelser*. Lund: Studentlitteratur, pp. 175–200.

Magnússon, Finnur 1996: *Janusansiktet: Vård och vardag på ett sjukhem*. Stockholm: Carlssons.

Morris, David 1996: Voice, Genre, and Moral Community. *Daedalus* 125:1, 25–45.

Nikander, Pirjo 2002: *Age in Action: Membership Work and Stage of Life Categories in Talk*. Helsinki: Academia Scientiarum Fennica.

Ojala, Hanna 2011: *Opiskelemassa tavallaan: Vanhat naiset ikäihmisten yliopistossa*. Tampere: Tampere University Press.

Ojanen, Karoliina 2014: Autettavasti mies? Mieheyksien rakentuminen ja avun pyytäminen laitoshoidossa. *Gerontologia* 28:1, 16–29.

Palola, Elina & Karjalainen, Vappu (eds.) 2011: *Sosiaalipolitiikka – hukassa vai uuden jäljillä?* Helsinki: THL.

Peltonen, Ulla-Maija 1996: *Punakapinan muistot: Tutkimus työväen muistelukerronnan muotoutumisesta vuoden 1918 jälkeen*. Suomalaisen Kirjallisuuden Seuran toimituksia 657. Helsinki: Suomalaisen Kirjallisuuden Seura.

Pietilä, Ilkka & Hanna Ojala 2011: Acting Age in the Context of Health: Middle-Aged Working-Class Men Talking about Bodies and Aging. *Journal of Aging Studies* 25:4, 380–389.

Ronström, Ove 1998: Pigga pensionärer och populärkultur. In: Owe Ronström (ed.), *Pigga pensionärer och populärkultur*. Stockholm: Carlssons bokförlag, pp. 1–25.

Salari, Sonia 2002: Intergenerational Partnerships in Adult Day Centers: Importance of Age-Appropriate Environments and Behaviors. *The Gerontologist* 42:3, 321–333.

Sandberg, Linn 2011: *Getting Intimate: A Feminist Analysis of Old Age, Masculinity and Sexuality*. Linköping: Linköping University Press.

Shuman, Amy 2005: *Other People's Stories: Entitlement Claims and the Critique of Empathy*. Urbana: University of Illinois Press.

Sihto, Matti 2013: Työllisyys- ja aktivointipolitiikan tulevaisuudennäkymiä. In: Vappu Karjalainen & Elsa Keskitalo (eds.), *Kaikki työuralle! Työttömien aktiivipolitiikkaa Suomessa*. Helsinki: THL, pp. 190–206.

Slevin, Kathleen 2006: The Embodied Experiences of Old Lesbians. In: Toni Calasanti & Kathleen Slevin (eds.), *Age Matters: Realigning Feminist Thinking*. New York: Routledge, pp. 247–268.

Slevin, Kathleen & Thomas Linneman 2009: Old Gay Men's Bodies and Masculinities. *Men and Masculinities* 12:4, 483–507.

Springer, Kristen W. & Dawne M. Mouzon 2011: "Macho Men" and Preventive Health Care: Implications for Older Men in Different Social Classes. *Journal of Health and Social Behaviour* 52:2, 212–227.

Townsend, Peter 1962: *The Last Refuge: A Survey of Residential Institutions and Homes for the Aged in England and Wales*. London: Routledge & Kegan Paul.

Turner, Victor 1974: *Dramas, Fields, and Metaphors: Symbolic Action in Human Society*. Ithaca: Cornell University Press.

Karoliina Ojanen is a researcher at the University of Helsinki. Her research interests include anthropological folklore studies, ethnographic fieldwork and knowledge production, and issues related to age and gender. In her earlier work, she examined girlhood, especially girl cultures and gender traditions in horse-riding stables in Finland.
(karoliina.ojanen@helsinki.fi)

SILENCING AND AMPLIFYING ETHNICITY IN ESTONIA
An Ethnographic Account from Tallinn

Elo-Hanna Seljamaa, University of Tartu

Drawing on long-term ethnographic fieldwork in the ethnically divided capital of Estonia, this article[1] suggests that the tacit norm of reciprocity and neighbourliness in Tallinn is to silence rather than amplify ethnicity. Silencing ethnicity is a continuous, context-dependent interactional process that includes linguistic strategies, as well as spatial orderings. The article discusses how residents of Tallinn negotiate and sustain distinctions between "Estonian" and "Russian" spheres by replicating particular trajectories and ways of doing things on a day-to-day basis. The ensuing separateness of Estonians and Russian-speakers is part of the local culture more than an expression of antagonism, though the two are not mutually exclusive. The article also reflects on the (im)possibilities of studying ethnic interactions at home.

Keywords: Estonia, Russians-speakers, ethnic interactions, everyday multiculturalism, ethnography

Caught Between Silenced and Amplified Ethnicity

Exploring the conditions and modes of recognition and contestation in multi-ethnic Tallinn, this article aims to contribute to a growing body of literature on the reception and performance of difference in quotidian urban life.[2] It also discusses meanings attached to ethnicity in a small post-Soviet nation-state with a considerably large Russian minority population as well as methodological challenges posed by tacit local rules of cohabitation, embodied by the native researcher belonging to the ethnic minority.

Between January 2010 and June 2011, I carried out ethnographic fieldwork in Tallinn for my disserta-tion on ethnic interactions, nationalism and integration in post-Soviet Estonia (Seljamaa 2012). Eighteen months of ethnographic fieldwork provided me with opportunities to interact with people representing different generations, diverse ethnic, linguistic and educational backgrounds, political views and levels of engagement in social affairs, all of which attested to the internal heterogeneity of the "Russian-speaking population" in Tallinn. The main methods for creating data were participant observation and interviewing.[3] In many cases, I used interviews to complement observational data and to follow up on particular issues. I found this approach to be particularly useful for interviewing people who were accustomed to speaking on behalf of minority groups, various institutions or the Estonian state, and consequently seemed to be giving well-rehearsed, politically correct answers that spoke little to their actual experiences and concerns. They were telling me what they expected me to hear, turning the interview into a ritual encounter that aimed to uphold a particular version of reality, while suppressing others.

One of the last interviews I conducted before returning to my university in the United States followed a similar pattern, at least to begin with. The interviewee was Maria, a Russian woman in her fifties. Maria was born and raised in Estonia and had been living in Tallinn for a long time. I interviewed her in her capacity as a representative of a Russian cultural organisation. This was our first personal encounter, though I had been to several concerts organised by her group. We communicated in Russian, starting out by talking about the association she was working for and about Russian culture in Estonia. Our topics became more personal and the tone of our conversation more dialogic towards the end of the interview. I asked Maria where in Estonia she was from, she responded, and continued by asking me about my reasons for studying ethnic interactions. Upon my mentioning the word "integration", Maria launched into a monologue about the "indecent" amount of attention given to ethnicity and ethnic differences in contemporary Estonia, blaming it on integration policy pursued by the Estonian state:

M: Integration has political motives. Because people who lived together and never thought that they had any problems started to live separately and understood that there was a problem. […] I was born here [in Estonia] and went to school and I never knew that there was such a thing as nationality/ethnicity [*национальность – natsionalnost*]. I found out about it only when I graduated from school. It wasn't that I didn't know. I knew what different languages sounded like […] But in the circle where I lived, only when I graduated from school did I realise that there were Estonians, Jews, Russians […] It was never declared. Nobody ever talked about it. It was indecent [*неприлично – neprilichno*]. […] There was a name and there was a person.

Maria argued in the same breath that what she saw as the foregrounding and commercialisation of ethnicity was symptomatic of a general loss of ethical norms and values in contemporary Estonia. She explained it by means of two different concepts of shame in the Russian language, an inner and external sense of shame:

Russians have two such concepts [of shame]: *styd* [*стыд*] and *sram* [*срам*]. […] *Sram* is an external concept [of shame]. For example, when you look bad in front of other people. But *styd* is an internal concept [of shame]. And when this internal concept ceased to exist, that something is *stydno* [shameful], and when [*natsionalnost*] became… a form of merchandise. *Natsionalnost* became a marketable good… [This is] madly *stydno*. What was earlier regarded as sacred, closed, no matter whether it had to do with physiology, love, something else, recognition of *natsionalnost*. It was a sacred, an inner thing. […] It used to be that nobody pointed a finger at you, that you were a Russian or an Estonian, we'll remove you or beat you. This was indecent. But now it is a normal thing: "We are national minorities! We are this and that!" All of a sudden it became a norm […]

In order to reiterate the defining importance of an inner sense of shame for humans, Maria concluded her statement by reverting to a children's rhyme about differences between animals and human beings, thereby equating the inability to remain silent to public defecation:

In my childhood, there was a saying: "It is good to be a cat, it is good to be a dog, I can pee where I want and I can poop where I want." But this is really characteristic of cats, not human beings. The human being has to distinguish himself [sic!] from animals by having styd [an inner sense of shame] and some sort of moral criteria. He must understand that it is not decent and good to talk about certain things. (June 13, 2011)

Maria's heartfelt and eloquent monologue pinpointed the intertwined paradoxes that had puzzled me most during my fieldwork in Tallinn. Representatives of ethnic minorities were encouraged to establish "their own" cultural associations and to take up their distinctive cultures as hobbies, yet discouraged from taking agency in shaping the Estonian society as *representatives of minorities*. Moreover, I noticed that Estonia likes to present itself as a home for over a hundred ethnicities, but this has the effect of downplaying the proportion of Russians, who make up a quarter of Estonia's population of 1.3 million. The share of Ukrainians, the second-biggest minority, is two percent and that of Belarussians, the third minority in terms of size, one percent of Estonia's permanent residents (Estonia.eu. Estonia at a Glance).

Maria's conviction that nationality/ethnicity should not belong to the verbal realm serves as the starting point for the following analysis of silencing and amplifying ethnicity in Tallinn. The focus of the article is on silence and silencing. Drawing on ethnographic fieldwork data, I discuss linguistic and other means used by residents of Tallinn to negotiate, sidestep and neutralise ethnicity and ethnic connotations in ways that bespeak and produce mutual recognition between Estonians and Russian-speakers[4] and facilitate daily co-existence, while maintaining their separateness. I describe this quotidian practice as *silencing ethnicity*, contrasting it with occasions when the ethnic framework is evoked and foregrounded, *amplified*. Amplifying ethnicity in daily communication may indicate conflict, but it also occurs in the context of what John Nagle (2009) has called "state-sponsored multiculturalism". In Estonia, state-sponsored multiculturalism finds its most characteristic expression in staged performances of ethnic particularity.

The analytical distinction between silencing and amplifying ethnicity emerges from fieldwork and this article is also an auto-ethnographic reflection on my experience of studying ethnicity in my native Tallinn. I realised in hindsight how Maria's somewhat attacking questions about my motivation for studying ethnic interactions and integration resonated with the hesitancy and anxiety I had so often experienced when trying to make contact with Rus-

sian-speakers in Tallinn or when asking them about ethnicity or matters that could be interpreted in ethnic terms. I knew – by virtue of having been brought up in Tallinn in the 1980s and 1990s – that by doing so, I was not acting in accordance with what is regarded as normal in Tallinn for an Estonian woman of my age. For example, I was aware that the questions I was asking or my very presence in particular places could be conceived of as a provocation or just odd in an alienating way. My broken Russian sufficed to conjure up my own ethnicity and that of my interlocutors. I could not help becoming the shameless animal peeing and defecating all over the place, breaching the norm that first comes the person and only later his or her ethnicity, if the latter issue has to be dealt with at all.

At the same time, it also dawned on me that my fears and sense of uneasiness, on the one hand, and the surprised and perplexed looks I was receiving in the field, on the other, pointed to a common ground, to the existence of tacit and embodied knowledge – "social habit-memory" (Connerton 1989) – shared by Tallinn's Estonians and Russian-speakers. Polemicising with Rogers Brubaker and others who call for indirect strategies for approaching ethnicity (Brubaker et al. 2006), I argue that ethnographers often cannot avoid contributing to the construction of ethnicity in the field, not least because they cannot shed their personal (ethnic) histories. These, in turn, are inseparable from continuous interplays between larger cultural, political, economic and other factors.

I am furthermore interested in the relationships between silence and agency and, in particular, the silencing of Estonian Russian-speakers in the context of Estonian-Russian relations. Russians and the Russian language occupied a central, unmarked and ubiquitous position in the Soviet system and it is questionable whether Volga Germans, Jews, Ingrian Finns or representatives of other non-Russian groups deemed "suspicious" by the Soviet regime would agree with Maria's claim that nationality only came to matter after the collapse of the Soviet Union (see Pihla Maria Siim in this issue). However, as I aim to show, such statements can be interpreted in terms of damaged reciprocity between the nation-state and minorities in the aftermath of drastic social changes.

The Tallinn of Ethnic Nationalities

Tallinn occupies an exceptional position in Estonia, due to both its size and the ethnic and linguistic make-up of its population. Over 430,000 people, or nearly one third of Estonia's residents, live in the capital. It is also the only major town where the proportion of Russian-speakers (45.8 percent) is roughly equal to that of native speakers of Estonian (50.9 percent) (Kuulpak 2015: 28). While Russophones tend to live in urban areas, in most other places in Estonia they are either clearly in the minority or constitute the majority.

Estonia's current ethnic composition took shape in the course of the Soviet era (1944–1991), when several hundred thousand people from various parts of the Soviet Union moved to and through Estonia. Most of these newcomers settled in the capital, in railway towns or in the rapidly growing north-eastern industrial centres. Many came with the military. Two peaks of immigration were in the 1950s and 1970s, with the geographical scope of countries of origin broadening over time: the newcomers of the first decades were mostly from the Russian SSR and European parts of the Soviet Union, while the late 1960s saw an increase in migration from the Volga region, Caucasus and Central Asia (Sakkeus 1999: 320; cf. Pettai & Pettai 2015: 332).

There was a chronic housing shortage, addressed by erecting Soviet-style blocks of flats on the fringes of older neighbourhoods. The most notorious of these new districts, Lasnamäe, was built on a flat limestone plateau above the older parts of Tallinn. Its construction began in the late 1970s and continued until the very end of the Soviet era, by which time Estonians had come to see it as an embodiment of the Soviet Russification policy. "Stopping Lasnamäe", as a popular song of the 1980s' national movement demanded, became a metaphor for putting an end to the Soviet rule, as well as to the influx of people from other parts of the Soviet Union. Yet only in 1990 did outmigration exceed immigration

for the first time (Hallik 2010: 10). It has been estimated that between 110,000 and 113,000 individuals of "non-Estonian nationality" left Estonia between 1990 and 2008, most of them in 1992–1993 (ibid.; Estonia.eu. Citizenship).

To make sense of the term "non-Estonian" (*mitte-eestlane*), one needs to know that more often than not, the noun "Estonian" (*eestlane*) does not refer to citizenship, but ethnic descent. The Estonian language lacks a widely used and generally accepted word to signify all residents of Estonia irrespective of their ethnicity. There is the word *eestimaalane*, which stresses connection to the Estonian territory rather than blood relations yet, for the time being, it serves as a euphemism for "non-Estonian". Even the authoritative online dictionary of the Institute of Estonian Language uses the following sentence to exemplify the meaning and usage of the word *eestimaalane*: "S/he was a resident of Estonia, but not Estonian" *("Ta oli küll eestimaalane, kuid mitte eestlane")* (EKSS). The prospect of having to detach nationality from ethnicity still seems to be inconceivable or unacceptable, something that is not to be talked about in the Estonian language.

The tendency to regard ethnicity and nationality as synonyms coincides with the Soviet nationalities policies, which treated nationality (in Estonian *rahvus*, in Russian национальность [*natsionalnost*]) as a category one was born into. Inherited from parents, nationality was attached to ancestral territory and language, but detached from one's actual place of birth or residency and sometimes even from one's ethnic self-identification. This particular notion of nationality as ethnicity is shared by most people in Estonia and constitutes a tacit starting point for the Estonian integration policy (Seljamaa 2013; see also Malloy 2009; Agarin & Regelmann 2011; Kuutma, Seljamaa & Västrik 2012; contributions to Cordell, Agarin & Osipov 2013).

For nearly two decades, the Estonian integration policy has propagated the idea of a multicultural Estonia and emphasised the importance of providing various ethnicities/nationalities living in Estonia with opportunities to preserve and develop "their own" cultures (Seljamaa 2013). Devising a national strategy for integrating minorities and the Russian-speaking population in particular was one of the preconditions for Estonia's accession into the European Union and NATO, not least because West European states feared the spread of inter-ethnic violence from Yugoslavia across post-communist Europe (see e.g. Cordell 2013). The number of non-profit associations representing minorities rocketed only after the Estonian state started to allocate funds to projects proposed by cultural associations of national minorities, which in turn depended significantly on the availability of resources allocated by the European Union and other foreign sponsors. As of March 2016, Russians had 98 such organisations, Ukrainians 31 and Belarusians 18, but there were also multiple associations representing Greeks, Koreans, Angolans and others, whose numbers are miniscule (Etnoweb.ee). Maria's criticism that post-Soviet Estonia was suffering from an overexposure to nationality ("We are national minorities! We are this and that!") could be interpreted as a commentary on this system that confines the agency of minority actors to artistic performances of ethno-cultural distinctiveness and turns ethnicity into a merchandise.

(Un)tellable Narratives and Lack of Agency

The emic nationality/ethnicity category reinforces groupist thinking and narratives that pose challenges for scholars such as myself who are anxious to avoid conflating the study and practice of nationalism (cf. Brubaker 1996). It has been common in Estonia to conceive of the Soviet era in terms of rupture and trauma, and to describe the restoration of independence as a return from abnormality to normality – meaning the West.[5] Conceptualising the Soviet era, a period of over 40 decades, in terms of rupture and trauma has framed Estonians as passive victims of the occupation regime, while framing as untellable experiences and events that contradict this nationalist narrative of victimhood.

The category of an Estonian communist, for example, is recognised, but excluded as something that should not have happened (cf. Shuman 2005: 19). The ethnologist Ene Kõresaar (2005) has extensively studied life stories written by Estonians born be-

tween the world wars. She describes how she and her colleagues were bewildered and alienated by a life story that was submitted to them in 1994 because it treated the establishment of Soviet power not in negative, but in positive terms: not as a rupture but as a new beginning. Kõresaar's argument that such "Soviet biographies" should be regarded "as part of Estonians' collective memory" (ibid.: 150) points to tensions between different ideas about what should or should not be talked about, as well as to the role of scholars as creators, supporters and breakers of silences that shape national(ist) narratives.

Repertoires of cultural analysts discussing Estonians' relationship to the Soviet regime and the Soviet era have broadened gradually to include topics such as Estonians' collaboration with and accommodation to the Soviet power and way of life, as well as other issues that cast doubt on the possibility of a total rupture and the feasibility of rupture as an analytic category (e.g. Annus 2012; Jaago 2014; Jõesalu 2005; Kapper 2016; Laanes 2009).[6] "Carving conventional 'periods' out of their historical surroundings is an artificial act and, as such, far from inevitable" (Zerubavel 2003: 95).

Soviet-era settlers, however, remain an understudied – untold – subject. Discourse on them appears to be predetermined by the rupture metaphor, which confines Soviet-era newcomers to Estonia and ethnic Estonians to mutually exclusive, yet mutually constitutive subject positions of perpetrators and victims. Within this framework, it is rather difficult *not* to treat Soviet-era settlers as henchmen of the Soviet occupation regime and Estonians as the injured party entitled to a privileged position. There is a recurrent pattern in public discourse of tying together ethnicity, rootedness, and agency in ways that question the right of Soviet-era settlers and their descendants to participate in the shaping of the Estonian society.

In October 2014, Estonia's long-term Minister of Finance reluctantly stepped down after having characterised the Minister of Education and Research as "a son of a settler" (*sisserändaja poeg*) who had no knowledge of what Estonia had been through and who consequently "should use utmost caution" when drawing conclusions about its current problems. The education minister, whose father is Russian and moved to Estonia towards the end of the Soviet era, had argued that Estonia's high emigration and poverty rates could not be blamed on Soviet power and the backwardness it had brought to the country (ERR Uudised). The finance minister's comments confirm Liisa Malkki's (1992) observation that uprootedness is often seen to result in and to be manifested in unacceptable behaviour and a lack of moral values, especially in the context of the nation-state. Some other examples following this pattern will be discussed below.

The (Im)possibility of Transcending Ethnicity

The episode involving ministers demonstrates that while "(c)ategorization is ubiquitous; ethnic categorization is not" (Brubaker et al. 2006: 237). Rogers Brubaker and his various co-authors have proposed the idea of "ethnicity as cognition". Rather than treating ethnicity as a "thing *in* the world" and talking about "ethnic groups", they propose approaching it as "a perspective *on* the world" and exploring when, where and how ethnicity becomes a salient or significant category for making sense of the world (Brubaker, Loveman & Stamatov 2004: 32; Brubaker et al. 2006: 169).

The book by Brubaker, Feischmidt, Fox and Grancea (2006) on nationalist politics and everyday ethnicity in the Hungarian/Romanian town of Kolozsvár/Cluj in Transylvania is the outcome of long-term quantitative and qualitative research, including open-ended and targeted interviews, group discussions and ethnographic discussions. The authors have described their approach as an indirect research strategy that avoided "asking directly about ethnicity, or signalling a special interest in ethnicity" (Brubaker et al. 2006: 15). Because ethnicity is always only one among many "interpretative frames", "(e)thnicized ways of experiencing and interpreting the social world can only be studied alongside a range of alternative, non-ethnicized ways of seeing and being" (ibid.).

The idea – or ideal – of avoiding contributions to the reproduction of ethnicity comes across as a dubious or hypocritical starting point to the extent that it implies that scholars are capable of detaching themselves from the flow of reification and essentialism that is everyday life (cf. Herzfeld 2005: 26). Brubaker and his colleagues do not reflect upon the successfulness or implications of their indirect research strategy: whether it enabled them – collectively as well as individually – to minimise their contribution to the (re)production and reification of identity in the field and at what cost. I wish they had done so because following their lead in Tallinn turned out to be easier said than done. For an ethnographer working at home, there seemed to be no way of avoiding contributions to the emergence and construction of ethnicity in the field.

When I first began fieldwork, I thought rather naively that being from Tallinn would make things easier for me. For example, in addition to knowing my way around, I would be familiar with local communicative practices and other norms of behaviour and would not have to learn them the hard way. Little did I know that in order to learn anything new in and about Tallinn, I had to become aware of what had been instilled in me over the decades, and go beyond ethnic and other borders I had been socialised to reproduce. Fieldwork took me, literally, to places I knew to be "Russian" by virtue of having been born and raised in Tallinn in an Estonian family. People I encountered in these places tended to see me as Estonian and sometimes demanded an explanation for my presence.

Occasions such as this one seemed to offer glimpses into Tallinners' social habit-memory, which is acquired by "living with people who habitually behave in a certain manner" (Connerton 1989: 30). Paul Connerton describes social habits as "legitimating performances" because their meaning "rests upon others' conventional expectations such that it must be interpretable as a socially legitimate (or illegitimate) performance" (ibid.: 35). I had to go against the grain of what was habitual.

My Estonian Tallinn

Estonia inherited from the Soviet regime a linguistically segregated educational system, with Estonian- and Russian-language kindergartens and schools operating in different facilities and teaching different curricula. Growing up in Tallinn in the 1980s, I went to an Estonian kindergarten, and later to an Estonian school, and had hardly any contacts with Russian-speakers. We lived in an older part of Tallinn, which, unlike Lasnamäe, was not an area used to accommodate the steady stream of settlers from other parts of the Soviet Union. Some of our neighbours were Russian, but we did not interact, though this was probably for class reasons rather than due to ethnicity. My parents socialised mostly with Estonian artists and intellectuals, many of whom were part of the Soviet counter-culture.

I went to the same school and studied with more or less the same people for 11 years. As far as I know, only one of my classmates came from a mixed family, but her father lived in Russia much of the time and she socialised with Estonians despite being fluent in Russian. Most of us had a much more complicated relationship to the Russian language. Like so many other Estonians of my generation, I started learning Russian in kindergarten and continued in school but never put it into practice – apart from the sentence *Ya ne govoryu po-russki* or "I don't speak Russian." I have distinct memories of rehearsing and using this phrase in the late 1980s in self-defence against Russian-speaking salespeople. Once a university student, I enrolled in yet another mandatory Russian course for beginners – and in another course in graduate school in the United States, but this time voluntarily.

Leaving aside differences between the Estonian and Russian languages and teaching methods (we learned to quote Pushkin by heart without having acquired the very basics of grammar first), our generation's slow progress in learning Russian must have reflected a broader state of mind in the Estonian society in the late 1980s and 1990s as well as the circumstances which made it possible for Estonians and Russian-speakers to live side by side with little or no interaction. For example, the art school I attended in the mid-1990s had separate Estonian- and Russian-language groups and we never communicated, even though we shared some of the teachers. Our separateness seemed to be a matter of habit and custom and could not be explained by language alone.

Towards the end of the 1990s, while taking English classes in a language school in Tallinn, I came across Russophone teenagers who were fluent in Estonian due to attending Estonian-language schools but whose parents spoke very little or no Estonian. By that time, an increasing number of Russian-language families had recognised the instrumental value of Estonian and had adopted the strategy of educating their offspring in Estonian (Vihalemm 1999). The percentage of Estonians who claim a command of Russian, however, is steadily falling (Tammaru 2016). Children growing up in Tallinn today, as well as their parents, have very different opportunities and challenges: my currently two-year-old daughter has the option of joining a language immersion kindergarten where Russian-speakers are taught Estonian and Estonian-speakers Russian. This is a huge change, though most kindergartens continue to use either Estonian or Russian.

In the course of my fieldwork, I encountered people of my age or older whose childhood, youth and much of their adulthood in Tallinn had been as Russian-centred as mine had been Estonian-centred. Some of them spoke very little or no Estonian despite having lived in Estonia their entire life or at least for decades. However, I also got to know many younger people who were fluent in both languages, often due to having attended Estonian-language schools. Thus, the experience of living side by side without much interaction is neither universal nor idiosyncratic. A lot of negotiation and planning takes place in Tallinn every day to maintain a co-existence that does not foreground ethnicity as a source of conflict.

To the extent that ethnographic knowledge is produced in the process of sharing time and conversation between the ethnographer and her interlocutors (Fabian 1990), it is inevitably shaped by individuals' subjective choices. In the words of James Fernandez, ethnography's "emphasis on extensive and enduring participatory and open ended interaction and extended life type consultation means that not all informants can be listened to and many must, in effect remain silent in the ensuing ethnographic account"

(Fernandez 2006: 162). He continues: "While we must assume the realist position that events, beliefs, entities, and so on exist independently of ourselves, we must also assume that we can not know them directly but must construe them" (ibid.).

For me, Lasnamäe with its up to 70 percent Russophone population (Kuulpak 2015: 25) seemed like an obvious starting point for an ethnographic study on ethnic interactions in post-Soviet Estonia. I began fieldwork by focusing on daily happenings and markers on ethnicity in this district and establishing contact with a circle of friends living there. At the same time, I started observing the performances and activities of various cultural associations of national minorities and interviewing their more active members. From fall 2010 until the end of my fieldwork in June 2011, I volunteered for and socialised with one particular organisation that united politically and socially active Russophone youths of diverse ethnic backgrounds. In addition, I participated in academic and other conferences and seminars that dealt with integration, cultural diversity and nationalism, as well as in events and ceremonies organised on the occasion of various official and vernacular holidays (e.g. Independence Day parades, Victory Day [May 9] and Shrovetide celebrations, Christmas and New Year concerts, Easter services in Orthodox churches, events organised on the occasion of the Day of Nationalities and Native Language Day, various annual festivals). Long-term systematic involvement in and exposure to these different public, semi-public and private venues of inter- and intra-ethnic interactions helped me to recognise certain recurring situations, arguments and patterns of behaviour.

Verbally Silenced Ethnicity

Language serves as the most obvious, visible and audible marker of ethnicity in Tallinn. Though Estonian is the sole official language, in reality Tallinn is bilingual and there are even neighbourhoods where Russian is the default language. While one is supposed to be able to use Estonian in all businesses and organisations, in practice the common language needs to be negotiated and agreed upon on a case-by-case basis. This holds particularly true for interactions that take place in residential areas with a significant Russian-speaking population, such as Lasnamäe.

In urban decor, the co-existence of official rules and vernacular practices is manifested in bilingual signs, among other markers. Looking for visual cues for ethnicity in Lasnamäe, I was particularly intrigued by signs on the doors of small shops and kiosks that combined typed Estonian-language information and handwritten Russian-language information. Estonian-language information about opening hours had been typed, printed out and displayed, as required by the Estonian Language Act. However, this formal presentation in Estonian had been complemented by means of handwritten information in Russian, so that next to the typed *avatud* stood the handwritten *открыто*, both of which mean "open". To the extent that information about opening hours can be comprehended without translation even by those who cannot read the Latin alphabet, the use and display of the Cyrillic script must have conveyed in this context messages of another kind, such as support or preference for the Russian language in an officially Estonian-language environment. The juxtaposition of typed Estonian and handwritten Russian seemed to stress the official status of the former language, on the one hand, and protest against the expulsion of the latter from the public sphere, on the other. As such, it made visible gaps between language policy and practice, between ideals and lived reality (Cook 2006).

Sales clerks in Tallinn supermarkets seemed to be fine-tuned to various non-verbalised cues for customers' linguistic identities. It sometimes happened that when I had Russian-language newspapers in my shopping basket, the cashier would address me in Russian. I observed on countless occasions how customers and sales clerks switched back and forth between Estonian and Russian. An Estonian customer would start out in Estonian, but switch to Russian when the salesperson's response was not quick or clear enough; however, the clerks would not necessarily follow the customer's lead but would continue in Estonian. Consequently, it was not uncommon for Estonian customers to speak Russian and

Russian-speaking clerks to respond in Estonian. At other times, Russian-speaking clerks and customers would speak Estonian among themselves.

The sociologist Triin Vihalemm has argued that Estonians' strategy of switching over to Russian serves the purpose of retaining the "symbolic divergence with regard to Estonian – not letting 'others' speak 'our language'" (Vihalemm 2007: 490; cf. Vihalemm 1999: 26). While this could be the case in certain contexts, ethnographic research in contemporary Tallinn suggests that switching over to Russian can also serve as a means of accommodating the other person and steering clear of evoking ethnicity as a potential source of conflict. This is more of a pragmatic choice and display of neighbourliness rather than a symbolic performance of distinctive identity. In fact, the potential for ethnicity-based tensions and conflicts appears to be greater when, for example, the salesperson is not capable of providing service in Estonian and the customer sticks to Estonian, demanding that the salesperson follow the law and speak the state language.

Approaching potential interviewees and interacting with fieldwork partners involved similar intricate linguistic negotiations. The first couple of months were particularly confusing as I did now know when I was expected to use Estonian and under what circumstances I was to choose Russian. While I did not want people to think or feel that I was being provocative or treating them condescendingly, I could not shed my broken Russian or the baggage of the minority–majority relationship. Whenever possible, I let my interlocutors determine the language of communication. Even so, the fear of making a phone call or writing an email and not knowing whether to use Russian or Estonian was at times paralysing, since choosing the "wrong" language could shut down the line of communication. I suspect that some of my emails went unanswered because I had written them in Estonian. At other times, I would receive a written response that had been composed in careful Estonian and with as few words as possible, as if to minimise the chance of grammatical and spelling mistakes and the ensuing risk of losing face. But at times my efforts to speak Russian were dismissed. I remember calling a Russian actress I wanted to interview and she interrupted me rather impatiently, demanding in fluent Estonian that I switch to Estonian.

Ethnicity could be furthermore silenced and prevented from becoming a problem by means of using Estonian and Russian in parallel. This was particularly evident in settings that brought together people who lived or worked side by side and in all likelihood were interested in reaching a mutual understanding. Every block of flats in Estonia must belong to a non-profit association uniting apartment owners of one or several buildings. Since all of the capital's districts and neighbourhoods are mixed to some degree, apartment associations constitute an important venue of inter-ethnic communication. The association I belong to in Tallinn sends me bilingual messages and our meetings have sometimes lasted longer because everything has been translated from Estonian into Russian and vice versa. I found the same strategy being used in the predominantly Russian-speaking district of Lasnamäe when on a couple of occasions my friends would kindly take me to the meetings of their apartment associations. Using both Estonian and Russian served as a means of taking ethnicity off the agenda and creating a neutral space accessible to all participants.

The same seemed to hold true in more public settings. On one particular occasion, the municipal government of the Lasnamäe district organised an information day for representatives of local apartment associations. While Estonian and Russian were used alternatively most of the time, one of the invited speakers spoke only in Estonian. Several audience members protested immediately. It was clear from their comments that they knew Estonian well enough to be able to follow the presenter. However, they insisted on using both Estonian and Russian. It was by virtue of not deciding for one language or the other that the situation could have been kept neutral and the ethnic connotations of language downplayed. Similar scenes played out at concerts and other events at the Lasnamäe cultural centre, which, as a rule, are bilingual and very often cater to a predominantly Russian-speaking audience.

Russian voices would call out for a translation into Russian, only to be hushed by other Russian voices. Occasions on which communication broke down or was damaged because the tacit expectation of bilingualism was not met illustrate how bilingualism can be a means of achieving mutual recognition.

The situation was different when there were more than two languages to contend with. This was not uncommon at concerts and other events organised by cultural associations of non-Russian national minorities that would use their native language alongside Estonian, that is the state language, and sometimes also Russian. For example, I saw disappointed faces at a Ukrainian concert whose programme alternated between Ukrainian-, Estonian- and English-language performances and speeches, while excluding Russian. Unlike the semi-private meetings of apartment associations, concerts of this kind belong to the public sphere. Organised by cultural associations of national minorities, they are designed to perform the distinctiveness of particular ethnic groups within the context of the democratic, multicultural Estonian nation-state and to reinforce mutual loyalty between minorities and the state.

Spatially Embodied Ethnicity

While language serves as an important means for silencing, amplifying and negotiating ethnicity in Tallinn, it rarely stands alone. Linguistic segregation becomes physical once it is mapped onto districts and buildings and people's daily routes, and it becomes structural once it is linked to greater or lesser mobility. The ability to travel and work abroad is tied to citizenship, which again depends on one's knowledge of the Estonian language. When Estonia restored its independence in 1991, it did not grant Estonian citizenship to Soviet-era settlers and their descendants, at the time roughly a third of the 1.5 million population. In order to be naturalised, these people had to pass a language exam, but most of them had little or no knowledge of the new state language.

Estonian citizenship policies have been said to have had "clear ethno-political motives [...] as well as stark ethno-political consequences": they addressed the dramatic decrease in Estonians' share of the population and cut the majority of Russian-speaking residents "out of the political system" (Pettai & Pettai 2015: 132). Their way back in has been slow and as of today, 6.1 percent of all permanent residents in Estonia remain stateless (Estonia.eu. Citizenship). Unlike citizens of Estonia and other member-states of the European Union, they cannot work in the European country of their choice, but are confined to Estonia and its restricted labour market. Several of my fieldwork partners in Lasnamäe belonged to this category of "people with undetermined citizenship" (ibid.). They were men, spoke hardly any Estonian, had not travelled widely and held manual jobs, meaning that their employment depended heavily on the health of the economy.

Lasnamäe being a residential district, its shops and businesses cater mainly to local residents, whose preferences are guided by their linguistic preferences, among other factors. I once went to get a haircut at a small beauty salon on the ground floor of a tall block of flats. When I sat down in the salon chair and tried to make myself understandable in my broken Russian, the hairdresser asked me, her voice filled with sincere surprise: *Как вы сюда попали?* – "How did you get here?" The hairdresser's question conjured up the invisible, practice-based borders that divide Tallinn into Estonian and Russian places and zones and categorise Lasnamäe as a Russian space. Tallinners sustain these distinctions by replicating particular trajectories and ways of doing things on a day-to-day basis. "The word *routine* is actually the diminutive of route, a small path," as Billy Ehn and Orvar Löfgren point out (Ehn & Löfgren 2010: 81). Ethnicity, like class, "happens on many levels" when "insignificant routines become an effective tool" of reproduction (ibid.: 211; cf. Connerton 1989). In asking me about my choice of hair salon, the hairdresser was also observing and commenting upon these routines. She pointed out to me that I was transgressing and it was our shared acknowledgement of my being in the "wrong" place that enabled her to demand an explanation, even if in a friendly manner, for she was clearly amused by the whole episode.

One time, on February 24, 2010, the Independence

Day of the Republic of Estonia, I was invited to the home of Alla, Andrey and their five-year-old daughter, along with Kostya, one of my key fieldwork partners from Lasnamäe. Both Kostya and Andrey spoke very little Estonian, were stateless and did manual labour. I had first met them at a concert of a Russian punk band in Tallinn in January 2010. I was with a friend of mine and we caught the attention of Kostya and Andrey because, as Andrey put it, "Splean is no Alla Pugacheva, whom Estonians would go to see," Pugacheva being a popular Soviet and Russian musical performer, whose concert in Tallinn in February 2010 was sold out and covered widely in Estonian-language media.

Upon our arrival to their home, Alla and Andrey joked that I was probably armed with secret recording devices. They returned to this joke and brought it to a conclusion towards the end of the evening when I was getting ready to leave, telling me that they had been the ones who had recorded our conversation. In the course of the evening, discussion had turned to politics and Andrey had asked me rather bluntly if I supported the Estonian Reform Party. Andrey was not the first or last Russian-speaker to ask me about my/Estonians' relationship to the Reform Party. In fact, many of them seemed to believe that *all* Estonians voted for the Reform Party and supported Ansip.

Andrus Ansip, at the time of my fieldwork the leader of the liberal Reform Party and Estonian prime minister, had played a key role in the Bronze Soldier crisis. In April 2007, the Estonian government decided to relocate from down-town Tallinn a Soviet-era World War II monument popularly known as "the Bronze Soldier".[7] Erected in 1947, the monument re-emerged in the mid-2000s as the site of Russian-speakers' newly discovered Victory Day celebrations. Observed on May 9, Victory Day celebrates the Soviet/Russian victory over fascism in World War II. Many Estonians, at the same time, had come to regard the monument and activities surrounding it as an anti-Estonian provocation and embodiment of the continuation of Soviet occupation. The polarisation peaked one day in April 2007, when the government began the exhumation of the remains of Red Army soldiers buried on the site of the monument. A large number of Russian-speakers gathered spontaneously at the monument to protest against this action. Later the same evening, this peaceful demonstration spilled over into a violent conflict between the protesters and the police, and gave rise to a wave of looting and acts of vandalism in down-town Tallinn. The statue was consequently relocated to a more secluded part of the capital. Estonian officials and authorities later claimed that the protests had been orchestrated from Moscow, but these charges could not be proven in court. However, this act of externalisation was significant in that it deprived Estonian Russian-speakers of agency, framing them as fifth columnists working for Russia, and Estonians, once again, as victims of Russian aggression (cf. Kaiser 2012).

Andrey had taken part in the demonstration at the Bronze Soldier and was among the more than a thousand persons arrested (Poleshchuk 2009: 9) by the police. While he was telling me about his ordeal, his wife Alla said that she had always been loyal to the Estonian state but wished that Estonians would let go of the past. Most obviously, the Bronze Soldier conflict revolved around "correct" interpretations of the past. By relocating the monument, the government erased from the centre of Tallinn commemorative practices that contradicted Estonia's official history, the insistence on having been occupied rather than liberated by the Soviet Union. Moreover, by means of locating the source of conflict in Russia, Estonian authorities denied the existence of "multiple pasts" (Zerubavel 2003) within the Estonian society and frictions between them.

Yet, April 2007 was not the only topic of conversation that evening at Andrey's and Alla's place. The TV was on and we watched a little bit of the live broadcast from the Independence Day reception hosted by the Estonian president and his wife. Watching this reception appears to be *the* ritual observed by most Estonians on the evening of Independence Day. Though Kostya and Andrey were participating in this ritual, they also seemed to be observing Independence Day from a distance. Kostya asked me how Estonians greeted each other on Independence Day and whether there was a particular wish or phrase used on this occasion. Andrey wanted to know if Estonia's foreign-born president Toomas Hendrik Ilves spoke bad Estonian. While these questions reflected Kostya's and Andrey's distance from the general life of Estonia, their lives were very much grounded in Tallinn and their criticism of the Estonian government sprang from their personal experiences and feelings. They had not been "brainwashed by Russian propaganda," to cite an argument often used by Estonians to dismiss the dissatisfaction of local Russian-speakers.

All of us transgressed our individual boundaries that evening. Alla and Andrey did it by inviting me into their home, and I would not have been sitting in Andrey's and Alla's living room had it not been for my research project. Together we opened up a space where we could discuss conflict-prone topics that focused on ethnicity and relations between Estonians and Russians in Estonia. Their questions – like my own – drew attention to the separateness of Estonians and Russians in Tallinn and, more broadly, to the lack of reciprocity between the state and Russian-speaking residents of Estonia. In this context, our ethnic identities were amplified. Our communication functioned as a magnifying glass, enabling us to scrutinise ourselves, each other and the society we were all part of.

On other occasions, I observed how Kostya and some other fieldwork partners of mine engaged in strategic acts of deconstructing my Estonian-ness. Thus, silencing ethnicity can also work by means of de-essentialisation. Several interviewees attached special significance to the fact that I was writing my dissertation for a foreign university: the Atlantic Ocean seemed to create a neutral space where my interlocutors could be critical of the Estonian state without being confrontational with me. Others asked me about my grandparents and focused on my Finnish roots. The fact that both of my grandfathers had fought in World War II, in the Red Army, was similarly emphasised. While I had little or no emotional connection to most of these pieces of information, the people I socialised and worked with in the field used these details to (re-)define me, at least for the purposes of the given situation, to make me

less of an Estonian. At one time, Kostya introduced me to a friend of his as somebody whose grandfather had fought in the Red Army. To my relief, his friend responded rather dryly "these things happen."

Indecently Loud Ethnicity

This article has so far focused on means of downplaying and negotiating ethnicity as well as on ways of giving it silent recognition. I will now proceed to explore the other end of the continuum: instances in which a person is defined through his or her ethnicity alone: "She is an Estonian. He is Jewish." Pondering Maria's claim that it is indecent to talk about ethnicity, I was reminded of another interviewee, Anna, who made a similar point by telling a story about her extended family. Like Maria, Anna was in her forties–fifties and lived in Tallinn. She was descended from Estonians and Estonian Russians, that is Russians who had been living in Estonia before World War II, and was fluent in Estonian. However, she sympathised very strongly with her Russian ancestors and heritage. She had raised her children in the same vein, while her cousins and their children had grown up identifying as Estonians. According to Anna, they formed a close-knit extended family until the attitudes of her Estonian relatives' began to change in the context of Estonians' national reawakening in the late 1980s:

Anna: But they changed so much, really to the point of becoming unrecognisable; it was truly astonishing. I'll give an example of a radical transformation of this kind, a crazy example, I would say. My older son was four or five years old, I think. It was the very end of the old era and the beginning of the new era. Right then. And one could already feel it. We were again all together at Granny's place, Estonians and Russians. And my boy, he speaks Estonian, maybe not that perfectly, and he has a little accent, but he speaks Estonian. But of course, we grew up more in Russian culture. My cousin's family was also there and his son was a little older than mine. Estonian. And I saw that my child was sitting in the sandbox alone and was looking somehow sad and yet there was this other boy, a little older, but nevertheless. So I went to him and said:

"Listen, Mart, please go and play with him a little bit. He is eager and very active; he wants to communicate and he likes to communicate, so please go to him."

And Mart looked at me and he was… he was around ten or eleven years old at the time. He said: "Now then…"

No, he was even younger, eight or something.

"Now then, why should I play with this little Russian?"

An eight-year old boy. I was about to… my mouth almost dropped open. I couldn't… I didn't know what to say. Actually I just said to him that

"Mart, why do you say such a thing? It doesn't matter who he is, we are all relatives and what difference does it make if he speaks Estonian a little bit, not as perfectly as you do, but he will teach you a little bit of Russian. Come on!"

"No, I don't want to."

But then I went to his dad, to my cousin, who is a very highly educated, well-known person in Estonia. And I said:

"Excuse me but what was this about. A child cannot make up such things."

"Did he really say such a thing?"

"Swear to God."

"You must have gone crazy. He said such a thing? He couldn't have said such a thing."

"How come when he did say it?"

I said… I tried to make it clear to him that he must have heard it at home.

"What's going on in your home; there's something wrong."

"Listen, don't be dramatic; don't take it like this." Something along the lines of "*Sama dura* [in Russian: you are the stupid one here]. Don't make a big deal out of this."

But I already regarded it with alarm. (July 8, 2010)

In this story, one child rejects another one on the basis of ethnicity, which in turn is defined in linguistic terms. The interaction of the boys, that are relatives, shows that in the process of Soviet Union's disinte-

gration, language became thicker than blood in Estonia. As such, this narrative shows the sinister side of the Baltic Singing Revolutions, nonviolent mass protests that began in 1987 and led to the restoration of independence, and contradicts the romanticised notion of Estonians as a "gentle nation singing of love" (cf. Šmidchens 2014).

Anna returned to the topic of inter-ethnic families later, stressing that mixed couples were under immense political pressure in the 1990s. Moreover, she used her extended family and what had happened to it as a model for describing societal changes in post-Soviet Estonia and relationships between Russians and Estonians:

Anna: The point of this whole thing [of the Soviet state] fell apart but the point of this thing was indeed wonderful. Each of us existed in our own culture and also together. This was an ideal model. They can say about this Soviet time whatever they want but this is the way it was; this is the way it was. I cannot see how we could have been Russifying those Estonians of ours. For instance, in giving the example of our family, I am talking about all these cousins of mine […]. They studied in Estonian schools during the Soviet era, and they received an excellent education from the University of Tartu. I don't know that anything was wrong with them. They were Estonians. They were Estonians and nobody was Russifying them. (July 8, 2010)

Anna's personal experiences and reasoning attest to conclusions reached by Uku Lember in his study on Estonian-Russian mixed families. Between 2009 and 2011 Lember conducted around 90 interviews with parents born in 1930–1950 and with children born in 1950–1970. He found, contrary to his expectation, that Soviet-era mixed families were not fraught with cultural and social conflicts. People "lived in a situation where they did not sense in their lives tensions between [Estonian and Russian] cultural worlds" (Lember 2015). Moreover, members of mixed families downplayed friction and used various means to contain, conceptualise and channel ethno-cultural differences (e.g. taking up cooking, folk singing and folk dance). Only in the late 1980s did some of them feel a need to take a clearer stand on political and social issues and to place family relations in the broader societal context. Silence, the absence of perceived problems, could turn into silencing, avoidance of conflicting issues, while an open discussion could lead to estrangement and divorce (ibid.; Lember 2016).

Damaged Reciprocity: The Case of Russian-Language Education

Anna and Maria both described the Soviet system as one characterised by mutual respect and perfect reciprocity between different ethnicities. The current undesirable state of affairs, on the other hand, was blamed on politics. This mode of thinking recalls Michael Herzfeld's concept "structural nostalgia" or the "idea of a time when state intervention was unnecessary for the conduct of a decent social life" (Herzfeld 2005: 147). One of the crucial features of structural nostalgia is that "the object of this rhetorical longing [...] takes the form of a damaged reciprocity": the allegedly decayed virtue longed for "always entails some measure of mutuality, a mutuality that has been, perhaps, irreversibly ruptured by the self-interest of modern times" (ibid.: 149).

The rhetoric of nostalgia obscures inequalities inherent in mutual relationships. As was suggested at the outset, Russian was the unmarked, default and taken-for-granted category in the Soviet Union, which may explain why back then Maria and Anna never experienced ethnicity as an issue. The regime change of 1991 along with its Estonian-centred nationalising citizenship and language policies pushed Russians and Russian-speakers into a marginal position that did not satisfy my interviewees. Maria's and Anna's reliance on the structural nostalgia model suggests that they felt themselves to be objects rather than subjects of politics and were looking for a more reciprocal relationship with the Estonian state.

For example, both women were concerned about the future of Russian-language education in Estonia. This was a hot topic in Estonia at the time of my fieldwork, since starting in fall 2011 Russian-language secondary schools (grades 10–12) were required to teach at least 60 percent of the curriculum in Estonian (see Estonia.eu. Russian-language schools' transition). Similarly to several other Russian-speakers I interviewed, Maria and Anna felt an urge to discuss this topic, bringing it up on their own initiative. They pointed out that partial Estonian-language instruction would have a detrimental effect on the Russian skills of young Russians, who in their estimation already did not know how to "speak Russian beautifully." Both women were furthermore concerned about the prospect of not being able to speak Russian to their grandchildren, about weakening ties between family members and, more broadly, about the continuation of Russian culture in Estonia.

Several younger interlocutors of Slavic descent – individuals leading active and successful lives in the dominant Estonian society – expressed similar fears. However, I also encountered parents who spoke very little or no Estonian, but were proud to have sent their children to Estonian-language schools. Estonian-born Anna referred to such people as *sovetskiye* or "Soviets", emphasising their immigrant background and her own moral superiority. Her argument that the blind loyalty of Soviet-era settlers made it difficult for "Estonian Russians", that is Russians whose roots are in Estonia, to negotiate with Estonian authorities, followed the same pattern of reasoning that links uprootedness to unacceptable behaviour (Malkki 1992).

Significantly, from the perspective of silence and silencing, the existential fears expressed by critics of the school reform were missing from treatments of this topic in Estonian-language media. While the problematics of Russian-language schools did receive quite a lot of media attention at the time of my fieldwork, it tended to be discussed in terms of human resources and figures: sufficiency of qualified teaching personnel and adequate materials or lack thereof, shrinking numbers of students and the average age of teachers, scores on national examinations and language tests, feasibility of deadlines, and availability of funding.

Moreover, the Estonian Security Police (KaPo)

discouraged open public debates about the school reform by presenting it as an urgent matter of national security that "should not be exposed to the normal haggling of politics but should be dealt with decisively by top leaders" (Buzan, Wæver & de Wilde 1998: 24). Thus KaPo claimed in its 2011 annual report that the "preservation of the Russian-language education system" in Estonia would be in the interests of Russia's "so-called compatriots policy" that misleads Russians and Russian citizens in Estonia "in order to influence the sovereign decisions" of the Estonian state (Kaitsepolitseiamet 2012: 9, 10). As in the case of the April 2007 crisis sparked by the relocation of the Bronze Soldier monument, local Russian-speakers were deprived of agency by means of treating them as executors of hostile plans originating in the Russian Federation.

Conclusion

In Maria's view, it was indecent to talk about ethnicity and yet it was beyond her capacity to control the amplification of ethnicity in public discourse and, in the case of school reform, what could be regarded as government intervention in family relations and intimate spaces. As an employee of a minority organisation, she was a cog in the very same integration system that was turning ethnic identities into merchandise. Examples discussed in this article point furthermore to a recurrent pattern of silencing Estonian Russian-speakers by means of ignoring their ability to act on their own initiative: criticisms of the school reform or government's handling of the Bronze Soldier case are sidestepped and discouraged by means of framing the critics as fifth columnists working for Russia. In this framework Estonians become, once again, victims of Russian aggression.

Ethnicity as a marketable good is a matter of national policy that serves the interests of minority activists, politicians, officials and possibly also scholars. Silencing ethnicity, on the other hand, is a local strategy of co-existence and survival that emerges from sharing urban space and daily transactions. Since language serves as an important marker of ethnic identity in Estonia, it is not surprising that residents of Tallinn have developed various strategies to avoid making a fuss about somebody's choice of language. Yet silencing ethnicity also operates through tacitly recognised notions of Russian, Estonian and shared spaces in the capital. It is based on knowledge that is bodily, experience-based, gendered, spatial and rarely verbalised. Borders and trajectories Tallinners inscribe on urban space through their daily choices and habitual ways of doing things are only put into words and only become visible when they are violated. One has to be prepared to step back, negotiate and re-negotiate. The existence of such tacit shared understandings points to integration and cooperation outside the realm of state-funded multiculturalism and it was in this sphere that I felt ashamed to be studying ethnicity and integration.

Notes

1 This research was supported by the European Union through the European Regional Development Fund (Centre of Excellence in Cultural Theory) and by the Estonian Research Council (Institutional Research Project IUT2-43). I would like to thank anonymous reviewers for their insightful comments and, last but not least, my fieldwork partners.

2 For example, Turam (2015); Valluvan (2016); Werbner (2013); Wise & Welayutham (2009, 2014).

3 In total, I conducted approximately forty interviews, some of which were group interviews; the interviews were in Estonian, Russian or in both languages. While the interviews included a relatively wide range of the population in terms of age, ethnicity, linguistic and educational backgrounds, political views and levels of engagement in social affairs, the analysis presented here does not make claims to representativeness, nor is selection bias a major concern in ethnographic studies.

4 Not all Russian-speakers identify as ethnic Russians. In this article, I use the term 'Russian-speaker' to refer to Russian native speakers irrespective of ethnic self-identification and 'Russian', 'Ukrainian' etc. to discuss ethnic identities. 'Estonian' is also used as an ethnonym.

5 Kõresaar (2005) analyses the rupture metaphor and Rausing (2004) the concept of normalcy; Lauristin and Vihalemm (1997) and Aarelaid-Tart (2006) employ the concepts of return and trauma, respectively.

6 Popular culture has likewise seen an increase in willingness to address these previously shunned complexities. Several recent films (e.g. the dramas *Purge* [2012] and *The Fencer* [2015], and the action war drama *1944* [2015]) show Estonians fighting in the Red Army and striving for self-fulfilment by means of taking advantage of ruthless Stalinist methods.

7 Literature on what happened in Tallinn in April 2007 is large, including Lehti, Jutila & Jokisipilä (2008), Kaiser (2012) and Poleshchuk (2009).

References

Aarelaid-Tart, Aili 2006: *Cultural Trauma and Life Stories.* Kikimora Publications. Helsinki: Aleksanteri Institute.

Agarin, Timofey & Ada-Charlotte Regelmann 2011: Status Quo Multiculturalism: The Crux of Minority Policies in Central Eastern Europe's EU Member-States. *Journal of Minority Studies* 5, 69–98.

Annus, Epp 2012: The Problem of Soviet Colonialism in the Baltics. *Journal of Baltic Studies* 43:1, 21–45.

Brubaker, Rogers 1996: *Nationalism Reframed: Nationhood and the National Question in the New Europe.* Cambridge & New York: Cambridge University Press.

Brubaker, Rogers, Margit Feischmidt, Jon Fox & Liana Grancea 2006: *Nationalist Politics and Everyday Ethnicity in a Transylvanian Town.* Princeton: Princeton University Press.

Brubaker, Rogers, Mara Loveman & Peter Stamatov 2004: Ethnicity as Cognition. *Theory and Society* 33:1, 31–64.

Buzan, Barry, Ole Wæver & Jaap de Wilde 1998: *Security: A New Framework for Analysis.* Boulder, Colorado: Lynne Rienner Publishers.

Connerton, Paul 1989: *How Societies Remember.* Cambridge: Cambridge University Press.

Cook, Susan E. 2006: Language Policies and the Erasure of Multilingualism in South Africa. In: Maria-Luisa Achino-Loeb (ed.), *Silence: The Currency of Power.* New York & Oxford: Berghahn Books, pp. 52–69.

Cordell, Karl 2013: The Ideology of Minority Protection during the Post-Communist Transition in Europe. In: Karl Cordell, Timofey Agarin & Alexander Osipov (eds.), *Institutional Legacies of Communism: Change and Continuities in Minority Protection.* London: Routledge, pp. 77–89.

Cordell, Karl, Timofey Agarin & Alexander Osipov (eds.) 2013: *Institutional Legacies of Communism: Change and Continuities in Minority Protection.* London: Routledge.

Ehn, Billy & Orvar Löfgren 2010: *The Secret World of Doing Nothing.* Berkeley, Los Angeles & London: University of California Press.

EKSS = *Eesti keele seletav sõnaraamat* [Estonian thesaurus]. http://www.eki.ee/dict/ekss/index.cgi?Q=eestimaalane&F=M. Accessed March 15, 2016.

ERR Uudised. Ligi palus vabandust, et nimetas "juurteta" Ossinovskit sisserändaja pojaks [Ligi apologised for calling "rootless" Ossinovski a son of an immigrant]. 23.10.2014, http://uudised.err.ee/v/eesti/828959f2-87a9-4c06-912d-bcd9e5559ab4. Accessed March 14, 2016.

Estonia.eu. Citizenship. *Official Gateway to Estonia,* http://estonia.eu/about-estonia/society/citizenship.html. Accessed March 15, 2016.

Estonia.eu. Estonia at a Glance. *Official Gateway to Estonia,* http://estonia.eu/about-estonia/country/estonia-at-a-glance.html. Accessed March 15, 2016.

Estonia EU. Russian-language schools' transition to partial Estonian-language instruction – What is happening and why? *Official Gateway to Estonia,* http://estonia.eu/about-estonia/society/russian-language-schools-transition-to-partial-estonian-language-instruction-what-is-happening-and-why.html. Accessed March 15, 2016.

Etnoweb.ee: http://etnoweb.ee/. Accessed March 15, 2016.

Fabian, Johannes 1990: *Power and Performance: Ethnographic Explorations through Proverbial Wisdom and Theater in Shaba, Zaire.* Madison: University of Wisconsin Press.

Fernandez, James W. 2006: Silences of the Field. In: Maria-Luisa Achino-Loeb (ed.), *Silence: The Currency of Power.* New York & Oxford: Berghahn Books, pp. 158–173.

Hallik, Klara 2010: *Koos pole lihtne aga eraldi ei saa* [It is not easy together but cannot do it separately]. Tallinn: Rahvusvaheliste ja Sotsiaaluuringute Instituut.

Herzfeld, Michael 2005: *Cultural Intimacy: Social Poetics in the Nation-State.* 2nd ed. New York: Routledge.

Jaago, Tiiu 2014: Nõukogude aeg elulugudes – 'katkestus' või 'järjepidevus'. [Soviet time in life stories – 'rupture' or 'continuity']. *Mäetagused* 57, 7–27, http://www.folklore.ee/tagused/nr57/jaago.pdf. Accessed March 14, 2016.

Jõesalu, Kirsti 2005: "The right to happiness": Echoes of Soviet Ideology in Biographical Narratives. *Berliner Osteuropa* Info 23, 91–99.

Kaiser, Robert 2012: Reassembling the Event: Estonia's 'Bronze Night'. *Environment and Planning D: Society and Space* 30, 1046–1063.

Kaitsepolitseiamet 2012: *Aastaraamat 2011* [Security Police of the Republic of Estonia annual review 2011], https://www.kapo.ee/et/content/aastaraamatu-v%C3%A4ljaandmise-traditsiooni-ajalugu-ja-eesm%C3%A4rk-0.html. Accessed March 16, 2015.

Kapper, Sille 2016: Post-Colonial Folk Dancing: Reflections on the Impact of Stage Folk Dance Style on Traditional Folk Dance Variation in Soviet and Post-Soviet Estonia. *Journal of Baltic Studies* 47, 93–111.

Kõresaar, Ene 2005: *Elu ideoloogiad: Kollektiivne mälu ja autobiograafiline minevikutõlgendus eestlaste elulugudes* [Ideologies of life: Collective memory and autobiographical meaning-making of the past in Estonian post-Soviet life stories]. Eesti Rahva Muuseumi sari 6. Tartu: Eesti Rahva Muuseum.

Kuulpak, Peeter 2015 (ed.): *Statistical Yearbook of Tallinn 2015.* Tallinn: Tallinn City Office.

Kuutma, Kristin, Elo-Hanna Seljamaa & Ergo-Hart Västrik 2012: Minority Identities and the Construction of Rights in Post-Soviet Settings. *Folklore: Electronic Journal of Folklore* 51, 49–76, https://www.folklore.ee/folklore/vol51/minority.pdf. Accessed March 14, 2016.

Laanes, Eneken 2009: *Lepitamatud dialoogid: Subjekt ja mälu* nõukogudejärgses Eesti romaanis [Unresolved dialogues: Subjectivity and memory in post-Soviet Estonian novel]. Oxymora 6. Tallinn: Underi ja Tuglase Kirjanduskeskus.

Lauristin, Marju & Peeter Vihalemm 1997: *Return to the Western World: Cultural and Political Perspectives on the Estonian Post-Communist Transition.* Tartu: Tartu University Press.

Lehti, Marko, Matti Jutila & Markku Jokisipilä 2008: Never-Ending Second World War: Public Performances of National Dignity and the Drama of the Bronze Soldier. *Journal of Baltic Studies* 39:4, 393–418.

Lember, Uku 2015: Rahvus, kooselu ja vaikus: Eesti-vene pered Nõukogude Eestis [Nationality, cohabitation and silence: Estonian-Russian families in Soviet Estonia]. *Sirp* 18.09.2015, http://www.sirp.ee/s1-artiklid/c9-sotsiaalia/rahvus-kooselu-ja-vaikus/. Accessed March 14, 2016.

Lember, Uku 2016: Inter-Generational Transmission of Pasts in Late Soviet Estonia: Oral History Perspective in Inter-Marriage Setting. In: Raili Nugin, Anu Kannike & Maaris Raudsepp (eds.), *Generations in Estonia: Contemporary Perspectives on Turbulent Times.* Tartu: The University of Tartu Press, pp. 159–187.

Malkki, Liisa 1992: National Geographic: The Rooting of Peoples and the Territorialization of National Identity among Scholars and Refugees. *Cultural Anthropology* 7 (1. Space, Identity and the Politics of Difference), 24–44.

Malloy, Tove H. 2009: Social Cohesion Estonian Style: Minority Integration through Constitutionalized Hegemony and Fictive Pluralism. In: Timofey Agarin & Malte Brosig (eds.), *Minority Integration in Central Eastern Europe: Between Ethnic Diversity and Equality.* Amsterdam & New York: Rodopi, pp. 225–256.

Nagle, John 2009: *Multiculturalism's Double Bind: Creating Inclusivity, Cosmopolitanism and Difference.* Franham & Burlington: Ashgate.

Pettai, Eva-Clarita & Vello Pettai 2015: *Transitional and Retrospective Justice in the Baltic States.* Cambridge: Cambridge University Press.

Poleshchuk, Vadim 2009: *The War of Monuments in Estonia: The Challenges of History and the Minority Population.* Report from the Åland Islands Peace Institute No. 1, 2009. Mariehamn: Åland Islands Peace Institute.

Rausing, Sigrid 2004: *History, Memory, and Identity in Post-Soviet Estonia: The End of a Collective Farm.* Oxford & New York: Oxford University Press.

Sakkeus, Luule 1999: Migratsioon. In: Jüri Viikberg (ed.), *Eesti rahvaste raamat: Rahvusvähemused, -rühmad ja -killud* [The book of Estonian peoples: National minorities, groups and fragments]. Tallinn: Eesti Entsüklopeediakirjastus, pp. 310–325.

Seljamaa, Elo-Hanna 2012: A *Home for 121 Nationalities or Less: Nationalism, Ethnicity and Integration in Post-Soviet Estonia.* Ph.D. dissertation. The Ohio State University, Columbus.

Seljamaa, Elo-Hanna 2013: Boosting Similarity and Difference or Only Difference? Soviet Nationality Policies and Integration in Post-Communist Estonia. In: Karl Cordell, Timofey Agarin & Alexander Osipov (eds.), *Institutional Legacies of Communism: Change and Continuities in Minority Protection.* London: Routledge, pp. 186–199.

Shuman, Amy 2005: *Other People's Stories: Entitlement Claims and the Critique of Empathy.* Urbana: University of Illinois Press.

Šmidchens, Guntis 2014: *The Power of Song: Nonviolent National Culture in the Baltic Singing Revolution.* Seattle & London: University of Washington Press; Copenhagen: Museum Tusculanum Press.

Tammaru, Tiit 2016: Millistes keeltes suudavad suhelda eesti ja vene noored? [On the ability of Estonian and Russian youth to communicate in different languages]. *Postimees* March 7, 2016.

Turam, Berna 2015: *Gaining Freedoms: Claiming Space in Istanbul and Berlin.* Stanford: Stanford University Press.

Valluvan, Sivamohan 2016: Conviviality and Multiculture: A Post-integration Sociology of Multi-ethnic Interaction. YOUNG 24:3, 204–221.

Vihalemm, Triin 1999: *Formation of Collective Identity among Russophone Population of Estonia.* Dissertationes de mediis et communicationibus Universitatis Tartuensis 2. Tartu: Tartu University Press.

Vihalemm, Triin 2007: Crystallizing and Emancipating Identities in Post-Communist Estonia. *Nationalities Papers* 35:3, 477–502.

Werbner, Pnina 2013: Everyday Multiculturalism: Theorising the Difference Between 'Intersectionality' and 'Multiple Identities'. *Ethnicities* 13:4, 401–419.

Wise, Amanda & Selvaraj Velayutham 2009 (eds.): *Everyday Multiculturalism.* Basingstoke: Palgrave Macmillan.

Wise, Amanda & Selvaraj Velayutham 2014: Conviviality in Everyday Multiculturalism. *European Journal of Cultural Studies* 17:4, 406–430.

Zerubavel, Eviatar 2003: *Time Maps: Collective Memory and the Social Shape of the Past.* Chicago & London: The University of Chicago Press.

Elo-Hanna Seljamaa is a researcher at the Department of Estonian and Comparative Folklore at the University of Tartu. Her Ph.D. thesis from the Ohio State University focused on nationalism, ethnicity and integration in post-Soviet Estonia, and she continues to explore these topics. (elo-hanna.seljamaa@ut.ee)

SELF-FULFILLING WORDS AND TOPICS NOT TO BE TOUCHED UPON
Noncommunication in Neo-Charismatic Rhetoric

Tuija Hovi, University of Turku

Uttering certain words with certain intention is understood as having performative power to produce desired outcomes in social life. However, a deliberate silence as well as words spoken out loud can function as an objectification of reality. With the help of Gregory Bateson's concept of noncommunication, silences are approached in personal narratives in the Word of Life congregation. Whereas explicit communication would alter the nature of ideas, *noncommunication* works by "keeping up sacredness", the unchangeable or untouchable. For believers, avoiding particular topics is an attempt to control the surrounding world and strengthen the feeling of safety and success in the spiritual as well as material life. The article studies four aspects of Neo-charismatic rhetoric as noncommunication: avoided topics, confirming, protection and meta-speech.

Keywords: noncommunication, Faith Movement, positive confession, performative speech, personal narrative

Silence is not the first thought that comes to mind when talking about Pentecostalism and Charismatic Christianity. On the contrary, noisy meetings with shouting evangelists, collective praying in tongues, ecstatic praising, amplified music and the oral traditions of sharing and witnessing give an impression of a culture where the human voice, talking, preaching, hearing and being heard are pivotal issues. Undoubtedly, they are essentially meaningful manifestations of faith in a ritual context, whereas stillness can cause confusion being that it is considered a completely strange element in the grammar of Neo-charismatic meeting practices (cf. Coleman 2007). Nevertheless, there are also situations and topics that require a believer to remain silent at times or to look for substitutive and euphemistic words. "Growing in faith" should be the goal for every believer, and since the use of language is said to make a great difference to the personal spiritual development, not all topics are accepted to be worthy of conversation. However, contextually meaningful silence can be more than mere speechlessness.

Introduction
In this article, I am returning to the interviews that I carried out among the adherents of a Neo-charismatic congregation called the Word of Life at the end of the 1990s. I have re-read the material in order to examine more closely the silent aspects of narration as rhetorical choices which are meant to keep up the

Tuija Hovi 2016: Self-Fulfilling Words and Topics Not to Be Touched Upon: Noncommunication in Neo-Charismatic Rhetoric.
Ethnologia Europaea 46:2, 44–57. © Museum Tusculanum Press.

desired reality. The Word of Life (Elämän Sana in Finnish) in Turku on the south-west coast of Finland was founded in August 1990. The founders were a group of Finnish members of the Livets Ord congregation, the Nordic centre of the (Word of) Faith Movement led by Pastor Ulf Ekman in Uppsala, Sweden. At this time, the Neo-charismatic Prosperity Gospel or the Health and Wealth doctrine, as it is often pejoratively called, was only paving its way to Finland and was facing strong criticism especially from the traditional Pentecostal community in the country. The Finnish Pentecostals were most displeased with all Neo-charismatic influences. Especially, they condemned the open teaching of the importance of money in religious life and the objective of being "successful" in all areas of life. In addition to that, the Finnish Pentecostals disapproved of doctrinal differences concerning the idea of miraculous healing, not to mention the "too American" meeting practices.

I interviewed 15 members of the Word of Life in Turku, including the pastor. The interviewees represented the first adult generation of the newly founded local community with a strong pioneer spirit. At that time, about half of the approximate 130 members of the congregation attended the Sunday service regularly. In addition to this main occasion of the week, there were several minor gatherings and thematic weekly meetings along with occasional team trips to evangelise in other towns. Most of the active meeting goers were 20–40 years of age, and fairly equally women and men. Such a gender balance was somewhat exceptional because, more often than not in religious communities, women have been found to be the majority (cf. Niemelä 2003: 187–189; Walters & Davie 1998: 641–643), not the least within Pentecostalism (e.g. Brusco 2010). According to my observations, the exceptional gender division in the Word of Life was due, at least in part, to the fact that the importance of marriage and partnership of women and men in religious life was emphasised. Moreover, prayers were made for the unmarried to find spouses and it was taken for granted that a husband and a wife belong to the same congregation.

I participated in several Sunday meetings of the congregation where most of the members used to attend. However, in actuality, I learned to know most of my interviewees through a "key informant", a 40-year-old woman whom I had met previously in a temporary job where she had enthusiastically told me about her faith and her active involvement in a new congregation. All the people whom I interviewed, nine women and six men, were actively involved in the congregational life and, accordingly, willing to share their experiences of faith with an outsider.

The discussions with the believers followed the principles of open-ended thematic interviews, typically used in an ethnographic study. It was my intention to discover how the believers themselves describe and explain their religious development. I asked them to tell me about their membership, involvement in congregational activities and their personal spiritual life in the Word of Life. Instead of a readymade and structured list of questions, I let the interviewees talk rather freely about the themes I was particularly interested in. I asked them to tell me about their experiences of guidance and healing, their understandings of prosperity theology, the role of the "gifts of the Holy Spirit" in their lives as well as their possible personal difficulties and challenges in faith. Studies at the Bible school of the congregation and the frequently read teachings of Ulf Ekman, the Swedish branch of the Faith Movement (Livets Ord) set the tone for the speech of the interviewees while they told about their beliefs and experiences as "born-again" believers.

For approaching the certain silences in the narration of the believers, I have adopted Gregory Bateson's (1987) concept of *noncommunication*. Essentially, noncommunication means saying nothing about negative and undesired things, or issues which may be too delicate to be shared. In addition to simply keeping silent by not saying anything about dubious issues, there are also other manners used, such as veiling and belittling things that are, for one reason or another, considered incongruous or even harmful. According to Bateson, whereas explicit communication would alter the nature of ideas, noncommunication works by "keeping up sacredness" (Bateson & Bateson 1987: 80). For a Word of Life believer, an attempt to avoid speaking about spiritually damaging themes is an attempt to control the surrounding world and strengthen the feeling of safety, well-being and success. Thus, noncommunication is a cultural practice that supports the idea of positive confession to keep up the Neo-charismatic reality (cf. Coleman 2000).

This article studies four aspects of Neo-charismatic rhetoric as noncommunication. These rhetorical aspects are avoided topics, silence as a confirming act, protection, and the meta-level of noncommunication. To be able to understand noncommunication and the faith-affirming role of personal narrative in the context of the Pentecostal-Charismatic social world it is necessary first to present an overview of some doctrinal and rhetorical principles of the tradition in question.

Prosperity Gospel and Positive Confession

The Healing Revival that emerged within Pentecostalism of the 1940s and 1950s in the United States promoted the idea of well-being and a healthy body being optimal for the Holy Spirit to manifest in the human life (Teinonen 1965: 109). The legacy of the Healing Revival became processed and refined later on in several forms of the so-called Third Wave Charismatic Christianity.[1] Especially the (Word of) Faith Movement, inspired by Pastor Kenneth Hagin's (1917–2003) teachings, is known for those principles. According to Hagin, a born-again Christian enjoys success and well-being in every area of life because, while accepting Jesus as the saviour, a person simultaneously gets emancipated from Satan's control and its negative outcomes in human life (Hagin [1966]1980: 18). As a result of this, health and wealth are said to be automatic divine privileges of true believers. Well-being may be procreated by faith as a part of the "salvation package", since the Atonement of Christ is said to include not only the removal of sin, but also the removal of sickness and poverty (Hunt 1998, 2000: 333). In the Faith teaching, receiving all these benefits preconceives controlling one's thinking, and heading it towards biblically acceptable ideas because negative thoughts and in-

correct faith are regarded as sin. The thoughts, be they positive or negative, are said to be self-fulfilling. Thus, by thinking in the "right way" – positively and following the biblical instructions – a person can receive all good things, like health, economic freedom and success.

The ideological roots of the self-fulfilling words and thoughts in the Prosperity Gospel have been traced back to the *mind cure* thinking[2] (Hambre et al. 1983: 35). There were certain elements that may have inspired the teachings developed by the Pentecostal Healing Revival, and further on, by Neo-charismatic teachers such as Hagin, for instance. Even though there is no straight connection between the healing doctrines of the nineteenth century in the United States and the Faith Movement of the twenty-first century in the Nordic context, it is in many ways likely that the ideas of the healing spiritualists assimilated in later Charismatic Christianity. The prominent authors of Christian Science of the nineteenth century shared the belief in the positive thinking as a reality changing power.[3] Correspondingly, the teachings of the Faith Movement emphasise the power of visualisation and the meaning of the "right confession". The idea of the right confession has even been compared to certain forms of shamanism, which, with the help of magic, seek to influence the supernatural powers (Coleman 1998: 248; Hunt 1998: 274).

Regarding the idea of success and well-being, the interrelatedness of speech, language and believer's lived reality is obvious in the Faith Movement. The roots of positive thinking come into sight in the notion that the words and actions are believed to directly affect people's mental and spiritual state. Presenting oneself as a successful person is understood as a means for changing the situation in a desired way. The "right confession" thus functions in the performative way and maintains the relationship between a believer and God as well as strengthens the cohesion in the community of believers. By contrast, talking publicly about one's failure or doubts is believed to cause failure (Coleman 1991: 13).

Anthropologist Simon Coleman has pointed out the importance of *positive confession* as a strategic mode of communication in the Faith Movement as a branch of Neo-charismatic Christianity. Positive confession as a way of speaking (and thinking) has virtually led this type of Christianity to be called Health and Wealth Gospel or Prosperity Theology. These attributes are given to the doctrine because of the idea of a true believer being materially rewarded by God already in this world, not only in the after-life, which typically is the basic idea, for instance, in old Pietistic revival movements. Especially in the Neo-charismatic Faith Movement, words spoken with certain intention – "in faith" – are regarded as objectifications of reality (Coleman 2000: 28). Even ritualising the everyday life by using conscious and intentional positive confession, also as silent and personal inner speech only in thoughts, aims at the same goal. For the believers in the Faith Movement, it is a holistic way of life that supports their "grow-ing in faith" (Coleman & Collins 2000: 323). As I also discovered while interviewing members of a Finnish Word of Life congregation, not only saying something out loud but also a deliberate silence as avoidance of uttering certain things, can function as an objectification of reality (Hovi 2007: 218). It is a method of excluding, marking the borders, and thus, protecting a believer's biblical reality from dangers of both "worldly" and "demonic" influences, which are not always easily separated.

Performative Power of Silence in Narration

According to Jerome Bruner, narration is a way of making personal experiences meaningful in a cer-tain social, historical and cultural context. It fills the past with meanings in relation to the present and frames the future orientation (Bruner 1987: 15). Moreover, as psychologist Brian Schiff argues, one of the primary functions of narrating is to make life experience and interpretations of life present again. Narrating brings experience and interpretations into play, into a field of action, in a specific here and now. It is a way of making sense of life experiences in a certain situation (Schiff 2012: 13). Such a contextual storytelling event may function as an important tool for identity formation. In a religious community, narration ritually creates and shapes social relation-

ships; a narrator can establish his or her identity as a believer by telling a story of a personally meaningful religious experience that follows the traditional pat-terns in a credible way (cf. Hydén 2010: 44–46).

In Pentecostal-Charismatic Christianity with the emphasis on personal spiritual developing or "grow-ing in faith", narration has a special role as "witness-ing". The tradition of witnessing functions as a ritual for carrying and transmitting this tacit knowledge within a group, not only by dealing with testimonies of conversion but also by narrating faith-affirming experiences of providence or receiving answers to the prayers. Believers are supposed, encouraged and expected to tell both each other and outsiders about their conviction and its developments (see also Piret Koosa's article in this issue). In the Bible, the true believers are instructed to be prepared to witness "in season and out of season" (2 Tim 4:2), in other words, to use every opportunity to spread the message, to evangelise. It is, as an elderly Pentecostal woman once clarified to me, a "chance for a lay person to speak like a pastor." Witnessing and preaching are, indeed, the two traditional speech acts for believers to speak the gospel most intensely (Harding 2000: 36). As the believers' personal experience is expected to match and be compatible with the doctrine and the community-specific tradition of interpreta-tion, there exists an inescapable social pressure for talking about the personal faith. By witnessing, the believers attempt to convince both the co-believers and the outsiders – the potential converts – of their true faith and the right choice to make (cf. McGuire 1979). Thus, personal narratives as a formulaic gen-re of witnessing are not only reflections of faith, but they function as catalysts for religious experience as well; the relationship between narration and experi-ence is inseparable.

As it is typical in social life, narratives emerge through interaction in a certain situation for certain purposes. A story about receiving an answer to a prayer told in an interview situation is, thus, built on different terms than a testimony in a revival meet-ing even though the topic of the story is the same; it is obvious above all in lexical choices and in the need for explaining the biblical rhetoric to an outsider (Hovi 1997: 330–331, 2007: 92–93). Despite the fact that my interviews were carried out for a non-religious purpose (i.e. academic research) in a documented situation, there were also situations where interviewees had a chance to talk about their faith to an outsider as it is proper according to the revivalist Christian traditions. Like Susan F. Harding has pointed out, witnesses are, of course, aware of this difference in understanding, but still, they aim at making their reality real also to a listener (Harding 2000: 37–38). The discussions during the interviews may thus be a kind of everyday speech, personal narrative that occasionally, however, moves to the register of witnessing.

Instead of being read as mere texts, personal narratives are meant to be interpreted holistically, by also taking into account the speech situation (the interaction in an interview), the Charismatic Christian speech culture and negotiation of subject positions (cf. Phoenix 2013: 73). Analysing interview speech as a situated narrative process, I want to point out how an individual expression of commitment to the doctrine and rituals maintains both collectivity among the believers and an individual's belief system. I have approached narration as *performative speech* that is used for creating or keeping up the desired situation. To summarise John L. Austin's idea of performative power of speech, the action that the sentence describes is, in explicit cases, performed by the utterance of the sentence itself. In his own words: "by saying something, we *do* something" (Austin 1978: 5–6).

The utterance changes the state of affairs when it is spoken out in a certain situation, by a certain person with a certain intention. Good examples of such performative power of the spoken word within religious contexts are ritual formulas, such as spells, incantations, blessings and absolutions. In the case of Faith believers, their formulaic narratives, like witness stories (or "testimonies"), are used for maintaining the desired states of affair, to establish the bonds between co-believers and the bonds between a believer and God. Witnessing has performative power to shape the identity and make a believer part of a religious community. Simultaneously, the pur-

pose of witness stories may be to change something in another person when they are told, with the hope of awakening the listener(s) (cf. Harding 2000: 57).

However, also a meaningful silence can have performative power. Expressions and silences may have such a function in a conversation with the intention of reproducing and maintaining the biblical truth in everyday life of believers. In her study of Catholic women who negotiate their unsatisfactory position as bystanders in the church, Laura Leming (2007) has investigated how the women use language to shift their positions in relation to the church authorities. In their "church talk", she points out the role of the strategic silence in certain situations while criticising the hierarchical policy. However, instead of not saying anything at all, the women used euphemisms and insinuation, and distanced themselves by referring to the church authorities as "others". Simultaneously, they included themselves as an elementary part of the church. According to Leming, they speak poly-vocally to negotiate the multiple positionalities of their identity as church persons. This agentic use of language allows them to give flexible expression to their dilemma of membership and the positions they claim, and gives voice to their opposition (Leming 2007: 84).

At the turn of the twenty-first century, the Word of Life was regarded as unusually radical and probably the most controversial group among the Christian communities in Finland because of its prosperity teaching and action-packed congregational life. However, as a new independent congregation ambitiously aiming at "conquering the world" it undoubtedly offered inspiring activities and meaningful personal and collective agency for every member regardless of gender or age. Thus, rather than expressing wishes for changing something in the policy of the community, like Leming's interviewees did in a hierarchical Catholic community, the adherents of the Word of Faith rather positioned themselves as democratic supporters of the "biblical order". When keeping silent or avoiding certain themes the interviewees in the Word of Faith did it mostly in order to maintain the ideal social dynamics within the congregation and strengthen their own faith and believer's identity. In the following section, I will examine how noncommunication indicates norms, values and wishes in the Neo-charismatic rhetoric used in the interviews.

Narrative Silence: Speechlessness and Evasive Speech

In the interviews of active Word of Life members, I have traced the themes that are covered by silence or passed over as less important or irrelevant matters, or perhaps even dangerous for the believer's identity. I have also looked for cultural models by which their faith is built up, and studied how those models can be verbalised at the individual level. The starting point is the hypothesis according to which the social interaction and communication construct and maintain the plausibility structure for faith at an individual level as well as at the social level. The religious interpretation of perceptions and experiences is supported by verbalisation that follows the traditional models of "canonic discourse", as Peter Stromberg (1993) argues. Speaking of conversion narratives, Stromberg has pointed out how a conversion narrative that is based on both referential and constitutive aspects[4] of canonic discourse facilitates the self-transformation of the narrator. Further on, for a believer in a religious community, the learned discourse has a significant role, not only in verbalising things but also in knowing what is supposed to remain unsaid. It is not always appropriate and relevant to say out loud everything that is meaningful for an individual's personal faith. In many cases, faith can rather be said to be based on noncommunication (Vesala et al. 2002: 21).

In the Faith believers' narration, there are meaningful aspects for the faith construction also when those aspects are not addressed explicitly, when they are avoided or when they are expressed through negation. I have found the social-psychologist Vilma Hänninen's concept of "inner story" useful while talking about personal narrative as means for faith developing. A person's inner story has been structured not only according to his or her personal experiences and memories but also according to the models of the cultural collective narrative tradition.

A person is never able or perhaps not even willing to put into words the inner story in its entirety. For instance, shameful experiences easily remain untold.[5] Furthermore, as Hänninen presuppose, among other things, the most sensitive memories or the most sacred experiences are protected by keeping them private (Hänninen 1999: 57). After all, a person's inner story is always fragmented and situationally constructed and, thus, can never be completed; instead, it is to be understood as a dynamic identification process.

Speaking about sensitive topics and ways of communicating them is a complex and multi-levelled theme. In a very illuminating way, Margareta Hydén has brought up the issue of sensitive topics in an interview conversation by pointing out how *any* topic can be a sensitive one depending on relational circumstances, namely relations between the teller and the listener (Hydén 2013: 226). Situational and contextual aspects are not without meaning either. Hydén has also pointed out how the circulation of narratives may cause harm by being reinterpreted afterwards in another context as well as the importance of the physical and discursive space of the narrative event (ibid.: 232–234). The themes that I discussed with the Word of Life people did not include traumatic experiences in the first place. On the contrary, religious conversion and "growing in faith" were described as constructive and empowering experiences as well as a means of overcoming personal obstacles such as accidents or emotional turmoil. Rather than seeing challenging experiences and difficult situations as unfortunate random events, the Charismatics take them as parts of "God's plan" that lead them, eventually, to positive changes (cf. Moberg 2013: 142). After all, what could and could not be told was dependent on relational circumstances and the space, both physical and discursive, that the interview situation presented to the participants.

Remaining silent may serve different purposes in social interaction. Depending on context, it may even have constitutive power in certain rhetoric. Following Bateson's thinking, protection, preservation and enablement can be identified as functions of noncommunication. Contextualisation is an essential factor in recognising what has not been said. In other words, we need to focus on the situation where the message is not transmitted as well as on the topic and the interlocutors (Ketola, Knuuttila & Mattila 2002: 8–9). While interviewing the believers I occasionally tried deliberately to chase after the things that were not expressed explicitly. As an outsider without the tacit knowledge of the right way to share the experience of faith, I had a good reason to ask for elaboration, to learn more about specific situations of not following God's will, for instance. This method did not necessarily generate exhaustive explanations concerning the themes that the interviewees did not spontaneously talk about. Nevertheless, there were some outcomes of negotiations, for example, explicit comments concerning the topics which should be avoided and the damaging effects of talking out loud about them. Considering those topics, it is obvious that noncommunication maintains and constructs social and cultural reality by being discussed – the significance of noncommunication was constantly contested and negotiated in the Word of Life. This aspect was not exactly taken into account in the first place by Bateson (cf. Ketola, Knuuttilla & Mattila 2002: 9). In an interview situation, noncommunication does not actually mean speechless silence but in various ways non-committal and reserved speech.

In the following, I demonstrate how noncommunication becomes constitutive in the discussion between a born-again narrator and an outsider interviewer in the way that can be understood as both constructing and expressing reality of the believer. I address four such aspects of noncommunication that emerge in the interviews.

Avoided Topics

When using the concept noncommunication in the context of Faith believers' narration, I mean basically saying nothing about negative things, or veiling and belittling them. I have tried to understand what has been veiled in silence or passed over as being less important or irrelevant, or even tabooed. In the speech of Word of Life members, noncommunica-

tion hides above all misfortunes and failures as well as difficulties in faith. They are themes that may be skipped over quickly or explicitly said to be "useless topics" as they are not supporting the personal spiritual development. In such a way, silence labels them as topics that are detrimental to faith. It goes without saying that misfortune, failure or doubts and scepticism do not fit the discourse of positive confession. Thus, noncommunication has performative power through negation. In certain situations, it is silence that protects the reality that a believer wants to live in or is actively aiming at by hiding undesired situations and emotions and excluding their negative influences, at least, at the rhetoric level.

The themes that definitely did not inspire the interviewees to produce long detailed narratives were failure, uncertainty in faith as well as the acts of Satan who is understood by the Word of Faith believers as a personified evil and the active antagonist of the benevolent God. Often, the interviewees used also other names denoting Satan, such as the Devil and the Enemy (of Soul). As a rule, these themes faded very quickly. However, there were significant differences in the precision and extent of narration between individuals. These differences were the most obvious in talking about Satan's impact on life. Three interviewees of the group of fifteen refused to discuss it at all, while the others referred to it in various manners. In the following excerpt, Linda[6], the 40-year-old female interviewee, who had accidently crashed into a pavement and hurt herself badly while she was cycling, insinuates by negation what is the origin of all evil, including her accident. Only after my definite question she indicates what she believes is the reason for misfortune – although she does so without spelling out the actual name – ending her story with the normative utterance of trust in God:

Linda: I know it so clearly that it is not God who sends this kind of accident and other things like it. …
Tuija: Do you think it was a situation like Satan's intervention?
Linda: Yes, yes. It always tries to harm people and God's work. And so on. You see it so clearly. It is

self-evident. You just have to trust God, and everything will be all right. (TKU/A/99/31:11)

As Bateson argues, noncommunication has the effect of altering the nature of ideas, maintaining sacredness (Bateson & Bateson 1987: 80). Thus, an attempt to avoid speaking about damaging themes is an attempt to control the surrounding world and strengthen a feeling of safety. In this way, noncommunication functions as a means of supporting the idea of positive confession in maintaining the Neocharismatic reality (Hovi 2014). Accordingly, Linda, cited above, aimed at emphasising God's goodness throughout the interview as well as pointing out the positive sides of the incident. However, for the actual cause of the accident, she accepted what I, as an interviewer, brought into focus. The theodicy, it is to say the dilemma of iniquity existing in the world despite of God's omnipotent benevolence, was negotiated in the interview situation while I seized the opportunity to interpret the accident by a theological assumption to complete the picture. Even though her answer confirmed the interpretation that I offered, the interviewee herself did not want to name the cause of the unfortunate event on her own initiative. Linda merely made a generalised notion about "it" always working in a harmful and damaging way and encircled the unspoken malevolent agent with her positive confession of God's impact on human life.

Silence as a Confirming Act

The interviewee cited above evaded my question on personal uncertainty and difficulties in upholding the faith. Her answer was made of a principled explanation at a fairly general level on how the Devil can "cause spiritual pressure" and "send demons" to harass the believers. However, if there was any personal experience of such things, it remained unanswered while she decisively adhered to the canonical teachings of the movement:

Tuija: What kind of situations have been the most difficult for you [to keep up the faith]?
Linda: Well, I actually talk about the situation that

has lasted a little longer, perhaps some months or so … Like … and it is like I said, in some situations it is possible that you really have done something wrong, that you just have not, if God has said that leave it, leave this and that, and you don't do so, then you have committed a sin if it is a wrong thing. I don't want to be more specific about it, but anyway, it is something that you know that it's wrong, you shouldn't do it but you just have not given it up, left it. So, it creates a barrier between you and God so that the contact is not quite open, because it is your fault, you have done wrong, but immediately when you give it up you can ask for forgiveness of sins and the blood of Jesus purifies you from all wrongdoing. It is said there [in the Bible], and it really is so. (TKU/A/99/31:34)

The hardships in maintaining the faith and developing it are intertwined with the concept of sin, in awareness of norm violation or, in other words, in the awareness of "actions against God's will." Linda explicitly refuses to reveal more specific details about her experience which she refers to, and instead, explains such hardships at a very general level. The negative connotation of doubts or unbelief becomes visible in the example above only through doctrinal principles, not as personal experiences. Linda expresses it by speaking in the second person equal to the generalising passive voice distancing herself as an active subject. The personal level in the form of the confessional "I" in narration is changed to speaking at the general level while the interviewee emphasises the positively charged power of normative repentance. The above example can be interpreted as an expression of commitment through noncommunication following the rule that the believers are not supposed to pinpoint their failures by reporting their former sins. Instead, the interviewee relies indicatively on the norm of grace and the authority of the Bible by pointing out how "it is said there" that the "blood of Jesus purifies the sinner." She holds onto the positive future orientation rather than trying to keep in mind what went wrong earlier.

Gregory Bateson's concept of *premise* corresponds to the concepts of worldview and self-image. It is a basic assumption that includes what people think of themselves, the environment and their relation to it. The creation of premises is necessary for all learning. Once the premises have been internalised they become self-fulfilling and confirming (Vesala et al. 2002: 23, interpreting Gregory Bateson 1972, *Steps to an Ecology of Mind*). For instance, the believers' premises of faith are the authority of the Bible and the necessity of following God's will, as well as offering in the form of giving money for the congregational activities and to fellow believers in need. In return, a believer can expect to receive God's blessings, for example, receiving money for a certain purpose or some other kind of help. The interplay of offerings and blessings is a typical motive in the healing and guidance stories. Thus, speaking out loud and normatively repeating these premises can be presupposed to strengthen the faith. Simultaneously, there is the tendency of turning away from the issues that may threaten "living in faith". As an essential part of positive confession, keeping silent about the personal norm violations refers to the principle, expressed by interviewees, of an unnecessary need to cling to the "bad things". The example above of narrating difficulties in keeping up the faith reveals how linking the confessional and normative speech to an avoided theme creates the faith performatively. By seeing such noncommunication as a faith-strengthening act, I return to the basic idea of speech and thinking as being self-fulfilling. In the context of the Faith Movement, it is a fundamental way of thinking – what is not said aloud is not given a right to exist.

Protection

The idea of the protective power of noncommunication also has much in common with the idea of the self-fulfilling speech and thinking. By avoiding harmful themes or by attributing them as external, perhaps even caused by the Enemy of the Soul, and thus wrong, a believer protects the reality that he or she wants to live in. By talking about their experiences, the interviewees also communicated their need for understanding what has happened as well as explaining it in a larger – biblical – explanatory system. For instance, a sudden and inexplicable accident finds its place in a plausible explanatory pattern when it is interpreted as an "attack", which can be attributed by a believer as being caused by an external malevolent agent. An attempt of a believer to protect the faith by avoiding speaking about harmful themes is simultaneously an attempt to control the environment and create the feeling of safety, which is an outcome of predictability of events, and to strengthen the positive self-esteem. It may give the sense of active agency instead of being a victim or only a passive receiver of grace.

While explaining to me the doctrinal principles, the pastor of the Word of Life congregation explicitly denied the Faith teaching being based on positive thinking. However, the idea of positive thinking becomes preferable for a believer in reverse as a definition of bad ways of thinking and speaking, and as withdrawal from such things. As the norm of the right way of thinking the pastor (male, 51 years) emphasised the importance of thinking according to "God's word", no matter what the circumstances are:

Pastor: We don't talk about positive thinking, but God is really a positive God, and his thoughts are positive but, but we don't talk about these human things, like a person being positive or to think positively. It is very good if a person does so, but it is not what is lasting and what helps a person in the end. Instead, it is God's word, the faith that God has given to you. And a very typical argument that describes it well... I have quite aggressively attacked the saying "I am a miserable sinner" ["minä vaivainen syntinen"; a typical expression in the old Finnish revivalist hymns].
Tuija: Mm.
Pastor: Because if I am a born-again God's child, so the Bible says, I am a completely new creation, all old things have passed away. But if this born-again person goes on and confesses that I am the worst sinner, so look, he will be what he says. (TKU/A/99/32b:11)

The pastor's instructive teaching strongly indicates that characteristics that are not explicitly expressed do not exist, or they are seemingly controlled and easier to be put aside in order to maintain and protect the desired identity of the believer. Uncertainty, giving up in the face of obstacles and inferiority are not characteristics that, according to the pastor, help a believer to succeed in his or her spiritual growth and earthly life. Simultaneously, by dissociating oneself from the idea of being an incurable sinner, it is possible to make a distinction between the image of dynamic and spiritually growing Faith believers and that of passive and surrendering traditional Pietism, of which the latter is a more common attitude in the Finnish revivalist scene.

Discussing noncommunication as hushed-up secrets in a Finnish folk ballad, folklorist Seppo Knuuttila has claimed that when certain communicative channels are closed, the informative dimensions of those propositions that still can be heard or seen will become more powerful (cf. Knuuttila 2002: 128). In the Faith rhetoric, the questionable "channels" that should be closed are expressions of inferiority, failure, and the instances where one is unable to give more space to the expressions of success and well-being as signs of God's care. Thus, noncommunication functions as protection for the stability of being a born-again believer by providing more space for the positive perspective.

Meta-Speech on Noncommunication

While interviewing the believers, I tried to approach the themes that they did not necessarily speak about with each other or the themes that are so self-evident that there is no need to explicate them within the inner circle of co-believers. Such conversations, which dealt with believers' personal views about issues that are usually silenced in the congregation, can be identified as a meta-speech of noncommunication. The interview situation was a frame for such a meta-level of communication (cf. Vesala et al. 2002: 25). The pastor's definition of the self-fulfilling character of speech in the excerpt above is a good example of the meta-communication that took place in the interview. It has an important role in the language of his sermons. The pastor had also determinately taught the "right thinking" according to the guidelines of

the Faith Movement by criticising the submissive attitude of the traditional Christian revival movements in Finland.

As a communication process, an interview defines the relationship between the interlocutors by giving the believers as interviewees an opportunity to talk to an outsider in another way than they would do among the co-believers while explaining their choices and experiences. Correspondingly, due to this frame, the allusive language of the inner circle does not work between a believer and an outsider in the same manner as it does within the community of believers. For example, success was a theme that the interviewees interpreted in a contradictory way. It is, after all, a concept that has a profoundly different significance for the members of the congregation than it does for the outsiders. Basically, instead of getting wealthier, success was defined by the Word of Life believers primarily in terms of harmonious domestic life, well-functioning social relations, health, adequate incomes and, above all, dynamic spiritual life, at both the personal and the congregational level (Hovi 2007: 178–179). For that reason, clarifying the concept of success to me was a relevant and motivating thing to do for the interviewees even though there was no point discussing it in the congregational context. With this respect, another female interviewee's comment on the unspoken rules in the congregation can be understood as meta-speech on noncommunication. Nora in her early thirties pondered situations that seemed as if the teaching about offering, blessings and success had been turned upside down in a community of believers. She wondered if she speaks about congregational attitude towards the idea of success in another way than her co-believers and she explains it with something she had realised while working temporarily abroad and thus got some distance from her home congregation:

I don't know really how to reify it. [...] This is, well, I don't know if anyone of other interviewees has talked like this (a laughter) but well... but for instance, one sees things like this in all communities, be they work communities, student communities, congregations, whatever, especially if one comes from outside. […] How should I say? But many times in the congregation… well, this is said really pointedly, and it's not exactly what I mean but, well, perhaps generally speaking, in a way, weakness is favoured like […] If we talk about this success, okay, we talk about economic success, we talk about success in work, so why are you more accepted in the congregation if you are unemployed? (TKU/A/99/49:19)

According to the teaching of the Faith Movement, believers can ask God for whatever they want or need, and they can expect to be privileged to get it. Furthermore, mundane success is regarded as a blessing for being a true believer. Nora continued on her personal experiences of being disapproved in the congregation because she dedicated too much time to her academic studies and her challenging new job instead of investing all that time in congregational work:

> [In the congregation] they criticise you awfully easily like, just as I said, and they warn you like "don't look for your own pleasure" and blabla-blabla, and like "studies can become a god for you." And when someone unemployed comes in, then everybody prays like "please, God, give this person a job," but no-one asks "what's going on, have you started to look for wrong things because there is no more blessing in your life and you have no work?" Nobody asks like this, but good heavens, if you have studies to do or a good and demanding job, it is criticised immediately. It is a little bit like a sign of being a half-renegade. (TKU/A/99/49:19)

The interviewee seems to question the Pauline logic of "sowing and reaping"[7] that was frequently referred to in sermons in the Word of Life meetings. However, the teaching about the economic success seems, in her reasoning, to be the other way around as the actual situation when the lack of blessings, for instance unemployment, is left without an interpretation within the community of believers because the interpretation would be far too negative.

It would rather communicate apostasy or committing a sin, getting away from "God's plan" because of not being ideally successful. The conceptual lens or a premise concerning the basic rights of a believer to make interpretations of reality actually defines what remains silent in a community. Following Bateson's thinking, it can be said that Nora had courage to enter a zone where the "angels fear to go." She put into words some silent premises in the congregation, but only in the company of an outsider.

Conclusions

Quietness as a sensory experience is, of course, the most obvious way of defining silence. In this article, however, I have approached the theme of silence from another perspective by discussing it as a certain absence of information in narration of interviewees who were committed adherents of the Neo-charismatic Word of Faith congregation. Neo-charismatic Christianity is typically well-known for its vivid and noisy worship culture and salient narrative tradition of witnessing as well as intensive preaching. In the Word of Life, the so-called positive confession is an essential aspect of the speech culture being based on the idea of spoken words as being self-fulfilling. Following this principle, members of the movement are advised to pay special attention to how they think and talk in order to promote their personal spiritual development. Accordingly, in her study on the Don Evangelicals, Piret Koosa shows how the converts' "proper talk" indicates their "proper deeds" and "proper emotions" as well (cf. Piret Koosa in this issue). By the right rhetorical choices the believers can make themselves credible in front of their faith community, but also draw the line between the "saved" and the "lost". The discussions regarding the lived religion with the members of the Word of Life revealed that there were certain situations and topics that required the believers to remain silent or to look for substitutive and euphemistic expressions. Such narrative choices appeared to be important for maintaining the reality they wanted to live in. I have approached such silences in the narration of the interviewees as *noncommunication*. In principle, noncommunication means saying nothing about negative, frightening or in some other ways undesired things that threaten in one way or another the prevailing equilibrium. However, contextual silence can be more than just speechlessness as it is revealed in the above analysis of the narration of the believers.

In the narration of the Faith believers, it is possible to recognise noncommunication in the form of certain narrative silences, such as veiling and belittling issues and situations which are, for one reason or another, considered inappropriate for a believer. Evasive speech occurs typically in the context of situations and topics that are regarded as negative for an individual's personal spiritual growth or for the public image of the congregation, such as personal failure or experiences interpreted as "Satan's harassment". Words and thoughts being self-fulfilling as they are in the world of the Faith believers, failures, sins and demonic interventions are, indeed, topics not to be touched upon. They do not fit the rhetoric of positive confession. However, it is obvious that what is regarded as a "sensitive topic" depends on the relationship between the discussants, on how familiar or distant they are to each other and what they expect from each other, for instance. While certain topics are, in practice, avoided or even considered taboo regarding the image of a born-again believer in the congregational context, they may sometimes be outspoken without hesitation in the company of an outsider. That is how an unspoken truth about the mind-set in the congregation could be spoken out loud in an interview situation, in another physical and discursive space where neither the credibility and status of a believer nor the prestige of the congregation was threatened.

As Bateson argued in his study of the nature and meaning of the sacred, whereas explicit communication would alter the nature of ideas, noncommunication works by keeping up sacredness. For a Faith believer, the decision of not addressing certain topics is an attempt to control the surrounding world and strengthen the feeling of safety and success as well as confirming the social cohesion within the community, keeping up the borderline between the saved and the unsaved. Thus, noncommunication is,

indeed, a functional aspect of religious communication. It is a performative practice that supports the Neo-charismatic reality.

Notes

1 I am referring to the historical development of Pentecostal and Charismatic Christianity often defined as three waves (e.g. Hunt 1997: 82; Poloma & Hoelter 1998: 258–259).

2 The general idea of the mind-cure doctrine of the nineteenth century was that a human individual should think "God's thoughts". The difference between mind cure and co-existent Puritanism lied in the idea of God's will. While the Puritans emphasised the significance of God's will, the mind-cure thinkers did not accept the idea of God's arbitrary will. Instead, all people were seen as able to get everything they need from God already during this life, here and now. However, the idea of God fulfilling people's hopes requires the people having only pure and virtuous wishes. It was an individualistic aim at personal spiritual development (e.g. Meyer [1965]1980).

3 These themes were dealt with in the spiritualisms which emerged in the nineteenth century, such as the New Thought by Phineas P. Quimby and the Christian Science by Mary Baker Eddy. The ideal of the New Thought was the "art of (authentic) living." According to Quimby, the reasons for illness were wrong beliefs and fear, which can be cured mentally. People are to themselves exactly what they think they are (Teinonen 1965: 76). Mary Baker Eddy, for her part, developed the idea of "malicious animal magnetism" which she claimed to prove that in case distant mental healing was possible, a human being was correspondingly susceptible to the influence of evil (Teinonen 1965: 84).

4 Referential communicative behaviour is based on a general consensus concerning the meaning of the expression in a certain social reference group, while constitutive aspects in discourse, rather, find their specific meanings in the (situational) contexts in which they occur (Popp-Baier 2001: 3; Stromberg 1993: 10).

5 Folklorist Elaine J. Lawless has pointed out that the physical pain experienced in the role of a victim is not easily told about by the battered women. Instead, the narrators whom she interviewed avoided the topic or refused to talk about it at all. Apparently, while talking about it, the narrator would be forced to live through the shameful situation again (Lawless 2001: 59–61).

6 The names of the interviewees are pseudonyms.

7 Apostle Paul's metaphor in the Bible (Cor 9:6) deals with the meaning and importance of offering for the congregational activities and spiritual work as "sowing" and receiving benefits of such investments as

"reaping the harvest." It is the principle that is frequently referred to in the Word of Life teaching about money; one receives the same thing in return that has been given, often even with interest (Hovi 2009: 163).

References

Archived material

Taped interviews by the author are archived in TKU-Archive of the School of Cultural Studies at the University of Turku:
TKU/A/99/31:11
TKU/A/99/32b:11
TKU/A/99/49:19

Bibliography

Austin, John L. (1962)1978: *How to Do Things with Words*. Second edition by J.O. Urmson & M. Sbisà. Cambridge: Harvard University Press.

Bateson, Gregory & Mary Catherine Bateson 1987: *Angels Fear: An Investigation into the Nature and the Meaning of the Sacred*. London: Rider.

Bruner, Jerome 1987: Life as Narrative. *Social Research* 54:1, 11–32.

Brusco, Elizabeth 2010: Gender and Power. In: Allan Anderson, Michael Bergunder, André Droogers & Cornelis van deer Laan (eds.), *Studying Global Pentecostalism: Theories and Methods*. Berkeley: University of California Press, pp. 74–92.

Coleman, Simon 1991: "Faith which Conquers the World": Swedish Fundamentalism and Globalization of Culture. *Ethnos* 56:1, 6–18.

Coleman, Simon 1998: Charismatic Christianity and the Dilemmas of Gobalisation. *Religion* 28:3, 245–256.

Coleman, Simon 2000: *The Globalisation of Charismatic Christianity: Spreading the Gospel of Prosperity*. Cambridge: Cambridge University Press.

Coleman, Simon 2007: When Silence Isn't Golden. In: Matthew Engelke & Matt Tomlinson (eds.), *The Limits of Meaning: Case Studies in the Anthropology of Christianity*. New York: Berghahn Books, pp. 39–61.

Coleman, Simon & Peter Collins 2000: The 'Plain' and the 'Positive': Ritual, Experience and Aesthetics in Quakerism and Charismatic Christianity. *Journal of Contemporary Religion* 15:3, 317–329.

Hagin, Kenneth E. (1966)1980: *Right and Wrong Thinking*. Broken Arrow, Oklahoma: Faith Library Publications.

Hambre, Christer, Marianne Hammar, Lars Hiding, Martin Lind, Ingemar Moritz, Sören Olsson, Carl Johan Rundman & Torbjörn Strand 1983: *Framgångsteologi: En analys och prövning*. Stockholm: EFS förlaget.

Hänninen, Vilma 1999: *Sisäinen tarina, elämä ja muutos*. Acta Universitatis Tamperensis 696. Tampere: Tampereen yliopisto.

Harding, Susan F. 2000: *The Book of Jerry Falwell: Fundamen-*
talist Language and Politics. Princeton & Oxford: Princeton University Press.

Hovi, Tuija 1997: Kääntymiskertomukset haastatteluissa – muotoutuvia muistikuvia ja neuvoteltuja merkityksiä. In: Katarina Eskola & Eeva Peltonen (eds.), *Aina uusi muisto: Kirjoituksia menneen elämisestä meissä*. Nykykulttuurin tutkimusyksikön julkaisuja 54. Jyväskylä: Jyväskylän yliopisto.

Hovi, Tuija 2007: *Usko ja kerronta: Arkitodellisuuden narratiivinen rakentuminen uskonliikkeessä*. Annales Universitatis Turkuensis C 254. Turku: Turun yliopisto.

Hovi, Tuija 2009: Sitä niittää, mitä kylvää: Raha suomalaisessa uskonliikkeessä. In: Minna Ruckenstein & Timo Kallinen (eds.), *Rahan kulttuuri*. Helsinki: Suomalaisen Kirjallisuuden Seura, pp. 162–175.

Hovi, Tuija 2014: Functions of Narrative Genres for Lived Religion. *Approaching Religion* 4:1, 80–88.

Hunt, Stephen 1997: 'Doing the Stuff': The Vineyard Connection. In: Stephen Hunt, Malcolm Hamilton & Tony Walter (eds.), *Charismatic Christianity: Sociological Perspectives*. London: Macmillan Press Ltd., pp. 77–96.

Hunt, Stephen 1998: Magical Moments: An Intellectualist Approach to the Neo-Pentecostal Faith Ministries. *Religion* 28:3, 271–280.

Hunt, Stephen 2000: 'Winning Ways': Globalisation and the Impact of the Health and Wealth Gospel. *Journal of Contemporary Religion* 15:3, 330–347.

Hydén, Lars-Christer 2010: Identity, Self, Narrative. In: Matti Hyvärinen, Lars-Christer Hydén, Marja Saarenheimo & Maria Tamboukou (eds.), *Beyond Narrative Coherence*. Studies in Narrative 11. Amsterdam: John Benjamins Publishing Company, pp. 33–48.

Hydén, Margareta 2013: Narrating Sensitive Topics. In: Molly Andrews, Corinne Squire & Maria Tamboukou (eds.), *Doing Narrative Research*. Second edition. London: Sage, pp. 223–239.

Ketola, Kimmo, Seppo Knuuttila & Antti Mattila 2002: *Puuttuvat viestit: Nonkommunikaatio inhimillisessä vuorovaikutuksessa*. Helsinki: Gaudeamus.

Knuuttila, Seppo 2002: Vaitiolo, salaisuudet, ilmaisukiellot: Nonkommunikaation kontekstuaalisia merkityksiä. In: Kimmo Ketola, Seppo Knuuttila, Antti Mattila & Kari Mikko Vesala (eds.), *Puuttuvat viestit: Nonkommunikaatio inhimillisessä vuorovaikutuksessa*. Helsinki: Gaudeamus, pp. 119–150.

Lawless, Elaine J. 2001: *Women Escaping Violence: Empowerment through Narrative*. Columbia: University of Missouri Press.

Leming, Laura M. 2007: Sociological Explorations: What Is Religious Agency? *The Sociological Quarterly* 48, 73–92.

McGuire Meredith B. 1979: Testimony as a Commitment Mechanism in Catholic Pentecostal Prayer Group. *Journal for the Scientific Study of Religion* 16:2, 165–168.

Meyer, Donald (1965)1980: *The Positive Thinkers: Religion*

as Pop Psychology from Mary Baker to Oral Roberts. New York: Pantheon Books.

Moberg, Jessica 2013: Piety, *Intimacy and Mobility: A Case Study of Charismatic Christianity in Present-Day Stockholm.* Huddinge: Södertörns högskola.

Niemelä, Kati 2003: Uskonnollisuus eri väestöryhmissä. In: Kimmo Kääriäinen, Kati Niemelä & Kimmo Ketola (eds.), *Moderni kirkkokansa: Suomalaisten uskonnollisuus uudella vuosituhannella.* Kirkontutkimuskeskuksen julkaisuja 82. Tampere: Kirkon tutkimuskeskus, pp. 187–220.

Phoenix, Ann 2013: Analysing Narrative Contexts. In: Molly Andrews, Corinne Squire & Maria Tamboukou (eds.), *Doing Narrative Research.* London: Sage, pp. 72–82.

Poloma, Margaret M. & Lynette F. Hoelter 1998: The Toronto Blessing: A Holistic Model of Healing. *Journal for the Scientific Study of Religion* 37:2, 257–271.

Popp-Baier, Ulrike 2001: Narrating Embodied Aims: Self-transformation in Conversion Narratives – A Psychological Analysis. *Forum: Qualitative Social Research* 2:3, Art. 16, http://www.qualitative-research.net/index.php/fqs/article/view/911. Accessed January 22, 2016.

Schiff, Brian 2012: The Function of Narrative: Toward a Narrative Psychology of Meaning. *Narrative Works: Issues, Investigations, & Interventions* 2:1, 33–47.

Stromberg, Peter 1993: *Language and Self-Transformation: A Study of the Christian Conversion Narrative.* Cambridge: Cambridge University Press.

Teinonen, Seppo 1965: *Nykyajan lahkot: Uusia uskonnollisia liikkeitä ja yhteisöjä.* Helsinki: Kirjayhtymä.

Vesala, Kari Mikko, Kimmo Ketola, Seppo Knuuttila & Antti Mattila 2002: Mitä enkelit pelkäävät? In: Kimmo Ketola, Seppo Knuuttila, Antti Mattila & Kari Mikko Vesala, *Puuttuvat viestit: Nonkommunikaatio inhimillisessä vuorovaikutuksessa.* Helsinki: Gaudeamus, pp. 11–41.

Walters, Tony & Grace Davie 1998: The Religiosity of Women in the Modern West. *The British Journal of Sociology* 49:4, 640–660.

Tuija Hovi, Ph.D., is specialised in the social-psychology and anthropology of Christianity, as well as qualitative methods such as ethnography and narrative inquiry. Her research interests focus on the global Pentecostal and Charismatic Christian trends accommodated in contemporary Finland, popular religiosity and healing. Currently, Hovi works as a university lecturer in comparative religion at the University of Turku, Finland.
(tuija.h.hovi@utu.fi)

EVANGELICAL SILENCE IN A KOMI VILLAGE

Piret Koosa, University of Tartu

Becoming an Evangelical Christian has much to do with mastering Evangelical rhetoric, but there are also non-verbal aspects that are substantial in constituting the Evangelical self. Focusing on a rural Evangelical community in the Komi Republic of Russia, this article discusses ways in which participation in distinctive Evangelical verbal practices can be challenging or even undesirable in a pro-Orthodox environment. By looking at how, when and what Evangelicals leave unsaid or convey by means of emotions and embodied practices, I analyse different silences that are created and employed by group members and also used as proselytising tools. I propose that the intertwining of emotional and embodied features of faith and the specific environment that is unwelcoming to non-Orthodox believers produce a kind of Evangelical silence.

Keywords: Evangelicals, Russian Orthodoxy, embodied faith, Evangelical silence, Komi Republic

Talking about becoming a Christian and testifying to one's conversion are considered to be of central importance among Evangelicals, and scholars and believers alike often conceptualise Evangelical Christianity as the religion of talk. However, while narrative forms of being a believer are conventionally emphasised and readily available, not all individuals have the confidence or willingness to follow these patterns. In this article, I explore how, in addition to refraining from particular words and narrative templates, Evangelicals conceptualise faith in terms of displaying certain emotions and embodied features. I suggest, furthermore, that these non-verbal manifestations can be seen as having priority over verbal claims of religious commitment, especially in a predominantly Orthodox environment that regards Evangelicals with strong scepticism. Under such conditions, a certain kind of silence can be a strategic choice: while it leaves a person on the fringes

of the Evangelical community, it also facilitates interaction with the wider community and movement between the two communities.

The ethnographic material presented in this paper[1] has been collected over the course of several short-term fieldwork trips to villages of the Kulömdin District in the Republic of Komi since 2008.[2] The Republic of Komi, with a population of about 900,000, is situated in the north-eastern part of European Russia. While the indigenous Komis constitute about 25 percent of the republic's overall population, they are a majority in the Kulömdin District. A small Evangelical congregation in the village of Don is the focus of my doctoral research. Don, with about 500 inhabitants, is situated some 15 km from the district centre. In 2003, a missionary team consisting of an American named William and the Russians Andrei (later to become the group's pastor) and Semyon settled in Don and a congregation formed around them.

Piret Koosa 2016: Evangelical Silence in a Komi Village.
Ethnologia Europaea 46:2, 58–73. © Museum Tusculanum Press.

About 10 to 15 people usually attend the weekly services in the Don congregation. A few more people are loosely tied to the congregation; for example people who say they have come to God in the group but now live elsewhere still sometimes visit, and there are also other random participants. It is somewhat difficult to pinpoint the exact size of the community as there is no formal membership and some churchgoers are affiliated with other churches as well. I consider it reasonable to regard people who say that they have come to God in this church, take part in the congregation's life and relate to the Evangelical message as a community. The majority of the members are middle-aged and elderly women, which coincides with the composition of Orthodox congregations. Apart from the missionaries, few other men have participated in the church life with any consistency. The churchgoers come from both Don and nearby villages, from where Andrei and Semyon bring them by cars. In addition to Sunday services held in a private house adjusted for this purpose, home Bible study meetings are organised in other villages.

In the Komi Republic, as in Russia more broadly, Russian Orthodoxy is considered a kind of "by default" religion popularly and often by officials as well. While the variety of churches and religious groups in the Russian religious landscape quickly multiplied after the collapse of the Soviet Union, many critical voices have accompanied this diversification. Religion is frequently perceived to be closely connected with ethnic and cultural belonging and thus foreign missionaries and people converting to a "non-traditional" (i.e. non-Orthodox) faith are regarded with scepticism and even hostility. People generally have little knowledge of different Christian denominations and most non-Orthodox religious groups are popularly referred to as "sects". The concept of "sect" has absorbed many of the negative meanings Soviet ideology projected onto religion in general and this word has ultimately come to signify the "dark other" of post-socialist religious life (Broz 2009: 21). Thus, in spite of the official religious freedom and plurality in post-Soviet Russia, different faith groups have not "competed" on an equal basis. Both the Russian Orthodox Church (ROC) and lay people often invoke the notion of tradition when justifying ROC's privileged position in Russia.

Evangelical Protestants, in turn, have frequently criticised the idea of traditional religion as in their view faith is not something one can inherit (see e.g. Elliott 2003). They disapprove of the common state of affairs in Russia that a person considers him- or herself to be Orthodox but has a vague comprehension of its teachings and never goes to church. High ritualisation in the Orthodox tradition and pervasive vernacular practices have also received condemning assessments from Protestants. However, the Don Evangelicals who are the focus of this study generally tend to avoid openly criticising Orthodox believers. That is to say, while there are occasional disapproving comments about certain aspects of (popular) Orthodoxy, critique of the Orthodox is not explicitly part of the mission discourse, nor is it routinely incorporated into sermons.

Indeed, in the Russian context, a quite distinct and remarkable feature of the Don congregation is their non-denominational ideology. Non-denominational Christian churches and congregations are historically Protestant but do not officially belong to any specific denomination. The character of the group is similar to the "new paradigm" or "free" churches increasingly common in America (see Miller 1998). Unregistered and called simply the Christian Community of Don (Donskaia khristianskaia obshina), the group welcomes Christians of all denominations. The congregation members usually refer to themselves as simply Christians or Evangelical Christians. Most of the people in the group have had some sort of personal contact with vernacular Orthodoxy and some still consider themselves Orthodox. The pastor has a background in a Charismatic church but does not regard himself as a follower of any specific denomination and strongly pursues an ecumenical approach. While open to different forms of worship, emphasis on the importance of individual and conscious conversion and mission activities places them firmly in the Evangelical tradition.

In my analysis, I draw on interviews conducted with nearly all of the people who have attended services at the Don congregation with some regularity, but also on casual conversations and personal observations at church events and other occasions. Most people have been interviewed more than once, both individually and in situations where several believers were present, whether in someone's home or at the church. In regard to recognising silences in social interactions, group conversations have sometimes turned out to be more informative than interviewing a single person. Situations where several group members are present provide an opportunity to examine the ways believers present their narratives to other believers and how they subtly guide each other in presenting these narratives. Analysing such situations also makes it possible to better detect when, in what circumstances and how silences are produced. It is important to note that silence does not mean only a lack of speech, but also noncommunication, avoiding saying certain things or saying things in a certain manner (see Tuija Hovi, this issue).

Conversion beyond the Narrative Lens

Within Evangelical Christianity, "conversion" is a central notion. While theoretically conversion can be understood to be any kind of religious change (Rambo & Farhadian 1999), in mainstream Evangelical discourse it usually has a rather specific meaning. Very often Paul's conversion on the road to Damascus as recounted by Luke in the Acts of the Apostles (Acts 9: 1–22) is taken as the primary model for conversion. This model combines ideas about sudden, dramatic revelation that leads to radical reversal of previous beliefs and is caused by external divine intervention (Bryant 1999: 181; Rambo 2003: 213).

Unlike the approach popularly conveyed by Evangelicals, scholars have tended to emphasise the processual character of conversion rather than viewing it as a distinct event (e.g. Rambo & Farhadian 1999). The process of conversion that leads to self-transformation takes place in the dynamic field of people and ideologies: it is not just a personal spiritual awakening but also an entry into a particular religious community, which makes it important to pay attention to the social and institutional dimensions of conver-

sion (Bryant & Lamb 1999: 12; Wanner 2007: 149). One element in the conversion process is the public display of commitment to the Evangelical faith and community (cf. Rambo & Farhadian 1999: 31). This commitment is most saliently mediated through a narrative form.

A conversion narrative or testimony is a story of one's life before and after conversion. It is supposed to present the total change in a person's life that is brought about by realising the truth about God and the acquired knowledge of being saved (cf. Lawless 1983). Being able to testify to how God has changed one's life can be viewed as a ritual expression of the person's new status as an Evangelical Christian (Hovi 2000: 375). Elaine J. Lawless (1983) has argued that the conversion is not actually complete until a narrative recounting of the experience is presented by the one who experienced it, as the narrative functions to articulate the belief. Telling the personal story or, especially, being asked to tell one's narrative to outsiders signals membership by conveying the sense of belonging strong enough to carry the message promoted by the community (cf. Cain 1991: 232).

Certain specific words and phrases are employed to describe one's new mode of understanding the world and how this comprehension came about. Because of "shared elementary language" (Harding 2000: 19), conversion stories are paradoxically both personal and stereotyped. Tanya Luhrmann (2004: 522) has pointed out that this combination of very personal and stereotyped narratives is not unique to Evangelical Christians. For example, the recruitment of shamans has been described as exhibiting an analogous combination of cultural expectations and personal experiences. Also, in a very similar manner, Carole Cain (1991) has described the way members of *Alcoholics Anonymous* learn to place the events and experiences of their lives into the general model provided by the group, and how telling the appropriate story makes it possible to demonstrate and gain validation for one's AA identity.

The conversion story as a specific genre or category can thus be said to provide a general framework in which individual stories can be seen as concrete examples that verify the group's general dogmas (cf. Cain 1991: 227). This framework for verbalising one's religious experiences and coming to God is acquired from the examples of more experienced believers who, by narrating their own stories, instruct novices on how it ought to be done. Certain stereotyped expressions help to formulate interpretations of individual experiences and convey these to other believers so that they can relate to and understand them. While common expressions can be appropriated in a personally meaningful way (cf. Lindquist & Coleman 2008), stereotyped language can also offer useful words to people who for some reason lack their own words or feel that these are somehow inadequate. As my case study of the Don congregation suggests, as people have very different motivations for joining the group, sometimes the formulaic following of stereotyped language stands alone and there is no active personal interpretation.

Scholars studying different branches of Evangelical Christianity have paid special attention to the role and importance of specific language practices in constituting the believer's identity. Whereas Lewis R. Rambo and Charles E. Farhadian (1999: 30), for example, see rhetorical practices as one feature of immersing the converting person in the new religion, other scholars have suggested that converting in essence can be described in terms of acquiring a new language (cf. Harding 1987, 2000; Stromberg 1993). Susan Harding (1987) has argued, based on the example of fundamentalist Baptists, that rhetoric is the principal vehicle of conversion.[3] According to Harding (2000: 59), speaking is believing: becoming a born-again Christian involves joining a particular narrative tradition to which one submits his or her past, present and future as a speaker.

Compared to the attention scholars have paid to Evangelical language ideologies and speech practices, the role and presence of silence along with sensuous aspects of Evangelical faith have received much less consideration. Still, several scholars have recently criticised approaches that ascribe a fundamental role to language in the process of conversion. Tanya Luhrmann has emphasised the importance of emotional and sensuous aspects of the conversion process. She claims that the transition from non-

believer to believer is not likely to occur simply by acquiring new concepts and words, suggesting that the convert must emotionally come to believe that those new concepts and words are true. According to Luhrmann (2004: 519; see also Luhrmann 2012: xxi, 131), "believers learn to identify bodily and emotional states as signs of God's presence in their life, identifications that imply quite different learning processes than those entailed by linguistic and cognitive knowledge."

Joseph Webster (2013: 107) has similarly questioned the contention that conversion occurs solely or even primarily through language, pointing out that this approach ignores the roles of embodiment and emotion. In his discussion of language in the construction of the Charismatic Protestant identity, Simon Coleman (2007: 167–168) has indicated that Harding's analysis leaves out two important elements of the conservative Protestant use of language. Coleman argues that, first, the deployment of language can reconstitute not only the listener but also the speaker. Second, language cannot be divorced from sensual forms, since the power of words is often demonstrated by their effects on and constitution of the material world, as well as on the born-again person.

This article aims to contribute to this recent body of scholarship that broadens perspectives on understanding conversion. I seek to demonstrate how the particularities of social and cultural context can influence the manner in which language is or is not used by members of a specific religious group, as well as the functions and meanings ascribed to nonverbal communication and expressions of faith. My suggestion is that, in addition to the general Evangelical ideology, conceptualising emotions and the use of language in the small group considered in this paper depend significantly on the environment that regularly challenges the acceptability of Evangelical mode of believing. Under such conditions, a certain kind of silence can be a strategic choice made to facilitate interactions with the wider community and movement between the two communities.

Challenging Narrative Templates and Deficient Language

In the Don group, a believer is often defined along the lines of "one who talks spiritual words and brings people to God by talking his word" (W, b. 1977)[4]. It is presumed that having been converted means that the person has to start working on converting others. And one of the central means by which adherents are expected to contribute to bringing others to God is by recounting their personal stories. However, despite this obvious and expected emphasis on the constant verbal articulation of one's faith, readily available narrative models remain inaccessible for some members of the congregation and conversion can be an ineffable experience.

Community members' conceptions of an ideal conversion narrative have been greatly influenced by one of the founding members of the congregation, the American missionary William. William's account is that of a man who was a hopeless alcoholic and a drug addict for years until quite suddenly his life was completely changed by converting and "taking Jesus into his life." As an American's presence in a Komi village is locally newsworthy, many non-Evangelicals of the Kulömdin District are aware of the Don group because of this curious connection. Stories about William have appeared in local media and spread among the villagers by word of mouth. Consequently, even though William left Kulömdin for another district in 2011, in the outsiders' perception he continues to function as a kind of emblem of the whole congregation due to his popularly known dramatic conversion story and "exoticism". In a way, his narrative is an archetypal example of its genre, being very similar to countless other Evangelical conversion stories. But for the Don Evangelicals William's decision to move to Russia and become a missionary, to dedicate his assets and abilities to serving the needy people in this specific geographic location, demonstrates in a very concrete and compelling manner the power of God and his care for people in Komi in particular (see also Koosa 2013).

Another often-referenced conversion story in the Don group is that of the local woman Nadya, who was an alcoholic for years but came to God in the Don church, repented and was able to quit drinking and drastically change her lifestyle. Such exemplar narratives are used to push into the background accounts that present conversion in less dramatic terms. Perceived to be more effective for proselytising purposes, they tend to acquire independent existence. Both William's and Nadya's narratives have become detached from the individuals whose experience they narrate: even when the central character is absent, I have often witnessed others using the stories to substantiate their own arguments. Moreover, excessive drinking is an acknowledged and often bemoaned problem in the villages and both William's and Nadya's stories convey the message that it is possible to get rid of alcoholism, which adds to their relevance in this specific social context.

Although William's story in particular is often repeated and referred to as an example, only a few members of the Don group actually attempt to present their personal narratives in similarly dramatic terms. While some do present the sins of their previous lives as if through a magnifying glass, more often than not people tend to speak of their lives in terms of continuity. That there is some kind of break from the previous life is often briefly remarked on or glossed over with the formulaic statement of now "going in a 180-degree different direction." While life after joining the Evangelical community is described in overly positive terms, this does not necessarily mean rejecting the former self or conceptualising the previous life in completely negative terms. As I will demonstrate in more detail below, this preference for continuity is also tied to the non-denominational character of the Don congregation and its members' self-positioning in a predominantly Orthodox society.

Even though giving testimony of the works of God is considered to be the duty of every believer, Don Evangelicals have ambiguous attitudes about the nature of human language and do not view verbal claims of one's faith in a straightforward way. To begin with, language can prove to be deficient in that it fails to offer sufficient vocabulary to allow for adequate expression of what one goes through by realising the divine truth and accepting Jesus in his or her life (cf. Tuija Hovi and Pihla Maria Siim in this issue).

> Nadya (b. 1976): The day of [my] repentance was for me…
> Inga (b. 1974) (interrupting): Unforgettable.
> Nadya: … unforgettable day.
> Inga: A spiritual rebirth. [You are] born again.
> Oksana (b. 1971): Yes, these processes, internal, deep, spiritual… it is not possible to convey in words.
> Inga: A person who has not lived through it can't understand it. He can't understand it.
> Oksana: And it happens not by your will, well, how to say, not simply because…
> Inga (interrupting): … because you want it.
> Oksana: Yes, yes. That you want or that it was your own will, your wish. You are drawn to God. But this process itself, how the Holy Ghost works, it is not possible to convey in words what is happening in the soul of the person.
> Inga: You come in front of all the people, fall on your knees, it's very interesting, yes (laughing), and you don't even feel ashamed. [You] throw such a burden off yourself…
> Oksana (interrupting): this lightness and joy, gratitude to God for releasing you from your sins, [from] wicked life. It is such a state, such a feeling that is not possible to convey.

In a sense then, the conversion experience is said to be clearly untranslatable to non-believers. In addition to demonstrating the idea that only insiders are truly able to grasp the meaning of conversion, there is another interesting aspect in this excerpt from a group interview. Namely, it is actually recently converted Nadya who has been asked to tell about her coming to God: the others urged her to do so. But as soon as there is a short pause in her narration, as she is looking for words, the more experienced congregants wade right in to help her to formulate her statement. In fact, most of her conversion experience is put into words by other women, while Nadya remains silently smiling and nodding in agreement. In addition to conveying the idea that the conversion experience is experienced similarly, this example demonstrates the implicit way in which the Evangelical discourse is taught to the newcomer, and the role of submissive silence in this process. But still, it cannot be seen only in terms of teaching the neophyte: the eagerness with which the women interrupt each other's sentences demonstrates the excitement they experience upon remembering their own conversion.

The somewhat ambiguous attitude towards language is also connected with the concept of empty words and with the idea that human words can be deceitful. Speaking properly is not enough; one must constantly substantiate his or her words by acting properly as well:

> [A believer is] one who believes and lives with God, and does not just talk. Well, how to put it: some say that they are believers but live in sin. [...] If I live with God then as God is holy, he makes me holy too and I can't sin. It seems to me that this is what a believer is like. That is, a real believer. [...] A human can't judge whether one is real or not real. Well, with some people you can see right away; it is clearly visible who is a believer. But otherwise only God can know whether someone has indeed given his heart to the Lord. (W, b. 1984)

> Faith without deeds is dead. [...] Only talking about being a believer, without deeds, then it is a dead faith. But when there are deeds, then the believer doesn't have to say anything at all. Because the other person can see it from the deeds. (W, b. 1971)

As words cannot always be trusted, the Don Evangelicals place significant importance on proper behaviour. Indeed, from the beginning, greatly influenced by William, their agenda has been to proselytise through practically reaching out to people (see also Koosa & Leete 2014). Intriguingly, direct verbal contact between William and the local people has been very limited as they lack a common language and the pastor Andrei has had to serve as an interpreter for William. Thus, most Komi Evangelicals are familiar with William's story not from a first person account but through translation. Moreover, William did not consider his oratory skills to be very good and thus wished to serve and witness for God through a social mission. This means that evangelising has been carried out with an emphasis on providing practical help to the socio-economically deprived. According to the Evangelical logic, this kind of work leads to the spiritual growth of the believer, as it is pleasing to God. Evangelicals' engagement in good deeds and selflessly helping the needy is also thought to cause non-Evangelicals to contemplate the motivation for acting and thus initiates a process of conversion.

Emotional and Embodied Faith

There is thus a certain tension around the idea of a verbalised account validating the conversion experience and the notion of language and verbal claims as being insufficient. Hence, great significance is attached to non-verbal communication through good deeds. Another important aspect of expressing the Evangelical self and conveying the Evangelical message concerns the managing of emotions. Luhrmann (2012) has thoroughly examined the ways Evangelicals learn to attend to their thoughts and emotions so as to experience the real and external presence of God in their lives. Among other techniques, she has identified specific emotional practices that believers employ to achieve this (ibid.: 111). Amy C. Wilkins (2008) has also focused on Evangelicals' conceptualisations of mental states by demonstrating how Evangelicals can come to perceive positive emotions such as happiness or peace as central to their Christian identity. According to Wilkins's analysis, happiness is understood to signal moral righteousness, and displaying positive emotions and friendliness is utilised as a proselytising tool. I have observed similar tendencies in discussing and conceptualising certain emotions among the Don Evangelicals as well, which attest to the need to examine non-verbal expressions of belief. In comparison to Orthodoxy, the Evangelicals frequently stress the importance of accepting faith consciously and with full understanding. At the same time, they often highlight the role of feelings and emotionality in the process of

coming to God. Women are conceptualised as being more emotional and this is thought to make accepting God easier for them:

> Because with his mind and with reasoning a person cannot logically accept these ideas and truths. (M, b. 1978)

> Women are kind of more sensitive emotionally and they evidently react to the fact that there is a living God. (W, b. 1966)

The emotionally and bodily felt aspects of faith are frequently discussed and emphasised. Accepting Jesus in one's life is commonly described in terms of experiencing the disappearance of a previously felt void in oneself or as getting rid of a physically felt burden. Moreover, the change brought about by conversion, although sometimes hard to put into words, is not understood to be exclusively internal or subjective: it is something that is possible for external observers to detect as well. Characteristically, the manifestation of genuine belief is described in terms of positive emotions. The person feels happy and calm, does not get agitated or angry about things that used to bother him or her before the conversion and the fear of the uncertainty of the future is gone.

> Before there was this anxiety. As if you're waiting for something bad [to happen]. But now you're as peaceful as a boa! I don't even worry what to prepare for dinner tomorrow or what to wear; [all] this somehow works out by itself. (W, b. 1959)

Evangelicals talk about how becoming a believer has not only transformed their behaviour and habits but has also given them a kind of special general appearance or "aura", which is said to be noticed by non-Evangelical people as well. For example, a woman described how she was able to remain calm when everybody else got upset in a tedious everyday situation:

> [T]here was this long, long queue, I stood there for two hours and the sales clerk said afterwards

that I was the only one to be so calm (laughing); everyone else was so angry and irritated. She said to me that I was so calm, [that] it's so interesting. You see – it is good that people already see the difference [in me] and it feels good too. (W, b. 1971)

From the discussion between two Don congregants quoted below it appears that the almost transcendent joy said to beam from a true believer is sometimes in fact judged to have priority over the verbal expressions he or she does or does not make:

Larisa (b. 1949): He [a Christian] never says a bad word...
Semyon (b. 1978): No, I think it's something else.
Larisa: No?
Semyon: The face – joy...
Larisa: Aa! Yes, the face.
Semyon: The person's eyes shine joyfully.
Larisa: Internal joy.
Semyon: Yes, one can see that this joy comes from within, a kind of love comes from within. At least I can tell the difference. Not always, but very often. Whether one is a Christian or not, it is visible.
Larisa: God is love and he gives this love to his children as well. This love even spills over. It is in the eyes and everywhere. They [Christians] love people.
Semyon: A person's face glows.

The excerpt illustrates how the more experienced believer – although younger in years – influences the discourse of the novice Evangelical. As Semyon interrupts Larisa and directs attention from the external to the internal, Larisa accepts this and subsequently only repeats and elaborates on the viewpoint Semyon has expressed.

On the one hand, the love of God is said to radiate from a believing person and the good emotions and proper way of behaving are sometimes described as automatically accompanying conversion. On the other hand, Evangelicals actually quite consciously make efforts to cultivate the Christian self. Part of this project is certainly controlling and silencing unwanted emotions in everyday situations as described

in the following quotation, where there is also a reflective remark on how it is consciously thinking differently that makes one feel different:

It's as if I'm not growing older, but rejuvenating with prayers. And I say that if it's because of self-suggestion, then thank God. I'm as glad as a little child. I've never been so happy [since coming to God]. And sometimes it happens that we argue, sometimes between ourselves; [my] husband tries to prove something – [then for me] it stops and that's it; my eyes are closed to all the bad things. And I said [to my husband] "come on, I will not argue with you over this nonsense." He turned around and went to his room. I say it is as if I could jump for joy that my life has turned out like this! (W, b. 1956)

As part of concentrating on positive emotions, one is supposed to refrain from or silence reactions and behavioural patterns that are perceived as negative and un-Christian. At the same time, to become a truly good Christian it is actually necessary not simply to avoid complicated or uncomfortable situations. In fact, it is the opposite: one must learn to cope and react in a way suitable for a Christian by not avoiding difficulties or possibly challenging encounters with other people. Pastor Andrei once explained at a service that this is one of the reasons one must participate in communal life:

Sitting on a couch, watching TV, and occasionally opening the Bible, it's easy to learn to love – no one irritates me, no one's socks or armpits smell and no one bothers me with their comments. You can't learn to love if you're torn away from the churchly communal life, sitting at home or fishing. [Or] Even [when simply] gazing at stars and contemplating God's might. (M, b. 1979)

It appears then that in addition to a certain pattern of talking "properly", there are also "proper" emotions that accompany conversion. Feeling and displaying good emotions is a sign of being a good Christian. Correspondingly, there are certain emotions a good believer is not supposed to feel or display. The mainstream discourse stresses a kind of instant, spontaneous change in emotional and behavioural conduct that coming to God brings about; at the same time, conscious and sometimes arduous efforts one does to achieve what is perceived as the good Christian self remain taciturn. Furthermore, it is my suggestion that in addition to the inner logic of Evangelical ideology that puts emphasis on certain emotional and embodied practices, the socio-cultural setting that complicates implementing the narrative mode of proselytising and expressing one's faith verbally also enhances focusing on these aspects of faith.

Difficulties in Speaking and Negotiating Continuities

When asked about their coming to God, several members of the Don group said that they "don't know how to speak (yet)." Different reasons and meanings of such a claim can be recognised. In some cases such a remark is indeed followed by few comments on (religious or other kind of) experiences. This is more likely to happen when a more seasoned congregation member is present. For example, during our first visit to interview Lidia (b. 1966), she suggested calling over another Evangelical woman, Albina (b. 1951). As Albina had started to visit the Don church through Lidia, this situation could be interpreted in terms of Lidia demonstrating her success in fulfilling the duty of bringing new people to God. We began by discussing briefly the aims of our work[5] and local religious life in general. Upon hearing that neither of us was baptised, Lidia started to talk about how life with God did not automatically make the hardships of life disappear but it did make them much easier to handle. She gave some examples from her experience and ended by indirectly urging us to consider our own spiritual state and also pointing out that such insistence was the duty of a true believer:

It is written that now is the time to repent, to be saved. One mustn't delay with repentance, as then it will be too late. And this is why we're called to witness about God and the gospel to all people (laughs).[6]

Lidia then paused and suggested that perhaps there were some more questions they could answer. When Lidia said that maybe Albina could add something, the latter promptly announced "I don't know how to speak yet. I cannot talk like this yet," to which Lidia responded by laughing kindly. In this instance, although otherwise quite talkative, Albina was apparently intimidated by the idea that she needed to present an account similar to Lidia's talk: well composed, combining references to the Bible, specific examples and more conceptual arguments. The few extended contributions Albina made during the conversation all generally followed directions prompted by Lidia. In comparison to Lidia's discussions, Albina's comments were more specific to the region's or her own family's history. Lidia for her part tended to place particular examples into the context of Biblical reality to make a more conceptual point. It seems plausible to assume that it was the presence of Lidia, fluently demonstrating the Evangelical discourse, that silenced Albina's less conceptualised and perhaps more ambivalent perspective.

Lidia: [...] It is written in the Gospels that Jesus said "I was persecuted and you will be persecuted." [...] That means that, indeed, true believers are not tolerated much, they are so-to-say persecuted. [...]
Albina: The Orthodox really were persecuted. You see, even here [...] they saved the icons [during Soviet times], these believers. [...] There were persecutions but there were always believers and they passed on everything, from generation to generation.
[...]
Albina: There was the revolution in [19]17. [...] And the mother and father [of my mother] died the same year. And they [the children] were given to different orphanages. But how, at that time, in [19]17, were they raised in orphanages? It was done without God. And that's how they grew up.
Lidia: Yes, yes, yes. Then there were those kinds of times.
Albina: Then there were those kinds of times.
Lidia: And now we ask what about those who

didn't know anything about living God [...] And in the Bible, there is a place [where it's written] that [they will be judged] according to deeds. They will be judged according to deeds, according to conscience. [...] These people who had not heard of Christ, they will be judged according to the conscience.

While Albina acknowledged Lidia's role in bringing her to the Don church and to God, she also declared some kind of continuity in her spiritual life. Although she was also baptised in the Don church, she did not articulate a clear break from her previous life, which rendered her religious identity somewhat ambiguous:

For about three years [Lidia Nikolaevna] spoke to me and I listened. And now I have been driving there [to the Don church] for two years already. And I'm very pleased that I indeed came to God. Through Lidia Nikolaevna. [...] I always considered myself a Christian, an Orthodox Christian. All your life you believe in something anyway. But I went there and listened and understood that God is one.

On the other hand, there are examples from my fieldwork where a statement about not knowing how to speak can be regarded as a disclaimer of performance (Bauman 1984: 21–22) for it is followed by a rich narrative account of a person's life. For example, when asked how she had become a believer, Matryona first announced that she did not know how to speak, but then quite smoothly went on to tell her life story, paying attention to different, including Orthodox, religious encounters throughout her life and to their significance. Finally, after speaking for over half an hour, she recalled:

Oh, I didn't tell you how I repented. In general, I went to the church for about a year. [...] But then William [the missionary] asked "if you die, where do you think you will end up?" I said, "well, I will go neither to paradise nor hell. I'm not that bad, and I will end up somewhere in between." He said

that there was no third option, no middle ground. Said, "repent!" I said "I'm not ready. How can I repent if I smoke and swear?" [...] [He told me] not to worry, that I'd manage. I said that I didn't even know what words to say. And William told me to repeat after him. So I thought I would try. And he talked and I repeated. And when I came out of the church I immediately quit smoking. Even though I had repented somehow without understanding. I mean, in words it was not understandable. I didn't understand a thing. And the Lord immediately cleansed me. (W, b. 1957)

During several conversations I had with Matryona, the above-described repentance experience did not seem to have too much importance in her everyday narratives about personal religious experiences and development. However, it seems she here tries to follow the example the "exemplar" members of the community have set by tying her conversion to a specific event. At the same time, Matryona refers back to her grandmother, who was the first to acquaint her with some religious principles, and she does not express any kind of exclusive commitment to the Don community:

[My] grandmother was Orthodox. But the Lord is anyway one and the same. I listen to the [Orthodox] Soyuz channel: Andrei teaches us exactly the same. The Commandments are the same, the Lord is the same, everything is exactly the same. [...] If our church weren't here, but there was an Orthodox church [in our village], I'd go there. (W, b. 1957)

From Matryona's account another interesting and ambivalent aspect of Evangelicals' attitude towards language emerges. In general, the Evangelicals try to avoid distinctly ritualistic formulas in their speech. Especially when addressing God in prayer, the emphasis is laid on using one's own words to make the utterances meaningful. However, in the situation described by Matryona it is apparent that sometimes certain words can be effective even when the speaker repeats them without deep comprehension.

Simply saying certain words – asking for repentance – proves to be sufficient for the divine force to bring about a transformation in the speaker.

Besides the more seasoned congregants, Evangelical literature, TV-programmes etc. also teach the new members of the group the specific style of conversion stories. Expressing hesitation about one's ability to narrate or to do it "properly", can be seen as a kind of meta-narrative device that establishes an interpretive frame according to which the listener should understand and judge the narrative (Babcock 1984: 70–71). As the group members are well acquainted with the genre of the conversion narrative, and it is recognised as performance, the speaker assumes responsibility for performing in a socially appropriate way (Bauman 1984: 11). In addition to creating an interpretive frame, proclaiming incompetence in speaking also reaffirms the idea that there indeed is a "correct" way and thus upholds the conventions of the genre (cf. Bauman 1984: 21). The Evangelical narrative pattern is not directly challenged.

In the case of Albina and Matryona, it can be said that the phrase "I don't know how to speak" signifies the worry that they have not learned to express their religious experiences in such a compact narrative following the kind of discourse that is understood to be the "proper" template. But at the same time they both seem to indicate a connection or continuity with the Orthodox tradition. The phrase thus seems to signify the fact that the individual has not actually personally felt the kind of drastic change in her life that she feels is somehow expected by the more experienced believers. Compared to the "exemplar" Evangelical conversion narratives, the overall nature of narratives in the Don group tends to be much more ambivalent, not presenting any sudden rupture in the narrator's spiritual life. Most people in the community understand their coming to God as a continuing process that began before they actively thought about religious matters and continues after the conscious decision to live with God. To an extent, there is a certain culturally motivated resistance to the specifically Evangelical form of being a believer. For people with an Orthodox background, articulating some kind of total break from the previous understandings of the world is not always considered desirable. Rather, people prefer to see and speak of their spiritual lives in terms of continuity.

Ambiguous narratives that do not follow the supposed Evangelical discourse are superseded by focusing attention on the "exemplar" narratives, such as William's or Nadya's. Narrators who find it difficult to formulate their experiences as well remain on the periphery of the community. However, while at the margins of the Evangelical community, these people are somewhat better positioned in the larger village community as they – at least partly – still carry the Orthodox identity and follow locally approved religious habits.

The ecumenical approach promoted by the Don group provides an accommodating environment for such a positioning. For example, while denominational Protestants (e.g. Baptists and Pentecostals) can be suspicious of attending even other Protestant churches, in the Don community it is quite acceptable that members also go to Orthodox services. It is the congregation's non-denominational character that allows space for somewhat ambivalent positioning and enables people to fit in even without a narrative stressing of a drastic change. But also, the diverse religious background of community members supports the non-denominational ideology.

Strategic Silencing

While there exists a generally acknowledged narrative form that a good Evangelical is supposed to follow, one aspect of this skill is learning what is not supposed to be talked about. Silencing can be used to fashion the Evangelical self, but being taciturn is also used with non-Evangelicals with the aims of proselytising, avoiding conflicts and finding common ground. A kind of strategic silencing serves multiple, sometimes overlapping purposes.

From the perspective of cultivating the Evangelical self, there are themes and words one is expected to avoid (see also Tuija Hovi in this issue; Hovi 2014: 86). First, there is an obvious stylistic side: a believer is not supposed to use swear words and foul language. Refraining from specific speech practices such as gossiping is part of becoming a good Christian. Certain things or processes perceived as negative are downplayed in believers' accounts in order to control the surrounding environment, and shape it according to Christian ideals (see also Tuija Hovi in this issue).

Compared to the clearly explicated need to renounce vulgar language and cursing, silencing or avoiding particular themes – doing things with silence – is somewhat more difficult to notice. One topic that is usually not addressed is lapsing from faith. Even when the community members admit that there are people who have joined the church and then left it, these occurrences are softened. For example, the aspect that even in their case the Evangelical message is still spread is emphasised:

> It seems to me that those people who were members and then left the church are a half-success [in evangelising] in the sense that now the people kind of know the other side, another alternative in life. (W, b. 1980)

Minimising and silencing negative or unpleasant things and highlighting positive aspects is used to see their activities as meaningful even when confronted with apparent failure.

Another important topic that is approached rather carefully concerns interdenominational problems. While most people have personal experiences of negative encounters and attitudes because of their belonging to an Evangelical community, it is quite common that these issues are not talked about – at least to outsiders – without being directly asked about them, and even when talked about, such difficulties are regularly minimised. For example, when recounting how the initial relationship with the local Orthodox priest was terminated by the bishop, the account is framed with softening remarks:

> Everything is good. […] We communicated with him very closely. […] Simply later on he was restricted by the bishopric. He was told that people had complained about him [for communicating with Evangelicals]. […] But otherwise we, we still

see him, everything is very good. In the beginning, we even drove around the villages with him. (M, b. 1978)

Actually, experiencing discrimination can also be utilised in identity building: encountering hardships because of their faith affirms Evangelicals' concept of themselves as true Christians (see Koosa 2015). However, in terms of aiming to create a positive image of the group, directed both to the members and outsiders, conflicts and problems are likely to be silenced and more positive aspects emphasised.

In the following excerpt, Lidia condemns the Orthodox followers who disdain Protestants but also emphasises that Protestants should not focus on problematic issues:

> If you believe in God, you must above all radiate this love of God, whether you're Orthodox or Protestant or Catholic. You must always love God and love your neighbour. And we have no right to turn people against each other. This is not in accordance with God. (W, b. 1966)

It seems that there is a dual logic behind avoiding mentioning conflicts and disagreements. This is supposed to avoid or lessen quite sharp confrontations with the Orthodox. Remaining taciturn about articulating problems helps to avoid the occasional accusations that the Evangelicals criticise the Orthodox and create discord in the community. Concentrating on the negative is also seen as hindering developing a good Christian self. Also, downplaying the interdenominational disagreements and difficulties is important in terms of the ecumenical agenda of Don Evangelicals as it helps to maintain the idea of overall Christian unity. As the different aspects are intertwined, it is not always possible to discern whether there are ideological or social reasons behind silencing certain issues.

But silencing of certain topics is also in a more straightforward manner employed to facilitate creating a suitable environment for proselytising and relating to non-Evangelicals. Conscious efforts are made to control language use so as not to utter specific words that are very likely to alarm their audience in the particular cultural context within which they operate. As a means of encouraging potentially sympathetic, or conciliating sceptical outsiders, and diminishing the felt estrangement concerning the non-Orthodox, the Evangelicals commonly prefer to avoid mentioning specific denominational names. Rather than speaking about being a Baptist for example, people identify themselves as (Evangelical) Christians or Protestants. While this use of words is certainly in accordance with the ecumenical mindset, it is also clearly determined by the specific cultural environment. The pastor commented on this strategy as follows:

> Basically, in the Protestant Churches there is now the tendency to get rid of this label of their names. It's because these labels are intimidating for many people. There's the First Baptist Church – [and the people would say] ooh, Baptist! – I will never go to a Baptist church! [Imitating an agitated tone of voice]. But if you call the Church, for example, I don't know, Church of the Home of God [Dom bozhii] for example or, well, I don't know, Church of the New Generation [Novoe pokolenie] or the Friends of Jesus Church [Druz'ia Iisusa], a kind of totally neutral name, for some people it is better. Apparently they would rather go there than to some Baptist church [...]. (M, b. 1979)

There is also a certain tension between the Evangelical assumption that one should verbalise his or her spiritual experience and locally conventional modes of self-expression. In the Orthodox tradition it is not customary to accentuate individual experiences of the transcendental or to seek a personal relationship with God; rather, God is addressed through different mediators. The concept of publicly conveying one's deeply personal experiences and thoughts also departs from Komi villagers' conventional practice. Furthermore, popular discourse interprets the dramatic change of a person as "brainwashing". Moreover, Orthodox critics sometimes speak of Evangelicals as if they "hypnotise" people with their talk. There is a widespread idea that Evangelical Chris-

tians are "zombified" sectarians who go about trying to lure new members into their sect. For example, a woman who was the only Protestant in Don before the missionaries' arrival characterised a typical reaction to her attempts to witness as follows:

> And as soon as you start to speak [about faith], everyone will point to their temples and say that you have gone mad, [that] Baptists are sectarians, Baptists are altogether horrible people [...]. (W, b. 1966)

Thus, in the Komi village environment the general opinion of their Orthodox neighbours is that Evangelicals are unwanted "sectarians" (see also Koosa 2015). Broadly, this has a twofold effect. By prohibiting "religious propaganda" in public space, unsympathetic officials restrict Evangelicals' opportunities to spread the Word of God.

> It's only possible for us to go from person to person; in this way you can evangelise without problems, that is, simply visit somebody. [...] But there can be no massive evangelising now, specifically here in this district. [...] And this all depends on the specific people in power there. As the boss says, so it is. Because of that, we of course continue the services; nobody prohibits you from believing, gathering in houses, at your own house. (M, b. 1979)

> In school, for example, one isn't allowed to talk [about faith] at all [...] A directive was issued. By no means can one say anything [about God]. Because of this one feels that if it is prohibited, then it is prohibited. You can speak at home, but at school you can't. (W, b. 1952)

While officially directives about religious activities in the public spaces concern all faiths, it is common practice that Orthodoxy is treated differently from the others. For example, it has not been unexceptional that representatives of the ROC visit schools or are included to official celebrations organised by local municipalities. Also, demonstrating one's adherence to Orthodoxy is unlikely to get negative attention while quite the opposite holds true for articulating Evangelical affiliation.

Furthermore, people have encountered similar restrictions from their superiors at work. For example, when a member of the Evangelical church became the director of the village's clubhouse, he was explicitly cautioned to abstain from any kind of "religious agitation". So, to an extent, the Evangelicals are forced to submit to the silencing imposed on them from outside in order to avoid direct confrontation with officials or employers. Under such conditions, other kinds of means are conceptualised and implemented as instruments of evangelising. Individual members of the group can also be discouraged from sharing the gospel with their neighbours and acquaintances as they have already experienced or anticipate unfavourable responses. This kind of self-censorship is only reticently admitted to as it is not thought to be in the spirit of being a good Christian.

Conclusions

Looking at how, when and what the Don Evangelicals say or leave unsaid, it is possible to discern different kinds of silence that are created and employed by the group members. The non-denominational character of the Don community allows space for quite a wide variety of personal dispositions in regard to talking or talking in a certain manner. While Evangelicals place great emphasis on narrative forms of being a believer, not all members of the Don congregation display confidence or willingness to participate in these narrative practices. In some cases people feel that they have not yet proficiently acquired the Evangelical language and are thus concerned with the possibility of saying something "wrong". But there can also be a conscious unwillingness to follow the Evangelical discourse that is demonstrated by the core members and, to an extent, expected by them. Even though the Evangelical message makes sense to people and they highly value their involvement in the congregation's life, they do not wish to conceptualise this belonging in terms of a typical Evangelical conversion narrative. As constancy and adherence to traditions are locally culturally valued, people can

find it undesirable to express their belonging to the group in a manner that accentuates discontinuity from the "tradition" or clearly contradicts it.

Furthermore, while talking is highly valued as a means of expressing one's identity and bringing new people to God, there are non-verbal aspects that are seen as important in constituting the Evangelical self. To a considerable extent, certain embodied practices and comportment are interpreted as reliable signs of people's religious commitment within the community. At the same time, these practices are employed as proselytising tools. Moreover, the emphasis on these embodied, non-verbal expressions of faith at least partially stems from the specific environment, which is often sceptical towards Evangelicals and their mission. These practices enable Evangelicals to better fit in with the pro-Orthodox environment and avoid conflicts with their fellow villagers, while approaching somebody with a straightforward proselytising discourse can often bring about hostile responses. Remaining silent in this context can be explained by the unreceptive stance of the potential audience and by the aim of maintaining good neighbourly relations and avoiding conflicts. It is a kind of constructive silence then, arising from recognising the implicit conflict and realising that reaching a compromise is unlikely. While refraining from explicit evangelising can help one to fit into the Orthodox surroundings and maintain friendly relations with neighbours, it remains a source of some tension for the Evangelicals, who see it as their obligation to testify. This tension is somewhat relieved through specific non-verbal forms of being and acting that are conceptualised as mediating the Word non-verbally. Practising these non-verbal forms involves consciously avoiding negative emotions and cultivating oneself to feel and react in a manner suitable to a good Christian. Excluding certain topics or even words from their discourse is also used to help establish the desired Evangelical self and to create a suitable space for approaching non-Evangelicals.

All of the members of the Don church assert the importance of embodied and emotional aspects of faith. However, while speaking constitutes the principal religious practice for core members of the congregation, people who tentatively remain on the fringe of the Don group tend to conceptualise and communicate their religious commitment and experience through non-verbal means. As the emotional and embodied features of faith and the specific environment of a Komi village converge, it produces a kind of Evangelical silence. It is important to note that while this is silence in the sense of not following the obligation to speak according to mainstream Evangelical ideology, it is conceptualised as communicative and still bears the Evangelical message.

Notes

1 This research was supported by the Estonian Research Council grant PUT590 and the ERA.Net RUS Plus programme's project 189 (CORUNO), as well as by the European Union through the European Regional Development Fund (Centre of Excellence in Cultural Theory). I thank Elo-Hanna Seljamaa and Pihla Siim, but also Tuija Hovi for their thorough comments on the draft of this paper.
2 Fieldwork was carried out jointly with Art Leete.
3 In the Russian context, Laur Vallikivi (2009: 76) has also found that for the formerly animist Nenets, the conversion to Baptism primarily has meant learning to express themselves in a new language: "Baptist Russian".
4 Sex (W for woman, M for man) and year of birth of the speaker are added to the excerpts from interviews.
5 My fieldwork partner, Art Leete, was also present.
6 Here Lidia's laughter functions to soften her statement, which could be seen as rather critical of us: even more so as I had only briefly met her once before and for Art Leete it was his first contact with her.

References

Babcock, Barbara A. 1984: The Story in the Story: Metanarration in Folk Narrative. In: Richard Bauman (ed.), *Verbal Art as Performance*. Long Grove, Illinois: Waveland Press, Inc., pp. 61–76.

Bauman, Richard 1984: *Verbal Art as Performance*. Long Grove, Illinois: Waveland Press, Inc.

Broz, Ludek 2009: Conversion to Religion? Negotiating Continuity and Discontinuity in Contemporary Altai. In: Mathijs Pelkmans (ed.), *Conversion after Socialism: Disruptions, Modernisms and Technologies of Faith in the Former Soviet Union*. New York & Oxford: Berghahn Books, pp. 17–37.

Bryant, M. Darrol 1999: Conversion in Christianity: From without and from within. In: Christopher Lamb & M. Darrol Bryant (eds.), *Religious Conversion: Contemporary Practices and Controversies*. London & New York: Cassell, pp. 177–190.

Bryant, M. Darrol & Christopher Lamb 1999: Introduction: Contours of Controversy and Commitment in a Plural World. In: Christopher Lamb & M. Darrol Bryant (eds.), *Religious Conversion: Contemporary Practices and Controversies*. London & New York: Cassell, pp. 1–19.

Cain, Carole 1991: Personal Stories: Identity Acquisition and Self-Understanding in Alcoholics Anonymous. *Ethos* 19:2, 210–253.

Coleman, Simon 2007: Materializing the Self: Words and Gifts in the Construction of Charismatic Protestant Identity. In: Fenella Cannell (ed.), *The Anthropology of Christianity*. Durham: Duke University Press, pp. 163–184.

Elliott, Mark R. 2003: Orthodox-Protestant Relations in the Post-Soviet Era. *Religion in Eastern Europe* XXIII: 5, 31–50.

Harding, Susan 1987: Convicted by the Holy Spirit: The Rhetoric of Fundamental Baptist Conversion. *American Ethnologist* 14:1, 167–181.

Harding, Susan 2000: *The Book of Jerry Falwell: Fundamentalist Language and Politics*. Princeton & Oxford: Princeton University Press.

Hovi, Tuija 2000: Textualising Religious Experience. In: Lauri Honko (ed.), *Thick Corpus, Organic Variation and Textuality in Oral Tradition*. Helsinki: Finnish Literature Society, pp. 373–400.

Hovi, Tuija 2014: Functions of Narrative Genres for Lived Religion. *Approaching Religion* 4:1, 80–88.

Koosa, Piret 2013: Sowing the Seeds of Faith: A Case Study of an American Missionary in the Russian North. *Journal of Ethnology and Folkloristics* 7:1, 31–48.

Koosa, Piret 2015: "Sometimes we'll have to prove that we're no crocodiles…" Evangelical Christians' Stigmatisation as Sectarians in a Komi Village. *Études finno-ougriennes* 47, 89–114.

Koosa, Piret & Art Leete 2014: Serving God by Being Neighbourly: Komi Protestants and Local Community Initiatives. *Suomen antropologi* 39:2, 39–57.

Lawless, Elaine J. 1983: Brothers and Sisters: Pentecostals as a Religious Folk Group. *Western Folklore* 42:2, 85–104.

Lindquist, Galina & Simon Coleman 2008: Introduction: Against Belief? *Social Analysis* 52:1, 1–18.

Luhrmann, Tanya M. 2004: Metakinesis: How God Becomes Intimate in Contemporary U.S. Christianity. *American Anthropologist* 106:3, 518–528.

Luhrmann, Tanya M. 2012: *When God Talks Back: Understanding the American Evangelical Relationship with God*. New York: Vintage Books.

Miller, Donald E. 1998: Postdenominational Christianity in the Twenty-First Century. *The Annals of the American Academy of Political and Social Science* 558:1, 196–210.

Rambo, Lewis R. 2003: Anthropology and the Study of Conversion. In: Andrew Buckser & Stephen D. Glazier (eds.), *The Anthropology of Religious Conversion*, pp. 211–222.

Rambo, Lewis R. & Charles E. Farhadian 1999: Converting: Stages of Religious Change. In: Christopher Lamb & M. Darrol Bryant (eds.), *Religious Conversion: Contemporary Practices and Controversies.* London & New York: Cassell, pp. 23–34.

Stromberg, Peter G. 1993: *Language and Self-Transformation: A Study of the Christian Conversion Narrative.* Cambridge: Cambridge University Press.

Vallikivi, Laur 2009: Christianization of Words and Selves: Nenets Reindeer Herders Joining the State through Conversion. In: Mathjis Pelkmans (ed.), *Conversion after Socialism: Disruptions, Modernisms and Technologies of Faith in the Former Soviet Union.* New York & Oxford: Berghahn Books, pp. 59–83.

Wanner, Catherine 2007: *Communities of the Converted: Ukrainians and Global Evangelism.* Ithaca & London: Cornell University Press.

Webster, Joseph 2013: *The Anthropology of Protestantism: Faith and Crisis among Scottish Fishermen.* New York: Palgrave MacMillan.

Wilkins, Amy C. 2008: "Happier than Non-Christians": Collective Emotions and Symbolic Boundaries among Evangelical Christians. *Social Psychology Quarterly* 71: 3, 281–301.

Piret Koosa is a researcher at the Estonian National Museum and a doctoral student at the Institute for Cultural Research and Fine Arts, University of Tartu, Estonia. Her current research focuses on the dynamics of religious life in post-Soviet northern Russia.
(piret.koosa@gmail.com)

FAMILY STORIES UNTOLD
Doing Family through Practices of Silence

Pihla Maria Siim, University of Tartu

Family history can be seen to be comprised of both told and untold stories and sentiments related to them, all of which affect family members. Drawing on interviews conducted with immigrants from the former Soviet Union living in Finland and their family members living in the country of origin (in Russian Karelia and Estonia), this article[1] explores the silenced aspects of family storytelling and analyses how the absence of narration can serve as a protector and maintainer of family as a set of relationships, or an enabler of "normal" family life. The focus of the article is on family past, and the continuum from tellable to silenced experiences will be analysed. However, the methodological side of studying unsaid or unsayable things is also touched upon.

Keywords: transnational families, storytelling, noncommunication, fieldwork, (re-)migration

Family Storytelling

Family stories, which are told as a part of common reminiscing about the sayings and doings of family members[2] in different times, have been one of my central research interests for years. Family stories rely on the experiences of one or several family members and through storytelling these experiences can become a shared past for the whole family. However, as Kristin Langellier and Eric Peterson have argued, family storytelling is a way of "doing things with words" rather than a collection of stories. Storytelling is one of the daily practices in which families are performed and produced. Within this performative perspective, families are narrative formations and imagined communities. The bits and pieces of family storytelling emerge within mundane activities of *doing family*, and are often invisible to family members as well as others (Langellier & Peterson 2004: 33–39). From this point of view, family is a set of relationships created, reconfigured and sustained through narrating and other practices.

Family storytelling concentrates on themes important for a particular family in a concrete situation. Family stories are not only about remarkable events, but tellability is also related to mundane meanings storytelling entails for participants (Langellier & Peterson 2004: 42). Stories are not always told as a whole; people may refer only to the main points or phrases of the stories they already are familiar with. Some of the family stories thus have the same characteristics as "small stories": they do not have to be long and coherent narratives to fulfil their function. Stories may be of shared (known) events, and include allusions to previous tellings, deferrals of tellings and refusal to tell (Bamberg & Georgakopoulou 2008). Entertainment is not the main function or value of family stories. In ways large and small, they matter to family members (Stone 1989: 5).

Pihla Maria Siim 2016: Family Stories Untold: Doing Family through Practices of Silence.
Ethnologia Europaea 46:2, 74–88. © Museum Tusculanum Press.

Family stories are a form of conversational storytelling (see Norrick 2007; Yerkovich 1983): stories are often told in turns and are negotiated. The situations of family storytelling are different depending on whether they deal with positive or negative memories and incidents. Positive stories, which make people laugh and feel good, can be told during bigger family gatherings and also to friends and acquaintances outside the family. Building and reinforcing the feeling of togetherness, these stories produce familyhood most explicitly. In terms of doing family, it is important to stress that people are selective while creating and recreating bonds with certain relatives. People may stress feeling close to some relatives, while saying nothing or telling negative stories about other relatives. Indeed, the interactional work of doing family can involve excluding some individuals from the set of valued relationships. Doing family involves construction and achievement rather than the enactment of a naturally existing set of relations (Naples 2001). For example, in the case of re-migration to Finland, it is more important to talk about the Finnish branch of the multi-ethnic family instead of concentrating on Russian relatives; this can actually be an important part of representing oneself as a proper return migrant (cf. Davydova 2004: 194). This article mainly deals with these kinds of descendant narratives: stories related to the (ethnic and religious) background of the family.

The storytelling situations of negative or sad stories are often slightly different. Negative stories are not repeated as often and can typically be told only in certain contexts, mostly confidentially, and one to one. There are also stories that are told only once; family members are aware of them, and later on they are only hinted at. Some family stories belong to the family circle only, and these are typically negative, sad or traumatic stories, or stories representing family (members) in a negative light. These stories include elements that are considered to be harmful in one way or another. They are the "family's own secrets", which are not meant to be understood by others. In addition, and the focus of this article, there are stories that are not repeated even in the family circle or not told at all.

This article concentrates on family past, and especially on untold stories, on the continuum from tellable to silenced experiences. Silence is a social process, involving different actions and agencies. It is not equal to forgetting, but rather refers to the absence of narration (Korjonen-Kuusipuro & Kuusisto-Arponen 2012: 113). In studying communication, people mostly pay attention to the communication process, and noncommunication is often perceived as a failure of communication rather than a functional and meaningful phenomenon (Vesala et al. 2002: 13). Not communicating something under certain conditions can also be intentional and purposeful. In introducing the concept of noncommunication, Gregory Bateson has stressed that in some cases communication is undesirable, because it somehow alters the nature of ideas (Bateson & Bateson [1987]2005: 80). More attention could thus be paid to situations in which noncommunication becomes meaningful (cf. also Tuija Hovi in this issue). Furthermore, as Seppo Knuuttila has stated, noncommunication can be seen as a method, a search pattern or a paradigm for studying things that are not explicitly stated (Knuuttila 2002: 119). In examining the practices through which family is performed and produced, the aim of this article is to pay close attention to silences and the absence of narration, and their role in doing family.

Research Context and Materials

The research material that this article is based on is comprised of field diaries and forty relatively open interviews conducted during the years 2001–2004.[3] Interviews were conducted among people who had moved to Finland from the former Soviet Union. Most of the interviewees who lived in Finland had come from Baltic countries and Russian Karelia. Only a few individuals originated from other parts of Russia, mostly from bigger towns. Further interviews were conducted with relatives who had stayed in the country of origin: in Estonia or Russian Karelia. If possible, I interviewed more than one person in the same family.[4] Interviewees were able to choose whether they spoke in Finnish, in Estonian or in Russian. During many of the interviews, two languages were used interchangeably.

People from Russia, Estonia or other parts of the (former) Soviet Union currently constitute almost 40 percent of all the immigrants in Finland.[5] The number of newcomers increased sharply during the 1990s, when former Soviet citizens of Finnish background – mostly persons of Ingrian decent – were able to apply for the status of returning migrant and for permission to move to Finland with their families.[6]

Return migrants from the former Soviet Union generally have Ingrian Finnish roots: they are descendants of people who migrated from the territory of present-day Finland to the easternmost part of the Swedish Empire starting in the seventeenth century. Today, this area lies in north-west Russia, in the district of Saint Petersburg. Due to wars, deportations and persecutions during the twentieth century, many people with Ingrian Finnish backgrounds ended up living in Estonia and in Russian Karelia.[7] Other groups of Finnish origin in the former Soviet Union are descendants of Finns who moved there between the years 1918 and 1939 and after World War II. Finns who moved to the Soviet Union before World War II were either "Red" emigrants, who escaped from Finland after the failed revolution of 1918, or people who relocated illegally at the time when there was a major depression in Finland. In addition, Finns from the United States and Canada resettled in the 1930s by invitation of the Soviet government. During the Soviet period, maintaining the Finnish identity and language was not easy, and in fact many of these families were multilingual and had mixed ethnic backgrounds.

Many of the people I interviewed moved to Finland in the 1990s or early 2000s and their families had at least partly (Ingrian-)Finnish backgrounds. However, often interviewees had multiple reasons for moving. Thus, the categories of – for example – student, worker, family member and return migrant may overlap.

In the case of migration, not all family members are equally mobile: some of them stay in the country of origin. Families thus become transnational through spatial separation (Huttunen 2010: 240), living some or most of the time separated from each other, yet holding together and creating something that can be seen as a feeling of collective welfare and unity, namely "familyhood", even across national borders (Bryceson & Vuorela 2002: 3). In studying transnational families, I was interested in the ways people did family: how family was negotiated, symbolically generated, and affirmed through everyday practices (see Körber & Merkel 2012). Narration and sometimes also its absence can help people to adjust to the challenges and changes they meet, and transnational families thus form an interesting entrance point for studying both doing family and cultural practices of silencing.

Silenced Themes during the Interviews

The interview situation can be regarded as a specific context for telling, with its own restrictions. Some experiences are difficult to put into words, or they are not presented to the researcher during the interview because of their intimate nature. Additionally, some stories do not fit into the picture people would like to present of themselves and their families to an outsider. For example, sometimes members of migrant families have stressed the close relationships between relatives in their extended families (in and by means of stories they have told about themselves), partly due to the wish to distinguish themselves from the families representing the majority of Finnish society, who in their view are more individualistic and nuclear family-centred (cf. Siim 2007).

As my material consists of field notes and recorded interviews with different family members, I can try to understand all that has not been said only by carefully studying that which has been said (see Klein 2006: 21–22). I have looked at the material and themes discussed during the interviews, paying attention to what has and presumably has not been talked about: which themes have been silenced or avoided during the interviews. This approach naturally has its limitations, and I do not claim to have knowledge of all silenced topics. However, it is clear that some of the themes related to present-day life were explicitly excluded. For instance, some interviewees did not want to talk about a spouse who had recently passed away, or about a spouse's serious illness. They also often did not want to talk about their difficulties in Finland (including difficulties in the workplace) or unsuccessful migration (see Siim 2014). My position as a researcher representing the majority may also have had an effect on how people decided to describe their integration into a new society. However, there were exceptions, and some interviewees told me quite openly about the difficulties they or their family members had faced. For example, 50-year-old Irina described the troubles her daughters had had in Finland after the relocation; in the second interview, she acknowledged that it may have been a mistake for her to come to Finland in the first place. "My life is really simple, and this is a sore issue for me. [...] I think my life in Russia was better" (H25: 30[8]).

People are also inclined to keep silent about problems in their marriages or other complicated family relations, especially when it comes to recent and ongoing matters. As one male interviewee stated when asked about his family and the meaning of family for him: "I'm not ready for this kind of question [...] when it comes to family, I don't want to answer those questions. I'm telling you frankly. At the moment there are relatively complicated problems, and this is why I would like to skip these questions" (H12B: 10). Also a woman in her thirties said to me directly that she did not feel comfortable talking about a taxing period of her life. She told me about her husband's serious illness, which changed their lives in many ways. At the time her husband fell ill, she was expecting their third child, and not only did she not feel comfortable talking about it, but indeed she did not remember the following year at all:

[...] and after that he got ill. When I was pregnant with our third child. As my time neared, it was a tough spot. I cannot remember that year at all. It's like a "black hole" (P: it has disappeared). It has disappeared. I can't remember my daughter being a baby. I guess I did everything automatically, but I cannot remember it like I remember the other kids: how I enjoyed it (P: yes). I cannot remember much. And my husband was not there at the birth; for the other two children he was

there, at their birth (P: yes) [small pause]. This kind of bad thing [the situation in the family] we have now; I wouldn't really like to talk about it (P: yes); it makes me feel bad [laughing a bit]. (H21: 35. Woman, moved to Finland from the Republic of Karelia[9])

These two interviewees were exceptional in stating directly that they did not want to talk about certain themes. More often people simply avoided talking about themes they felt uncomfortable with or themes that were too emotional. Sometimes I realised people had been avoiding certain themes on the basis of interviews done with other family members. The emotions the topics under discussion may evoke could not always be anticipated and they may have taken interviewees by surprise. Some of the interviewees were wiping tears from their eyes during the interviews, and these situations caught me by surprise. Since the strong emotions questions may produce in the interviewees cannot often be anticipated, one responsibility of the interviewer is to help interviewees to narrate through these situations. A researcher can turn the discussion to other themes, for example by talking about how the interviewee has made it through the difficult times (Rosenthal 2003: 920). One should also keep in mind that the therapeutic impact of narration or interviews cannot be taken for granted (cf. Strandén-Backa 2013: 85–89). The skill of listening to the silence related to fraught experiences and memories can be useful (cf. Peltonen 2003: 18). While analysing the life-history interviews she conducted in the 1990s with Ingrian Finns in northern Ingria (in the current Saint Petersburg district), Armi Pekkala noted that she reacted with silence to strong emotional expressions of anxiety, stress or grief in order to give interviewees time to compose their thoughts, either to continue with the same topic or to change it (Pekkala 2007: 184).

When it comes to problems, people usually talk about them only when some time has passed or the problems have been resolved. For example, one may be ready to talk about the problems with a spouse only after a divorce. Interviewees are rather keen to talk about how they have made it through tough times. One function of these kinds of survival stories (see Benmayor et al. 1987; Zeitlin, Kotkin & Cutting Baker 1982: 46) is to encourage the younger generation(s) to successfully make it through difficult times in a new, foreign society. It is also possible to laugh at difficult things afterwards in the family circle: these stories include a kind of self-irony and can increase the feeling of togetherness among family members.

In the following, I explore the dynamics of talking about and the silencing of experiences and themes that seemed for various reasons to be sensitive among the families I studied. I begin by analysing stories that were transmitted among family members, despite the fact that they touched on somewhat difficult topics, and then I move on to untold stories.

Stories about Persecution and Survival

The family histories of the descendants of Finns I interviewed often included repeated relocations, deportations, persecutions and fear. Families with other ethnic backgrounds also experienced persecutions, especially during the Stalin regime. Sometimes stories about these incidents were passed along to later generations, particularly stressing the survival and endurance of family members.

Alma, a 34-year-old woman, stated that her grandparents talked about the past "quite a lot, about the war times and, although we were little, very little, they still talked about everything" (H21: 50). She mentioned, for example, stories about her great-grandfather going to Saint Petersburg to do construction work, about her grandfather being imprisoned by Russians and forced to help rebuild an airport, even while it was being bombed, about her grandmother driven away from home, and the relationships of ordinary people, that is Ingrians, to Russian and German soldiers (H21: 51–54). Alma introduced the background of the storytelling in the following way: "it bothered [my grandfather], and that is why he told us. About what it was like, what happened (P: mm). I guess he thought that we children should also know" (H21: 52).

In my experience, the stories that are told about

difficult times are of an informative nature, concerning the different phases in the lives of family members. They do not dwell on unpleasant details, in spite of being quite specific at times. Nevertheless, emotional and troubling experiences or descriptions seemed to stick more strongly in the minds of listeners. This seems to also be the case with the following detailed description that Alma offered about her father's childhood experience during World War II, when Germans occupied the southern and western parts of Ingria. The story had been told by Alma's grandmother. While talking about the most difficult themes in their lives, people often describe them through narratives conveying the experiences of others, for example their children (cf. Miettinen 2004: 429; Siim 2007: 238). For Alma's grandmother, it may have been easier to talk about the war time and fears related to it through the actions of her son.

Pihla: Has someone told you about what your grandparents or parents were like when they were little? Alma: Yes, my grandmother told me about my father, when he was two years old. The Germans came to the village, chased the family into the cellar, and took up residence in the house. [...] I can't recall how long they had to stay there in the cellar, but granny said they didn't have the courage to go up and ask for anything. The children were very hungry, and so my two-year-old father [nicknamed "Kostja"] jumped up from his mother's lap and ran up the stairs from the cellar. Grandma said she was terribly afraid that they would kill the boy and went to watch through a chink in the door what they would do. The Germans were sitting around the table; they had a big, round loaf of bread on the table, and granny's jam jars. [...] [she] said Kostja went to the table and pulled on one German's trouser leg. [...]My grandma said her heart was about to stop, she was so afraid for the boy, but she was too frightened to go and get him. [...] The German looked at the boy, took the bread and cut a big slice with a big knife [...] and put a lot of jam on it, and gave it to him. When Kostja came back, [granny] tried to take the slice away from him, because he hadn't eaten anything for a long time and might get a stomach-ache. But he started to scream, made so much noise, that she gave it back [laughing]. She thought that otherwise the Germans might come down and start shooting because of the noise they were making [laughing]. And the boy ate the whole piece of bread. (H21: 59. Woman, moved to Finland from the Republic of Karelia)

Some interviewees stressed that children, while growing up after World War II, were aware of the roots of the family and of the family history, including sufferings, deportations and other war-time experiences. However, it seems that these kinds of stories were not often repeated. Sometimes the younger generation may explicitly ask older members of the family to tell them about the past in more detail, but these inquiries were not always fruitful. It can also be difficult for a family member to ask about these emotionally very loaded experiences. As one interviewee with an Ingrian Finnish background stated: "My mother always cried if you asked her something. Those years were so tough" (H31C: 9). By this she was referring to difficult phases in her mother's life, including displacement. If stories stir up difficult memories and negative feelings, people may avoid telling them. They may be afraid that the listener will not understand their experiences in the way they would like them to be understood (cf. Kaivola-Bregenhøj 2003). Talking about nightmarish experiences and suffering may sometimes feel like minimising the experiences (Miettinen 2004: 71, 428). The authenticity of experiences can thus be protected through silence (cf. Knuuttila 2002: 121).

Some interviewees mentioned that as adults they turned to different archives and authorities to find out more about their families. Lempi, a woman in her sixties, had a long-time dream of compiling a family tree or a family history. At the time of the interview, she knew a little about the past of her family, but she had had to push hard to find out about it. Her parents were both born in Finland, at the beginning of the twentieth century, but ended up living in the Soviet Union. In the repressions of the 1930s, tens of thousands of Finns, considered to be politically unreliable, were deported to as far away as Central Asia, Lempi's father being one of them. Her mother is not eager to talk about her father's fate. Apparently, Lempi's mother lived for a long time without knowing exactly what had happened to her husband. The same was true for many families: people were not sure about the fate of their family members.

Lempi: My grandfather and grandmother were an ordinary Finnish couple. Grandpa participated in the activities of the Social-Democratic movement here in Finland. In the 1930s when there was high unemployment here, a crisis, remember […] they went to Russia. My mother was 14 at that time, she was born here [in southern Finland] […] Father was born in Karelia […] in a place that became part of the Russian territory after the war. As a young man he moved to America, in the 1930s, looking for a job, and then moved on to Canada. Then there was a campaign; they were told that in Russia there was work available, and that you'd receive housing, everything. And he moved to Russia as a young man. So both of my parents were born in Finland, but met there in Russia. And got married. I was born in 1936, before the war. During the war, or rather in 1937, they started repressions against Finns in Russia. My father was deported to Central Asia […] We didn't know about that. I got to know about it quite recently, when they opened the archives. […] He was in Central Asia, and then, when World War II started, he was first taken into the Red Army. So the archive documents revealed. I think he was there for two months, and then he was kicked out of the army and sent to [a labour camp in the Urals] because he was a Finn. He was there the whole wartime and died in 1944. In the beginning, after the war, my mother made inquiries about him through archives and […] found out that he allegedly died of tuberculosis. Maybe because the living conditions there were worse than in prison. That kind of fate was suffered by many Finns, even my acquaintances; many fathers were repressed that way […] I also have documents saying he suffered repression. Well, my father is dead, and my mother is alive; she returned to Finland after 60 years [...] Pihla: Do you know this history well, and talk about it a lot at home?

Lempi: No, my mother does not like to recall it. It's simply that when they started to open the archives in Russia, I started to look for my dad's roots. My mother didn't know anything about him, after the arrest. And, only after leaving for Finland [from the Republic of Karelia], I received notification from the archives. About the fate of my father. But until then we didn't know what happened to him, where and when; we knew nothing. (H12A: 21–22. Woman, moved to Finland from the Republic of Karelia)

Here Lempi stated that her mother was not aware of the events taking place after the arrest of her husband. Later in the interview, Lempi talked in more detail about her wish to collect her mother's stories for future generations and about her mother's unwillingness to narrate. All she managed to get were small pieces of recollections, mainly about her mother's childhood and youth.

It can be claimed that sad and in some way undesirable or inappropriate family experiences can be erased from memory and it can be difficult to differentiate between intentional silencing and unintentional forgetting. Some stories, however, which at first glance may be categorised as untellable, can be transmitted after all, thanks to a changed societal context or because of the function these stories of persistence and strength of family members have in encouraging other family members to cope. Additionally, difficult personal experiences can be described by projecting emotions related to them onto others (cf. Lawless 2000: 76–77). In studying exiled Estonians, Jürgenson (2009: 137) has noted that some traumatic events are retold as if they are holy stories requiring utmost respect from both the teller and the listener. "Holiness", with its emotional charge, can also mean that one cannot talk about the incidents, but has to remain silent (cf. Bateson & Bateson [1987]2005; Tuija Hovi in this issue). Next, I will analyse the experiences and topics people have kept silent about, as well as the functions of these silences.

Protective Silence

Concealing their ethnic or religious background from people outside the family was important for Finns living in the Soviet Union – especially under the Stalin regime – as was the case with many other ethnic and religious groups. There were certain themes that the authorities also wanted people to keep silent about. Talking about ethnic or religious affiliations or relatives living abroad could cause problems or unpleasant reactions, which is one of the reasons why Finns internalised a "culture of silence" during the Soviet time, stressing that keeping silent could not hurt you (cf. Miettinen 2004; Raudalainen 2014: 386). Many interviewees recalled how they had been advised to conceal their family's ethnic background: "my grandmother on my father's side also said not to tell anyone you were Ingrian" (H36B: 70). Also religiousness was to be kept hidden: "My brother and I were baptised. When we were little. But we were not to talk about it at school, or we would have been expelled" (H21: 58). Several interviewees also mentioned that they did not speak the Finnish language, sometimes not even at home: "We were afraid to speak it" (H36B: 72). "My mother knew Finnish very well. But at home we never spoke Finnish. [...] If they spoke it in some families it was a secret; no-one should know" (H12A: 27). People were afraid to keep in contact with (Finnish) relatives living abroad, for example answering their letters or meeting them while they were visiting the Soviet Union.

Depending on the conditions at hand, silence and secrets could contribute to family survival as surely as telling family stories (Langellier & Peterson 2004: 51). Keeping some things hidden from outsiders under a totalitarian regime may not be that surprising, but it is intriguing that some things were hidden even from family members. In this case, there is no clear difference between public and private sharing of family memories. For example Anni, a 30-year-old woman I interviewed in Russia, told me that she became aware of the ethnic background of her family at school: it had not been talked about at home. After being "accused" of being a Finn at school, she first was upset and wanted to deny it; calling someone a Finn was a term of abuse, as far as she knew.

Anni's parents had not directly talked about the ethnic background of the family at home (or its importance was not stressed; cf. also Elo-Hanna Seljamaa in this issue) and she was not aware of it, in spite of having heard her grandparents speaking Finnish.

> Pihla: What was the position of Finns in general in the Soviet Union?
> Anni: I don't know; our [relatives] lived [near Petrozavodsk] [...] and in school they were praised because they were so determined and knew the Russian language even better than Russians. The teacher always noted that Finns could sit still, and write without mistakes. Also when I studied at school, generally it was normal, and there were no such ethnic problems. Only once at school, it was necessary to mark your nationality everywhere; there was this grouping, and maybe it was a necessity in that system. [It was then] I for the first time found out that I was a Finn. From childhood I had heard my grandfather and grandmother, and all the people around them speaking Finnish. When I came to Petrozavodsk, everything was in Russian, and for me there were no problems. Whether there were Russian or any other people. There was just this incident at school, before classes. On the table there was a teacher's book with some information written down [about the pupils], like where the parents worked, their nationality, and the nationality of the child. I remember the children also said "Huttunen, she's a Finn." I was so upset, calling me that [laughing]. "It is not true." I just didn't understand what they were talking about; it was said in such a tone of voice. I think they also didn't understand, seven–eight years old. My only friend was also an Ingrian Finn. We didn't have problems and still don't. (H33: 43. Woman, living in the Republic of Karelia)

Ethnic background was sometimes deliberately concealed even from one's own spouse, as Salme, a woman in her fifties, said. The motivation to hide things from those close to you may be a desire to protect family members, and to keep the family together. While interviewing Salme and her husband Tarmo (with Ingrian Finnish and Estonian backgrounds, respectively), we talked about reasons for remembering and not remembering the family past. Tarmo claimed that women were more inclined to remember family-related things, since "men worked more in Estonia." He also noted that their families were cut off from their "roots" after moving to town. Salme, on the other hand, stated that the main reason for the rupture experienced inside the family was her Ingrian Finnish background:

> Salme: And for me it was cut off because I had an Ingrian-Finnish background; on my mother's side many relatives had died in Siberia [...] they were dispersed.
> Pihla: We talked about that a bit, yes, that people were afraid to talk.
> Salme: Yes, people were afraid to say that they were Ingrian Finns and my mother didn't have the courage to tell my father, and he was offended by that and maybe it was also one reason for their divorce. My father felt wounded that she hadn't dared to talk to him [...] didn't trust him in that sense. But life... I have started to think that no matter what kind of secret, it can come out somewhere, by accident; it doesn't need to be intentional. That it is really good to keep that kind of big secret to yourself.
> Tarmo: But well, surely your parents felt tension, since your mother was still, in 1994 and 1995, when there was independence, she was still afraid to tell everything; there was still a kind of fear, anxiety [...][The fear] kind of went inside, maybe it's still there.
> Salme: Yes, people were too afraid to say [aloud] even that God existed (P: mm). Before her death, my grandmother said that God did exist. But otherwise people kept those things to themselves.
> Tarmo: Well I said that we also had cantors [in our family], but no-one talked about that.
> (H36A & B: 69. A couple, moved to Finland from Estonia)

People justified not communicating certain things by referring to the protective effect of unawareness:

things that you knew nothing about could not harm you. Silence in this case was intentional: stories fallen into the wrong hands would entail the alteration of the intended message (cf. Bateson & Bateson [1987]2005: 80). Thus, the motivation for not telling stories was often to save the kids or other relatives from unpredictable consequences. There seems to have existed also a more general wish to protect children from negative memories or feelings, a desire to stress positive stories (cf. also Raudalainen 2014: 386). As told by a 28-year-old woman, who has a partly Ingrian and a partly Karelian family background, neither of her parents were very keen on talking about negative things:

> Ilona: Stories, I didn't hear them. I don't know why my parents didn't tell us anything. Or was it just hard to talk about these things. Because there were a lot of bad [things], and for sure all parents don't want to tell all the bad things to their own children. [...] Once I asked [my father] and he said that the reason why older people didn't tell us anything was that maybe if something bad happened to a person and he had all of this in his soul, when he calmed down, he wouldn't want to talk about it any more, because it was difficult, difficult for him, and he wouldn't want this evil to touch others, especially his own kids. He wants to [...] spare his children from all the negative sides. But, well I was interested in all these things because I was interested in history, and I started to ask all these little things. [...] And then he started to tell me, but usually [parents] don't say too much. (H29: 7, 80. Woman, living in the Republic of Karelia)

Sometimes silenced and repressed stories are brought to the surface due to a societal or personal change of situation. This can be illustrated by the story of the 45-year-old Oksana, talking about the past of her family. She only came to know about the deportation of her family after finishing her university studies. That is when her parents thought it was ineluctable to inform her about this part of her family history, since she had been offered a job in the KGB (the foreign intelligence and domestic security

agency of the Soviet Union). Being aware of her family history made her think that she, too, needed to be ready for anything that could happen in life. Recognising this made her stronger: she said that she was not afraid of anything anymore.

> Oksana: [...] my grandfather was murdered when Stalin rose to power. [...]And my grandmother was sent to Kazakhstan with five children [...] I was born in Kazakhstan but after that I came back. When my grandmother received a document saying that my grandfather was innocent, she was able to return. But she had a difficult period in Kazakhstan: no food, no medicine, nothing. And five children [...]
>
> Pihla: When you think about your oldest son, have you told him or has your grandmother told him, for example, about this period in Kazakhstan? Does he know?
>
> Oksana: Yes, well I was told about this happening to us when I graduated from university. Because I was offered a good job in the KGB and when I told my mother [about that], she said "You better not go there." That is how I know my own history. But when the new era began and perestroika and everything, and everything was open, I frankly told the boys what happened. [...] And it was funny since I knew what happened to our family. Then I decided I had to be able to do everything I could. I study, I knit, and I can do anything, milk the cow, or work in a shop. I think my grandmother had such big problems because she was rich and we had a house, our own house [...] she was well off. So she was not ready. And I think I had to know everything in life. I didn't want people to come and send me to Siberia, for example. It is interesting, and now I can do everything. I'm not afraid of anything. (H3: 9, 33. Woman, moved to Finland from Russia)

As Helena Miettinen (2004: 429) has noted, Russian Finns are not very keen to talk about their relationship to Soviet ideology. This narrative silence took a slightly different form in a family where the grandfather, 81-year-old Viktor, besides being Ingrian also had a communist background, which he did not hide – quite the opposite. However, his family members that I interviewed claimed that generally they did not talk very much about the past in the family circle. But if the grandfather talked – to the grandchildren while they spent time at the summer cottage or during parties when he may have had a little too much to drink – then the topic was the war time, and memories of childhood. Even though he had managed to avoid the most hideous fate during the war, there were painful aspects of his life history he deliberately avoided. It seemed that the destiny of other Ingrians had left a mark on him. He talked about deportations in quite a laconic tone of voice: "It was quite a hard time, in the 40s and 50s. All the Ingrians were sent to Siberia. Had to move away from Tallinn, so I went to Leningrad. In the Tallinn railway station there was a long train full of Ingrians. It headed towards Siberia. I went to Leningrad" (H28: 31). When discussing the stories related to the past, his daughter said that many things were hidden from her. Viktor himself stated that he had talked about "necessary things", but additionally he implied that under the new social order there was no need to know about the old one (H28: 71). According to his granddaughters: "there are a lot of stories he could still not talk about some time ago. […] Since he has a communist past […] he is not used to talking freely […] he is always a bit on edge" (H26A & B: 22). He himself also claimed that the position he had held during the Soviet time set certain restrictions on him: he had to refrain from talking about his past and his job, and avoid contacts with relatives living abroad. In a way this seemed to have affected the practices of later generations: they were not very interested in the past, but rather lived in the current moment.

As these examples show, there was reluctance to talk about certain themes among the families interviewed. When the narratives contained information that could cause problems if spread outside the family, silence was protective. Telling can have damaging effects and silence can be protective in certain societal or political contexts, which makes not communicating meaningful under these circumstances (see Bateson & Bateson [1987]2005: 89; Knuuttila 2002:

120). However, there is not necessarily a consensus among family members regarding the untellability of particular stories, especially in changing societal situations.

(Un)told Stories and Sentiments Related to Them

Societal changes or the "new era" do not always change the practice of keeping silent about some aspects of family history. At least certain aspects of the past were still regarded as taboo during the time of the interviews and people preferred to avoid those topics, concentrating instead on living in the present, coping with everyday routines, and being oriented towards the future. Lilia, in her twenties, described her husband's family, which has an Ingrian Finnish background, still avoiding talking about the past:

> My grandmother told quite a few stories […] but [in my husband's] family they don't usually talk about this at all, because in the Soviet time, and especially in Stalin's time, a lot of relatives were sent to Siberia and executed. […] a lot of relatives died during Stalin's time. And in their childhood, no one ever talked about this; it was forbidden. Because if someone said something, he could be arrested the next day and sent to Siberia. That's why I think this [habit] remained, from bygone times, the tradition not to talk about things. (H7: 53. Woman, moved to Finland from Lithuania)

According to Lilia, her own family likewise preferred to talk about recent events. When I asked what kinds of stories they told when she visited her parents in Lithuania, she said that they concentrated on present-day incidents:

> Well, of course I prefer to hear what is going on now rather than about the past. Because it seems to me that all who were born in the Soviet Union, who were influenced by Stalinism and all the negative phenomena in Soviet Union, there was already this habit of avoiding the past, refraining from talking about what happened many years

ago, you know. [...] However, now people have probably started to think about it more. Although, I don't know; my parents don't think about it. I don't know why it doesn't bother them; maybe they would be happy to know about the past, about family secrets and all sorts of things, but I don't know why they don't want to; there's no real desire. They live more in the present and the future than in the past. [...] When the Soviet Union fell apart, a new time began; people changed rather quickly and forgot about all that had happened in the past. For Lithuanians, it is painful. What happened during the Soviet time is often a big taboo. [...] What happened during the Stalinist times, people don't want to talk about. (H7: 64. Woman, moved to Finland from Lithuania)

Sometimes the past, for example the experience of childhood, is not considered worth talking about or remembering. People may also belittle the value of their own life story, thinking it's just typical, and that there's nothing special in it, or experiences are just too depressing to be repeated. For example, when I asked Lempi, a woman in her sixties, if she had told her children about her childhood, she answered:

They do know a little, because when the [Second World] war started, my mother was a student at the university. [The university] was then evacuated to Komi. [...] I ended up in an orphanage. [...] And it basically happened that we – that I went missing. Only after the war did my grandfather find me. All of the war time I spent in an orphanage, and after the war was brought to [my home-town]. And I lived together with my mum for several, long years, just the two of us (P: yes) [pause]. Well that is what my childhood was like: hungry, cold, without parents [pause]. Of course my children are aware of the main points. (H12A: 24. Woman, moved to Finland from the Republic of Karelia)

Ulla-Maija Peltonen, who has studied remembering and forgetting the 1918 Civil War in Finland, has stated that the desire to keep silent and to forget is common. People are reluctant to go through traumatic events again. Of the people she studied, some had not told their relatives or children what happened to their loved ones in 1918. Silence was a way to keep incidents out of daily routines, making daily life easier (Peltonen 1996: 28–29). Silence could thus be seen as an enabler of "normal" family life, making it easier to concentrate on present-day challenges. Nevertheless, information and emotional attitudes can also be passed on through silence (Jürgenson 2009: 141). Concentrating on positive aspects and trying to ignore negative ones is thus not always enough to forget unpleasant things. There may be fears or other strong emotions that are linked to these stories, despite their apparent remoteness (cf. Miettinen 2004: 205). In many cases it seems that the images, associations and fears related to stories have been transmitted from one generation to another, although sometimes in slightly different forms. These emotions sort of run in the family, regardless of the fact that realistically there should not be many reasons for anxiety any more, in the changed societal situation. However, my interviewees talked about their recent fears, which, in a way, were related to the family history they were aware of. For example, in one group interview with siblings of Ingrian Finnish background and their spouses in Russian Karelia, one couple in their late fifties reflected on their feelings related to the recent relocation of their children, expressing the fear that the border between Finland and Russia may close.

Terttu: [...] In the beginning it was terrible, to be honest [...] because we knew what happened to our parents. [...] All of a sudden they could close the border: such fears we had. [...]
Arvi: The fear still remained from our parents, at least for our generation. The way they were treated – that is why they passed on the fear to us. (H31A & D: 34. Group interview in the Republic of Karelia)

Being aware of family history made interviewees think that something similar may happen to them or to their loved ones. This is also discernible in the interview with Oksana (cited earlier): she wanted to be ready for everything, to be able to cope in any situation which she could possibly face.

Some fears were also carried over to the interview context. A few interviewees in Russia were afraid of potential consequences from the interviews for their relatives living in Finland, or of how their relatives would react when they heard about the interviews. For example, one 81-year-old man I interviewed in Russian Karelia insisted that I should not give the interview material to the folklore archives in Finland. He was afraid that his relatives living there would suffer if the recordings ended up in the hands of the "enemy" (Field diary, April 2003). This fear seemed irrational to me; he also commented after the interview that he had not talked negatively about Finland. Looking at his request through the prism of his life history, I respected his wish not to archive the material.

Family history can thus be seen to be comprised of both told and untold stories and sentiments related to them, all affecting family members. There are family traditions or experiences that are rarely verbalised but the ideas and feelings related to them nevertheless affect the thoughts and actions of family members. Additionally, as Aivar Jürgenson has noted, if a person starts to talk about an event only after years of silence, the previous silence can acquire a dimension full of information. Keeping silent about certain incidents can thus be far more expressive than actually talking about them. Silence passes on feelings, convictions, desires and judgements (Jürgenson 2009: 138–141).

Conclusion

Storytelling is one of the practices through which families and identities are created and maintained. People are selective about what kind of events and people they talk about, and to whom. When talking about the negative experiences of a family, focus in the stories is usually on the survival and persistence of family members. Emotionally difficult themes are often depicted through the experiences of other family members, for example from a child's viewpoint. Storytelling situations involving negative experi-

ences are typically quite different from more cheerful remembering, and these painful stories may be kept strictly within the family circle. This poses methodological challenges for a folklorist interested in communication inside families, both shared and silenced experiences of family members.

The interactional work of doing family can involve excluding some relationships or experiences, and stressing others, depending on the situation. The absence of narration is also part of doing family. In this article, I have drawn attention to noncommunication as a protector, maintainer and enabler (cf. Ketola et al. 2002: 9). The interviewees are members of transnational families whose history goes back to the Soviet Union, and the families' past often includes persecution. For families with Ingrian Finnish backgrounds, it has been vitally important to keep silent about certain things, including ethnic and religious background. Sometimes these themes have not been discussed even within the family circle. Silenced stories can sometimes emerge abruptly, when the (societal) situation changes, but certain themes may remain taboo, the habit of keeping silent about certain things is persistent.

When experiences are silenced because of fear, it is possible to talk about forced noncommunication. Reasons for keeping silent about certain experiences can include a need to protect others by keeping them in the dark. Additionally, people may not want to burden their loved ones with negative feelings, may think their stories are not worth telling, or prefer to forget about negative experiences. However, silence cannot be assumed to be a space for forgetting: cultural silences do not necessarily mean that the events are forgotten. Rather, silences may illustrate that there is something there, but the words to convey it are lacking (see Korjonen-Kuusipuro & Kuusisto-Arponen 2012: 121–122). Some experiences and emotions are also difficult or even impossible to verbalise and the authenticity of experience is protected through silence.

A family's past is comprised of both told and untold stories, and emotions related to them, all affecting family members. There are family experiences that have rarely or never been verbalised, but the knowledge and feelings connected to them are nevertheless transmitted to other family members and affect their lives. In studying storytelling in families, we should thus try to find ways to also investigate silences and emotions, which are often strongly intertwined.

Notes

1 This research was supported by the Estonian Research Council (grant no. 9271 and Institutional Research Project IUT2-43), and the European Union through the European Regional Development Fund (Centre of Excellence in Cultural Theory).

2 By "family" I am not referring only to the nuclear family, but also to the set of people a certain individual consider to be family. While studying the family under conditions of increased mobility, the characterisation of a nuclear family by settledness and geographical proximity becomes questionable (Körber & Merkel 2012: 5–6).

3 I have collected this material for my Ph.D. dissertation on narrative practices of transnational families. For more detailed information about the interviews, please see the "Interviews" section.

4 In ten families I interviewed two or more family members. In addition, I interviewed six individuals (no other interviewees from the same family). Not all family members were willing to be interviewed. Some said they felt everything had already been said by their spouses, for example, and in the case of post-divorce families I did not contact the ex-spouses.

5 According to Statistics Finland, in 2014 40.5 percent of foreign nationals permanently living in Finland had Russian or Estonian citizenship and 37.3 percent were Russian- or Estonian-speaking. Of foreign-born inhabitants, 34 percent were born in Estonia, Russia or the former Soviet Union (Statistics Finland 2015).

6 For the moment, the right to apply for the status of returning migrant has ceased. The system of return migration for Ingrian Finns will be abolished after a transition period, with some exceptions (Act on the amendment of the Aliens Act 57/2011, confirmed on March 25, 2011 [Laki ulkomaalaislain 48 §:n muuttamisesta 57/2011]). The relative proportion of labour migration from Estonia to the old EU member states, including Finland, increased significantly after Estonia's EU accession in 2004 and the global economic crisis that started in 2008.

7 Ingria was a multicultural area: in addition to Ingrians, also Votian, Izhorian, Russian, German and Estonian people lived there. At the end of the nineteenth century, Ingrian Finns were the largest Finnish-speaking group in the Saint Petersburg area. During the first half of the twentieth century, Ingrian Finns experienced serious political, social and economic changes. When the Civil War started in 1917, thousands of Ingrians fled, mainly to Finland. During the years 1928–1936 approximately 40,000–50,000 Finns, considered a politically unreliable segment of the population, were deported from Ingria to as far away as Central Asia. At the same time, Finnish-language schools and media were abolished, and Lutheran churches were closed. During World War II, Leningrad and the northern part of Ingria were controlled by Russians, and approximately 20,000–30,000 Ingrians were deported to Siberia. Germans occupied the southern and western parts of Ingria and the siege of Leningrad lasted over two years. Approximately 63,000 Finnish-speaking people were evacuated to Finland in 1943–1944. After the armistice, Finland returned most of these people to the Soviet Union. However, they were not allowed to return to their home district, and were scattered instead to different parts of the Soviet Union. After the war and again in the 1950s, some of them moved back to Ingria, Karelia and Estonia. Karelia and Estonia were appealing locations, because of their kindred languages and their closeness to Ingria (Anepaio 1999; Hakamies 2004; Miettinen 2004; Nevalainen 1991).

8 I use pseudonyms when referring to the interviewees. In the text, the combination of the letter H and a number refers to a certain numbered interview and the number after the colon to a certain part of this interview.

9 The Republic of Karelia is a federal subject of Russia, located in the north-west Russia.

References

Interviews

The research material consists of field diaries and forty relatively open interviews conducted in 2001–2004. Eight of the interviews were group interviews in which at least two of the family members were present. In total 31 women and 14 men were interviewed, 6 of the women repeatedly. 15 of the interviewees were under 30 years old, 12 were 30–49 years old and 18 were over 50 years old at the time of the interview. The interview material and field diaries are in the possession of the author. Interviewees cited in this article (reason for moving to Finland or current place of residence mentioned):

H3   Woman, 40–49 years old, from Russia. Marriage.

H7   Woman, 20–29 years old, from Lithuania. Studies/marriage.

H12A   Woman, over 60 years old, from the Republic of Karelia. Return migrant.

H12B   Man, 30–49 years old, from the Republic of Karelia. Return migrant.

H21	Woman, 30–39 years old, from the Republic of Karelia. Studies/marriage, Ingrian background.
H25	Woman, 50–59 years old, from the Republic of Karelia. Return migrant.
H26A	Woman, under 20 years old, from the Republic of Karelia. Return migrant.
H26B	Woman, 20–29 years old, lives in the Republic of Karelia. Ingrian background.
H28	Man, over 50 years old, lives in the Republic of Karelia. Ingrian background.
H29	Woman, 20–29 years old, lives in the Republic of Karelia. Ingrian background.
H31A	Woman, 50–59 years old, lives in the Republic of Karelia. Ingrian background.
H31C	Woman, 50–59 years old, lives in the Republic of Karelia. Ingrian background.
H31D	Man, over 50 years old, lives in the Republic of Karelia. Ingrian background.
H33	Woman, 30–39 years old, lives in the Republic of Karelia. Ingrian background.
H36A	Man, over 50 years old, from Estonia. Return migrant.
H36B	Woman, 50–59 years old, from Estonia. Return migrant.
H39	Woman, over 60 years old, lives in the Baltic States.

Literature

Anepaio, Terje 1999: Soomlased. In: Jüri Viikberg (ed.), Eesti rahvaste raamat: *Rahvusvähemused, -rühmad ja -killud*. Tallinn: Eesti Entsüklopeediakirjastus, pp. 437–445.

Bamberg, Michael & Alexandra Georgakopoulou 2008: Small Stories as a New Perspective in Narrative and Identity Analysis. *Text & Talk* 28–3, 377–396.

Bateson, Gregory & Mary Catherine Bateson (1987)2005: *Towards an Epistemology of the Sacred*. Cresskill, NJ: Hampton Press.

Benmayor, Rina, Blanca Vázquez, Ana Juarbe & Celia Alvarez 1987: Stories to Live By: Continuity and Change in Three Generations of Puerto Rican Women. In: Ralph Samuel & Paul Thompson (eds.), *The Myths We Live By*. London: Routledge, pp. 184–200.

Bryceson, Deborah Fahy & Ulla Vuorela 2002: Transnational Families in the Twenty-First Century. In: Deborah Bryceson & Ulla Vuorela (eds.), *The Transnational Family: New European Frontiers and Global Networks*. Oxford: Berg Publishers, pp. 3–29.

Davydova, Olga 2004: *Etnisyyspuhe Suomen kynnyksellä: Paluumuuttajien suomalaisuuden muodostuminen*. An unpublished licenciate thesis in Folklore. University of Joensuu, Finland.

Hakamies, Pekka 2004: Finns in Russia, Russians in Finland: Remigration and the Problem of Identity. In: Anna-Leena Siikala, Barbro Klein & Stein R. Mathisen (eds.), *Creating Diversities: Folklore, Religion and the Politics of Heritage*. Studia Fennica Folkloristica 14. Helsinki: Finnish Literature Society, pp. 43–53.

Huttunen, Laura 2010: Emplacement through Family Life: Transformations of Intimate Relations. In: Thomas Faist, Pirkko Pitkänen, Jürgen Gerdes & Eveline Reisenauer (eds.), *Transnationalisation and Institutional Transformations*. COMCAD Working Papers No. 87. Center on Migration, Citizenship and Development. http://www.uni-bielefeld.de/tdrc/ag_comcad/downloads/workingpaper_87_TRANS-NET.pdf. Accessed March 1, 2016.

Jürgenson, Aivar 2009: Escape to the West in the Memories of Estonians in Argentina: The Historical, Social and Psychological Context. *Acta Historica Talliensia* 14, 125–145, http://www.kirj.ee/public/Acta_hist/2009/issue_1/acta-2009-14-125-145.pdf. Accessed March 1, 2016.

Kaivola-Bregenhøj, Annikki 2003: The Narrator's Emotions. In: Lotte Tarkka (ed.), *Dynamics of Tradition: Perpectives on Oral Poetry and Folk Belief*. Studia Fennica Folkloristica 13. Helsinki: Suomalaisen Kirjallisuuden Seura, pp. 329–342.

Ketola, Kimmo, Seppo Knuuttila, Antti Mattila & Kari Mikko Vesala 2002: *Puuttuvat viestit: Nonkommunikaatio inhimillisessä vuorovaikutuksessa*. Helsinki: Gaudeamus.

Klein, Barbro 2006: Introduction. Telling, Doing, Experiencing: Folkloristic Perspectives on Narrative Analysis. In: Annikki Kaivola-Bregenhøj, Barbro Klein & Ulf Palmenfelt (eds.), *Narrating, Doing, Experiencing: Nordic Folkloristic Perspectives*. Studia Fennica Folkloristica 16. Helsinki: Finnish Literature Society, pp. 6–28.

Knuuttila, Seppo 2002: Vaitiolo, salaisuudet, ilmaisukiellot: Nonkommunikaation kontekstuaalisia merkityksiä. In: Kimmo Ketola, Seppo Knuuttila, Antti Mattila & Kari Mikko Vesala, *Puuttuvat viestit: Nonkommunikaatio inhimillisessä vuorovaikutuksessa*. Helsinki: Gaudeamus, pp. 119–150.

Körber, Karen & Ina Merkel 2012: Imagined Families in Mobile Worlds: An Introduction. *Ethnologia Europaea* 42:2, 5–11.

Korjonen-Kuusipuro, Kristiina & Anna-Kaisa Kuusisto-Arponen 2012: Emotional Silences: The Rituals of Remembering the Finnish Karelia. In: Barbara Törnquist-Plewa & Niklas Bernsand (eds.), *Painful Pasts and Useful Memories: Remembering and Forgetting in Europe*. Lund: Centre for European studies at Lund University, pp. 109–126.

Langellier, Kristin M. & Eric E. Peterson 2004: *Storytelling in Daily Life*. Philadelphia: Temple University Press.

Lawless, Elaine 2000: Transformative Re-membering: Describing the Unspeakable in Battered Women's Narratives. *Southern Folklore* 57:1, 65–79.

Miettinen, Helena 2004: *Menetetyt kodit, elämät, unelmat: Suomalaisuus paluumuuttajastatukseen oikeutettujen venäjänsuomalaisten narratiivisessa itsemäärittelyssä*. Sosiaalipsykologian tutkimuksia. Sosiaalipsykologisia tutkimuksia 11. Helsinki: Helsingin yliopisto, sosiaalipsykologian laitos.

Naples, Nancy A. 2001: A Member of the Funeral: An Introspective Ethnography. In: Mary Berstein & Renate Reimann (eds.), *Queer Families, Queer Politics: Challenging Culture and the State.* New York: Columbia University Press, pp. 21–43.

Nevalainen, Pekka 1991: Inkerinmaan ja inkeriläisten vaiheet 1900-luvulla. In: Pekka Nevalainen & Hannes Sihvo (eds.), *Inkeri: Historia, kansa ja kulttuuri.* Suomalaisen Kirjallisuuden Seuran Toimituksia 547. Helsinki: Suomalaisen Kirjallisuuden Seura, pp. 234–299.

Norrick, Neal R. 2007: Conversational Storytelling. In: David Herman (ed.), *The Cambridge Companion to Narrative.* Cambridge: Cambridge University Press, pp. 127–141.

Pekkala, Armi 2007: Persuasion or Coercion? Striving for Understanding in Conducting Open Interviews. In: Bente Gullveig Alver, Tove Ingebørg Fjell & Ørjar Øyen (eds.), *Research Ethics in Studies of Culture and Social Life.* FF Communications No. 292. Helsinki: Suomalainen tiedeakatemia, pp. 167–191.

Peltonen, Ulla-Maija 1996: *Punakapinan muistot: Tutkimus työväen muistelukerronnan muotoutumisesta vuoden 1918 jälkeen.* Suomalaisen Kirjallisuuden Seuran toimituksia 657. Helsinki: Suomalaisen Kirjallisuuden Seura.

Peltonen, Ulla-Maija 2003: *Muistin paikat: Vuoden 1918 sisällissodan muistamisesta ja unohtamisesta.* Helsinki: Suomalaisen Kirjallisuuden Seura.

Raudalainen, Taisto 2014: *Oma maa ubina äitsen: Ingerisoomlased 20. sajandil.* Tallinn: Argo.

Rosenthal, Gabriele 2003: The Healing Effects of Storytelling: On the Conditions of Curative Storytelling in the Context of Research and Counselling. *Qualitative Inquiry* 9:6, 915–933.

Siim, Pihla 2007: Äidit ja heidän lapsensa: Perhesuhteista neuvottelua ylirajaisissa perheissä. In: Tuomas Martikainen & Marja Tiilikainen (eds.), *Maahanmuuttajanaiset: Kotoutuminen, perhe ja työ.* Väestötutkimuslaitoksen julkaisusarja D 46/2007. Helsinki: Väestöliitto, pp. 218–244.

Siim, Pihla 2014: Üle piiride liikuvad pered: lood mobiilsusest ja paigal püsimisest. *Mäetagused* 56, 127–154, http://www.folklore.ee/tagused/nr56/siim.pdf. Accessed March 1, 2016.

Statistics Finland 2015: *Statistics Finland's PX-Web databases.* Population Structure, http://pxnet2.stat.fi/PXWeb/pxweb/en/StatFin/StatFin__vrm__vaerak/?tablelist=true&rxid=b871bb23-3c74-41c7-b548-a1c727b68e70. Accessed March 27, 2016

Stone, Elizabeth 1989: *Black Sheep and Kissing Cousins. How Our Family Stories Shape Us.* New York: Penguin Books.

Strandén-Backa, Sofie 2013: Dealing with Emotions. In: Camilla Asplund Ingemark (ed.), *Therapeutic Uses of Storytelling: An Interdisciplinary Approach to Narration as Therapy.* Lund: Nordic Academic Press, pp. 85–100.

Vesala, Kari Mikko, Kimmo Ketola, Seppo Knuuttila & Antti Mattila 2002: Mitä enkelit pelkäävät? In: Kimmo Ketola, Seppo Knuuttila, Antti Mattila & Kari Mikko Vesala, *Puuttuvat viestit: Nonkommunikaatio inhimillisessä vuorovaikutuksessa.* Helsinki: Gaudeamus, pp. 11–41.

Yerkovich, Sally 1983: Conversational Genres. In: Richard M. Dorson (ed.), *Handbook of American Folklore.* Bloomington: Indiana University Press, pp. 277–281.

Zeitlin, Steven, Amy Kotkin & Holly Cutting Baker 1982: *A Celebration of American Family Folklore.* Tales and Traditions from the Smithsonian Collection. New York: Pantheon Books.

Pihla Maria Siim is a research assistant at the Department of Estonian and Comparative Folklore, University of Tartu. She is finishing her doctoral studies in folklore at the University of Eastern Finland. In her Ph.D. dissertation, Siim explores questions of identity and belonging among transnational families living in Estonia, Finland and north-west Russia. In the framework of two research projects led by Prof. Laura Assmuth, she continues her research on multi-local families in Estonian-Finnish transnational space.
(pihla.siim@ut.ee)

Open issue contribution

ENTANGLED GENEALOGIES
History and the Notion of Tradition

Anne Eriksen, University of Oslo

Growing reflexivity within folklore studies has established an understanding of tradition as a key-word of Western modernity, and of folklore studies as part of the modernisation processes. The article explores this field by examining how processes that produced a modern idea of *history* also gave birth to the notion of tradition. The contention is that as twin products of a uniquely modern temporality, history and tradition are mutually constitutive concepts. A temporalised notion of History as an overall process, and as a "collective singular", had its parallel in the understanding of Tradition as a separate but related mode of temporality with its own processes of change and transformation. The discussion is based on British and Nordic examples.

Keywords: tradition, folkloristics, temporality, history, nineteenth century

Entangled Genealogies: Concepts of History and Tradition

From their very beginnings as academic disciplines in the nineteenth century, tradition was a core concept in both ethnology and folklore studies. It referred to empirical material as well as to major research questions about continuity, change and distribution. During the twentieth century, the importance of the term decreased in both disciplines, and at present it seems to have been more or less eclipsed by the new and powerful notion of cultural heritage. Heritage studies now attracts the attention of scholars from a wide range of disciplines. To ethnologists and folklorists, this new field comes with an echo of older terms and of the concept that once defined their disciplines. At this conceptual crossroads, the present article seeks to investigate the genealogy of the concept of tradition. On a general level, this approach refers back to the works of Michel Foucault.

More particularly, the discussion will be based on Reinhardt Koselleck's argument that the emergence of a modern experience of temporality, traced by him to the period 1750–1850, created a new concept of history (Foucault 1975; Koselleck 1985). I will argue that the notion of tradition was stamped by the same processes. As twin products of the modern experience of temporality, history and tradition can be seen as parallel and mutually constitutive concepts. The temporalised notion of history as an overall process or force was accompanied by an understanding of tradition as a parallel, but different type of temporal process. Tradition represented a separate kind of transformations, changes and continuities. The conditions of possibilities that created the modern notion of history were equally significant for the concept of tradition.

Tradition is a term with many meanings, both as a scholarly concept and in vernacular language. It can refer to practices of communication and transmission, to shared cultural property and to ideologies and cultural norms (Ben-Amos 1984; Eriksen 1994; Bronner 2000; Oring 2013). The growing reflexivity within folklore studies from the 1970s onwards has established an understanding of tradition as "a keyword of Western modernity," as Dorothy Noyes has expressed it. Out of this has grown a deepened insight into how folkloristics, with its interest in tradition, itself has been an integral part of modernisation processes (Noyes 2009: 234). Its role in nineteenth- and twentieth-century nation-building has been well established by now, but what Noyes and others point out is that tradition, even on a more fundamental level, is a part of modern mentality (see for instance Shils 1981; Hobsbawm & Ranger 1983; Blank & Howard 2013). Examining the theoretical aspects, Pertti Anttonen has analysed how "the concept of tradition is inseparable from the idea and experience of modernity, both as its discursively constructed opposition and as a rather modern metaphor for cultural continuity and historical patterning" (Anttonen 2005: 12). Anttonen's seminal work clearly demonstrates how modern experience as well as theories of modernity rely heavily on a notion of tradition for their articulations.

The present article will explore how processes that produced a modern idea of history, also were highly significant for the notion of tradition during the nineteenth century. The nineteenth century's interest in collecting and studying folk culture was not only part of the processes of modernity on a more general level, but represented an active reinterpretation of specific cultural forms. The material that emerged from this process of transformation as "tradition" was neither discovered nor invented in the period. What happened was rather that it was inscribed into new ways of conceptualising time and temporality. This gave rise to new terms embedded in a new discourse. What had long been known as "popular antiquities", "superstitions" or "peasants' beliefs" re-emerged first as "folklore", and then as "tradition".

These terminological changes can be traced empirically. This article will argue that they are also integral to more fundamental changes in the experience of temporality and understanding of history. British and Nordic material supply the empirical basis for the following discussion.

The aim of these investigations is not to mine the empirical material for the origins of the term 'tradition', but to explore its conditions of possibilities in a field of entangled concepts, ways of speaking and ways of understanding. When knowledge about the past gradually came to be identified with the new discipline of history, what happened to those parts of the past that could not be disciplined within these frames? Oral narrative, material remains, customs and old ways of living also reflected "the past", but did not fit into this concept of history. And equally important: Their ways of existing in time did not fit in either. The empirical material in this study will be explored to detect how this type of temporality was articulated and conceptualised.

Shipwrecks of Time – Popular Culture in the Early Modern Period

Peter Burke presented his influential thesis about the "discovery of the people" in the now classical study *Popular Culture in Early Modern Europe* (1978). Burke's well-known argument was that elite culture had separated itself from popular culture in a process of gradual withdrawal that took place from the end of the Middle Ages until the middle or late eighteenth century. When popular poetry, tales and customs finally attracted new attention, this process meant that the elite were largely in the dark about them, so that they subsequently "discovered" popular culture and inserted it into cultural and political programmes of Romanticism, nation-building and cultural criticism. The model has considerable appeal, not least because nineteenth-century collectors and editors themselves frequently used a very distinct terminology of discovery and salvage.

However, as Burke himself also makes clear, the culture that was "discovered" was not totally unknown. Antiquarian collection and knowledge production, reaching back to the Renaissance, included a constant interest in popular culture. The role of these activities should not be underestimated. Moreover, this kind of work contributed significantly to the creation of a notion of modernity and change during the early modern period. Bauman and Briggs have argued that "the gap between the past and the present that is constitutive of the advent of modernity" relied heavily on antiquarian discourse and the erudite interest in popular antiquities during the seventeenth and early eighteenth centuries (Bauman & Briggs 2003: 70). Antiquarian studies of what later came to be known as folklore held "a key role in defining modernity through this negative or alteric process," they claim (ibid.: 72). Their investigations of antiquaries from Aubrey to the Grimm brothers demonstrate how the tales, beliefs and customs of rural populations were conceptualised and collected as fragments and relics from the past. To Bacon, antiquities were remnants of history, casual escapes from the shipwreck of time. Bauman and Briggs take this further and argue that "antiquities, by definition, can only exist in a damaged state," as "emblems of absence, decay and loss constructing and underscoring the gap between past and present" (ibid.: 74). With his efforts to save the relics, the antiquarian conjured the past into the present, bridging, but also affirming, that gap between the past and the present which Bacon understood as constitutive of modernity.

Taking the antiquarian work of John Aubrey as their first case, Bauman and Briggs present a meticulous investigation of what they term the "antiquarian constructions of modernity and the discursive Other" (ibid.: 72). A warm admirer of Bacon and his ideals for a new science, Aubrey very explicitly let his work echo the baconian understanding of antiquities as shipwrecks of time. Bauman and Briggs are nonetheless emphatic that to Aubrey, the disjunction of past from present was no mere theoretical stance or abstract philosophical principle, but directly based on his personal experiences of the radical changes of mid-seventeenth-century England. His references to "the past" correspond to the "before" of his own boyhood and the period before the Revolution. In that period, according to Aubrey, old women told tales of ghosts and walking spirits, of Robin-good-fellow and the fairies, while "nowadays", all such

fables and stories are gone. People read histories in printed books instead of listening to the old wives, and the phantoms have disappeared. Bauman and Briggs remark that Aubrey "reads historical and cultural disjunction out of a change in discursive and metadiscursive practices; the displacement of particular speech forms and speech practices becomes an index of a fundamental contrast between the old times and the present" (ibid.: 75). At the same time, they underscore, the disjunction is not complete. Aubrey's separation of past from present is couched in a "purifying rhetoric" that is itself producing this contrast or break. Furthermore, the older forms have not fully disappeared. They remain in memory – Aubrey's and others' – and they are cited and referred to by antiquarians and collectors. However, they live on merely as fragments (ibid.: 76f.).

Similar notions of antiquities as remains or "vestiges" can be found in the works of the seventeenth-century Danish physician, collector and antiquarian Ole Worm. In his efforts to read the runic alphabet he did not only collect ancient inscriptions from all over Denmark and Norway, but also drew on contemporary peasant culture in his interpretations of them (cf. Svestad 1995; Mordhorst 2009). One reason for this was that close to Worm's own time, runic letters were still in some cases used for the peasants' wooden calendars. Even far more generally, however, Worm referred to the customs and sayings of the peasant population to give an interpretative context to his readings of the old Norse and Mediaeval inscriptions. This approach was important in his first antiquarian work, the *Fasti Danici* from 1626, as well as in his large *Danicorum Monumentorum Libri Sex* from 1643. In both cases, the investigations relied heavily on reports from local clergy and other collaborators in answer to a royal missive from 1622, requesting all bishops in Denmark-Norway to send in "antiquities" of every kind from their respective regions.

One of the small collections of drawings and descriptions that was sent to him may serve to elucidate the comparative approach and its tendency to regard all "antiquities" as equally ancient. From the diocese of Oslo, Worm received fourteen watercolours made by the laywer and philosopher Peder Alfssøn of the Oslo cathedral school. Most of them depict runic stones, situated in churches and churchyards in the region. On each of them Peder Alfssøn has noted that he has asked the local peasant about the meanings of the inscriptions, but that "nobody" is able to read them or has any information about the stones. Three other images present rock carvings at sites close to the medieval churches where the runes were found. Alfssøn reports that nobody has been able to tell him more about these "inscriptions" either. He presents his own theory that the rock-carvings are pastime works by the masons who built the churches (Moltke 1958). That rock carvings and runes have been made in very different periods does not seem to occur to him, neither the idea that the stones are far too old for any living peasant to have direct knowledge about them.

A similar strategy of juxtaposition of ancient and peasant customs are found a century later in the work of the Norwegian antiquary Iver Wiel. Investigating an ornate drinking horn and an old dagger at the farm Strand in Hallingdalen, Wiel presents an elaborate antiquarian argument. For horns, he says, nothing fits better than to derive the Latin word *cornu* from the Greek *keras*. The reason is that Xenophon relates that the Thracians drank wine from horns after having greeted each other at feasts. This has obviously also been the custom in Hallingdal. The connection is proved by the dagger, which probably has been a pocket weapon "used at banquets, which seldom took place without murder and manslaughter." Wiel presents his argument in the following way:

When they arrived at a banquet, they are said first to shake hands, and to take drink from a horn. Then they sat down, and the drinking merrily went on. When all were drunk, they started to quarrel and fight: *Inqve repentinos convivia versa tumultus / Assimilare freto possis, qvod svæva qvietum / Ventorum rabies motis exasperat undis*

(You might compare the banquet, changed into a sudden tumult, to the sea, which, first calm, the

boisterous rage of the winds disturbs it by raising its waves)

Then they drew their daggers, the lights went out, and everyone hit those he could, whence a large loss of both friends and foes frequently followed. (Wiel 2005: 115f.)[1]

Today, the peasants in Hallingdal use wooden bowls instead of horns and knives instead of daggers. Apart from that, nothing has changed.

The structure of these comparisons is quite complex. On the one hand, Wiel compares local customs in "ancient" and present times. The ancient is represented by the somewhat unspecified past that produced the horns, while the "present" is the life of contemporary peasants. At the same time, Wiel also compares Norwegian customs to what Xenophon says about the Thracians. Nonetheless, this is not a case of modern ethnography. The past tense in the passage above is somewhat unspecified, as are also the actors. It is not obvious when these customs were in use, neither *who* actually behaved in these ways. The obvious reason is that the words are not Wiel's own. The paragraph is partly a paraphrase, partly a quote. Wiel takes his description from Worm, who builds on Xenophon. The Latin inserted words are from Ovid. Consequently, nothing of what is being said originally concerned peasants in Hallingdal, in the past or present. The passage refers mainly to Xenophon's description of the ritual banquets of the Thracians (in *Anabasis*), while the Ovidian quote is taken from *Metamorphoses*. What is remarkable is that Wiel inserts these quotes and phrases so seamlessly into his own text that all difference in time, place and actors dissolves, most specifically, in relation to the actors. The word "they" slides unnoticeably between referring to the inhabitants of Hallingdal in ancient times, to the present inhabitants of the same valley and to the Thracians of Xenophon's Greek world. Apart from the use of Latin and some Greek in the quotes, there are no grammatical traces to whom the word "they" actually concerns. Thracians and the peasants from Hallingdal merge into one (Eriksen 2014b: 42).

A precondition for this kind of juxtaposition of more or less contemporary popular customs with ancient inscriptions and other material was an understanding of their shared nature as "antiquities". This made them comparable and relevant to each other, independent of any more detailed discussion of their respective age or origin. According to this argument, then, what defined antiquities to seventeenth-century scholars was not their age as such, but their dislocation and survival in a fragmented state. Antiquities belonged to a "before" of some kind, but this temporal dimension was not conceptualised as one of progress, development or even of causal chains of events. What created antiquities was rupture, break and temporal disjunction – Bacon's "shipwreck of time."

Antiquities, History and Exemplarity

Arnaldo Momigliano has pointed out the existence of two separate but parallel lines of knowledge about the past during the early modern period: antiquarianism and history (Momigliano 1990). Antiquarianism was based in a study of material remains from the past, including coins, inscriptions and documents. It was largely a work of collecting and inventorying. Antiquarian publications, often in the form of catalogues of collected material or descriptions of a specific locality, tended to be systematic rather than chronological in their structure, and to focus on typologies, categories and forms. History, on the other hand, is described by Momigliano as largely rhetorical. Chronology gave it its structure, while the grand epic style distinguished its form as well as its content. These two lines did not really converge until the nineteenth century, when they both contributed to the modern discipline of history as critical, source-based investigations into the past.

The strict dichotomy of this model can be criticised, but its perspectives have nonetheless proved highly fruitful (Jensen 2003; Miller 2007). The older interest in collecting or inventorying the popular antiquities of a certain region or locality fits well into Momigliano's description of antiquarianism, and with the fact that even if they were understood to be old, even "ancient", popular antiquities were not normally treated as parts of regular history. Like material findings, tombs or inscriptions, they might in some cases *contribute* to the knowledge of this or that historical hero or event, but they were not ascribed independent historical value. Antiquities might supplement history, but did not belong to the realm of rhetoric and epic style. Representing "the wisdom of the ancients," they could nonetheless teach useful lessons.

In 1695, the Danish clergyman and linguist Peder Syv published his book of two hundred ballads, an extension of the collection of one hundred old ballads published by the antiquary Anders Sørensen Vedel about a hundred years earlier (1591). In a dedicatory poem, Syv presented the ballads as containing moral lessons: They will teach us to follow the path of virtue and demonstrate the detestable effects of evil deeds. The ballads present ancient stories about the pious and the wild, the hard and the mild, about good deeds and misdeeds. With elaborate and playful alliterations, the poem was obviously intended to entertain and amuse, as well as to demonstrate the author's linguistic proficiency. But despite the light note, Syv was vehement in his presentation of the ballads as both instructive examples and vestiges of great antiquity (Syv 1695: dedication). This was the staple argument of early modern antiquarianism. Ballads, like other antiquities, were *additions* to history. They told stories about ancient kings, and heroes, about memorable deeds and great courage. In this way, they reflected the same world as did the work of Saxo and other medieval chroniclers. However, their prime value as historical supplements lay in their being material remains of this ancient world, not merely referring to it or describing it. Antiquarians were frequently accused of being mere collectors of meaningless fragments and dusty shreds, neither presenting the synthetic analyses nor having the rhetorical elegance of the historians. The oft repeated defence was the claim that antiquarian work gave more substance to historical narrative: It supplied history with a sound material base (Sweet 2004: 2).

Momigliano's portrait of history, on the other hand, reflects an understanding similar to that of Koselleck in his description of the *magistra vitae* topos, the idea of history as a teacher of life. Koselleck argues that this notion, going back to Cicero, dominated historical writing in Europe for nearly two thousand years. What defined history according to this way of thinking was that it presented ethically valid and politically relevant narratives about memorable persons and events, and that these stories could work as models and examples. Pragmatic history of this kind therefore often occurred in the plural as "histories". Taken as a whole, history consisted of a large repertoire of stories that could be used to judge, understand and interpret not merely the past, but also the present and the future, and thus work as practical guides for action and lessons for thought.

This was the understanding of history that dissolved with the new experience of temporality during the latter part of the eighteenth century. Koselleck describes its novelty as both fundamentally modern and as genuinely historical – the realisation that the present differs from the past in profound ways, and that the future is open-ended and will always be unknown and new. A gap emerged between the space of experience and the horizon of expectation, in Koselleck's terms, and with it the understanding that narratives from the past could give no guidance for the future. In the place of histories as a plurality of exemplary narratives, History (with a capital H) emerged as a collective singular and as an overall transformative and temporal process (Koselleck 1985: 31).

Other scholars have argued that the dissolution and disappearance of pragmatic history was not as uniform and straightforward as implied by Koselleck (Jensen 2009). In his investigation of historical writing in Britain 1740–1820, Mark S. Phillips finds an extension rather than a dissolution of pragmatic history in this period. He argues that new reader groups with considerable "sentimental competence" required new kinds of historical narratives to identify with and learn from. History could no longer be merely lessons in politics and statecraft, relevant for the training of a male elite of princes and leaders. Readers from the new middle classes and the bourgeoisie wanted to read histories that concerned their own situations in life. According to Phillips,

this contributed significantly to widening the field of historical writing, which now came to include dimensions of civil life and society, from commerce and trade to art and literature (Phillips 2000).

The Aesthetic Fragment

During the latter half of the eighteenth century, fragments dramatically changed their role: They became aesthetic objects. Ruins are a case in point. Michel Makarius has pointed out that in European art the meaning of ruins changed in this period. From being an allegory of heathendom in Nativity scenes and images of the lost world of classical antiquity in landscapes, they became aesthetic objects in their own right, appreciated for their "sublime" qualities and as symbols of worldly transitoriness (Makarius 2004). A leading figure in this development was Denis Diderot. As an art critic he began to mix his description of the works exhibited at the annual *salons* with more general reflexions on philosophical and aesthetic questions, thus creating a "poetics of ruins" (Bukdahl 1995: 5ff.). Makarius also argues that this new poetics became a productive force far beyond the world of painting. It worked to transform the ruins, and more generally the fragment, into an autonomous philosophical and aesthetic object (Makarius 2004: 111; Eriksen 2014a).

Even before Diderot had written his most influential texts on ruins, a similar transformation could be seen to change the role and significance of popular antiquities: An aesthetic evaluation of the fragment made popular antiquities leave the dusty realm of antiquarianism to be incorporated into the sphere of art and artistic appreciation. Popular antiquities – per definition fragments – became objects of independent aesthetic enjoyment and of new interest. Book titles like MacPherson's *Fragments of Ancient Poetry* (1760), and Percy's *Reliques of Ancient English Poetry* (1765) fully demonstrate this change. Both men, in their respective prefaces, emphasise the fragmentary character of the material they present. Percy embedded it in a comprehensive aesthetic program:

To atone for the rudeness of the more obsolete poems, each volume concludes with a few modern attempts in the same kind of writing: and, to take off from the tediousness of the longer narratives, they are everywhere intermingled with little elegant pieces of the lyric kind. Select ballads in the old Scottish dialect, most of them of the first-rate merit, are also interspersed among those of our ancient English minstrels; and the artless productions of these old rhapsodists are occasionally confronted with specimens of the composition of contemporary poets of a higher class; of those who had all the advantages of learning in the times in which they lived, and who wrote for fame and for posterity. (Percy 1765: x)

The defining qualities of the "reliques of antiquity", as they are presented in this text, are their simplicity and artless grace, which make them speak directly to the heart of the reader. These values are aesthetic rather than historical. Moreover, they are not about classical harmony, balance and completeness. The pleasure of fragments lies in their capacity to address sensibility and imagination, to evoke strong emotions. To enjoy the kind of artless art that popular antiquities are taken to represent, the reader will therefore have to be trained in romantic sensibility, and to have developed a competence for being moved, for taking part in the typical eighteenth-century "cult of sensibility" (Damsholt 2000; Krefting 2003). These values, embodied in the natural simplicity and somewhat rugged character of the material – according to Percy – are so important that he has sought to enhance them through his own creative adaptations. Samples of contemporary poetry were included to produce a variegated, lively and colourful composition, tossing the reader incessantly from one fragment of poetry to another. Percy thus staged a cult of fragments, adding new ones to the ancient, thereby amplifying their aesthetic appeal. These editorial principles represent the very opposite of an attempt at restoring the poems to a more complete state.

From these perspectives it becomes clear that the fragmentary nature of antiquities was not a defect to be mended, but rather an ideal to be emulated by Percy and his contemporaries. As "Naturpoesie" – to

use Herder's term – popular poetry came to represent an aesthetic alternative to (overly) sophisticated works of art produced according to classical patterns. Its simplicity and presumed artlessness was one reason for this, but the broken and fragmented forms also added to it significantly. As fragments, popular poetry did not only represent samples in the antiquarian's collection, but also examples to be followed in poetic work. In the Norwegian contexts, the poetic works of Henrik Wergeland supplies an example. He did not collect folk songs himself, but published poems with the title of folksongs, imitating the simple and "natural" style of oral poetry (Wergeland 1849).

As was the case with the ruins, this new evaluation of popular antiquities invested them with a new temporality. What distinguished these fragments – ruins and popular culture alike – was no longer merely a rupture between "before" and "now". They came to invite sorrowful but also pleasingly melancholic meditations on decline, dissolution and death. Antiquities – material and immaterial fragments – embodied the inevitable transitoriness of all human greatness. To antiquarians of all kinds this brought a new awareness that change and disruption not only had taken place in the past, but that it was still going on and probably would continue to do so. Change was not tied to definite events, like the Revolution with its impact on British antiquarianism, or the Reformation that created a similar divide between a Catholic, superstitious "before" and a pious, Lutheran "now" in the northern countries (cf. Pontoppidan [1736]1923). It rather appeared as a constant and all-compassing process, intrinsic to time itself. The metaphor of the shipwreck that h*ad taken place* was changed for that of a devouring fire *going on*. By the same token, rescue work became more urgent as well as more heroic. The Norwegian collector M.B. Landstad compared medieaval ballads to old family jewels, and declared that his strenuous efforts had saved them as "from a burning house." Though "ancient, venerable and golden," they also carried the traces of the devouring forces of fire (Landstad [1853]1968: iv). Moreover, work of rescue also brought with it the drive towards reconstruction of the lost whole. The influential theories of the Grimm brothers saw fairy tales in oral tradition not only as fragments that could be saved by eager collectors, but also as remains of an ancient mythology to be reconstructed through diligent scholarly work.

The romantic aesthetication of fragments in the late eighteenth century added new dimensions to the exemplarity of popular antiquities, far exceeding those that had been called upon by Syv and other antiquarians a hundred years earlier. Their presumed simplicity, innocence and general artlessness that left the fragments models to be imitated by romantic poets, also turned them into examples of emotional expression of a profoundly "natural" and therefore ideal kind. One reason for the popularity of Macpherson's Ossian was, according to Linda and Alan Burnett, that the poems were "permeated by a tenderness and sensibility that appealed directly to 18th century readers looking for literature that was instructive but also touched their hearts" (Burnett & Burnett 2011: 31). The new appreciation can easily be compared to the situation Phillips described for historical narrative (above): New and competent groups of readers wanted stories, images and poems that addressed their sensibility and desire to be moved (Damsholt 2000). Fragments of popular culture, or contemporary artistic reworkings of them, fitted well into this wish for strong feelings and emotional identification. They were integrated into the vocabulary of forms and expressions distinctive to the "cult of sensibility" of the late eighteenth and early nineteenth centuries.

New Terms, New Times

When the work of the Grimm brothers inspired a more systematic collection, research and publishing of "popular antiquities" in the early nineteenth century, this old term seems to have been found increasingly unsatisfactory. Early collections often did without any overarching generic term and contented themselves with an enumeration of the different "species" – legends, tales, folksongs, proverbs, customs, superstitions and so on. The term used by the Swedes E.G. Geijer and A.A. Afzelius for their collection of ballads, published in 1814–17, was

"ancient folksongs" (*folkvisor från forntiden*). The stories published by Andreas Faye in 1833 bore the title *Norwegian legends (Norske Sagn)*. In his introduction, explaining the value of books like this, Faye also used the word folk legend (*folkesagn*). Contrary to that of the two Swedes, Faye's term suggested nothing about age. However, even in his choice of words, which probably was directly influenced by the Grimm brothers, the older notion of the "popular" (*allmue*) had been replaced by the more fashionable epithet "folk".

William John Thoms' new term "folklore", launched in 1846, was expressively intended as an alternative to the older notion of popular antiquities, or, as Thoms emphasised, to the expression "popular literature" (Thoms 1846, here from Dorson 1968: 52). The new field of collection and systematic study that this proposal was intended to designate was still dominantly literary in nature. Folklore could largely be found in books, for instance in Shakespeare. Thoms' scholarly ideal was the Grimm brothers' methods for reading ancient mythology out of the collected material (cf. above), but the practical work that he advocated seems to have been conceptualised as largely literary and archival (Bennett 1994: 30). Dundes has also pointed out that Thoms' choice of term reflects the nationalistic sentiment that was intrinsic to the new field of study. As an alternative to the Latinate "popular antiquities", the new term was "a good Saxon compound" (Dundes 1999: 10; see also Mazo 1996).

It corroborates Dundes' perspective that in Norwegian, Danish and Swedish the corresponding generic term came to be "*folkeminner*", literally meaning folk memories. At the beginning of the nineteenth century, the word was used in the singular (*folkminnet*) and referred somewhat loosely to the field that could be mined for bits and pieces of mythological information and ancient poetry (Bringéus 1962). From the middle of the century, the plural form became the accepted form, and the meaning changed from the location or site of collection to the material that was being collected. Used mainly as a noun, "folkeminne" referred thus to objects rather than to activities, processes or mental faculties. The plural form furthermore indicates the collectability of these objects. They appear as separate items rather than as pieces of an organic whole. In the same way as the English "folklore", the new generic term signalled an attempt to delimit a new field of collection and scholarly investigation. The national folklore archives that were established in Scandinavia during the early twentieth century all came to have the word "folkeminne-" in their names.

When P. Chr. Asbjørnsen and Jørgen Moe published the second edition of their collection of Norwegian fairy tales in 1851, the original work (1841–1844) was equipped with a long introduction written by Moe. The text is now regarded as the earliest scholarly investigation of folk narrative in Norway. Its main aim was to argue the distinctly national character of the tales, though without hiding their connection to similar tales found in other countries. The list of literature as well as the argument indicate that Moe and his colleague were well read on the emerging field of comparative folklore research. Most important in the present context is the fact that Moe on this occasion used neither the Nordic term "folkeminner" nor the English "folklore", but instead chose the word "tradition". It is largely used in the plural, as "traditions". Moreover, Moe also speaks about "folk literature" or "folk poetry" *(folkedigtning)*. Occasionally using the plural form even here, he indicates that each "folk" has or has had its own (oral) literature – or traditions.

As Moe employed it, the word "tradition" was thus not invested with a meaning that differed significantly from that of "folklore" or *folkeminner*. All these terms referred to objects or items, objects that could be collected from the folk, largely the peasant populations, and be categorised, analysed and eventually published according to the scholarly methods and ideals that were being forged on this new field of comparative erudite work. Used in this way, traditions worked as a collective term, even if it did not yet represent a unity. Nonetheless, the term did have significant potential. Contrary to the words "folklore" and *folkeminner*, "tradition" was not irrevocably locked to an understanding of popular culture as a patchwork of single items. The word proved to

be open to some very interesting shifts of meaning.

Complementing the plural form with the singular, "tradition" gradually evolved into a generic term. In the work of Moltke Moe, Jørgen Moe's son and Norway's first professor of folklore studies, expressions like "the tradition" or "foreign tradition" appear as a matter of course (see for instance Moe 1888). Similar wordings are found in the work of Moe's contemporary, the Danish professor Axel Olrik (for instance Olrik 1908). These expressions refer to unities, to the sums of the folklore items, traditions (in the plural) or popular antiquities that can be found within a group or nation. These items, on their hand, could now be described as traditional, indicating that they shared an identity and possessed specific qualities stemming from this overarching category. Contrary to the somewhat older terms, tradition thus proved to be a concept that could refer to cultural processes, not merely designate cultural items. Moreover, it proved to work on a theoretical level as well as on the empirical.

During the same period, the notion of folklore partly followed another path. In her investigation into "the Science of Folklore" in Britain, centred on the Folklore Society and its leading figures, Gillian Bennett has argued that during the earliest years of the life of the Folklore Society, its perspectives were efficiently redefined from the older (antiquarian) approach to the new theories of evolutionary anthropology. The man behind this adaptation – or revolution – was the society's young secretary Georg Laurence Gomme. By his manoeuver Gomme secured the "science of folklore" a central position in current cultural theory, Bennett contends. Folklore was no longer the antiquities renamed by Thoms, but came to be seen as cultural "fossils" – or survivals, according to Andrew Lang – and as such as extremely valuable witnesses to the understanding of primitive man. The only problem was that this happy situation did not last long. Hardly had Gomme succeeded in his redefinition before cultural theory and the interest of anthropologists started to change. Bennett writes that by the 1880s, many British folklorists "saw anthropology and folklore simply as different aspects of a single study. But the catch was that folklore could only be a part of anthropology if classic cultural evolution was the dominant theory. Unless the 'folk' could be transmogrified into 'primitives' using the 'space-becomes-time' formula, the materials of folklore were not relevant to the understanding of primitive society" (Bennett 1994: 32). The implication of this "formula" was that folk culture – taken to represent the culture of a primitive past – could be equated with the culture of "primitive" people living in the present. The historical distance of the one corresponded to the cultural distance of the other, and the two – folk culture and primitive culture – could thus shed light on each other. The "folk" of the folklorists equalled the "primitives" of the anthropologists, and scholars in the two fields could work hand in hand.

In this way, evolutionary theory forged a link between anthropology and archaeology. Folklore studies had conceptualised itself as the very embodiment of this common ground. When changes in cultural theory drew the two disciplines apart, folklore studies "simply fell through the gap" (Bennett 1994: 33). As the losing party, the "science of folklore" found itself turned into what it had claimed folklore to be: fossilised remains of older ways of thinking.

Bennett's argument sheds important light on the development of folklore studies in England. In the Nordic context, however, the notion of folklore or *folkeminner* was incorporated into that of tradition. Put simply, it can be said that folklore remained the itemising designation of particulars of expressive culture, while tradition came to be used both as a similar designation (often in the plural) and as a – frequently normative – term for cultural processes that shaped these particulars and gave them their meaning and value (cf. Kverndokk, forthcoming).

Tradition and History as Entangled Concepts

How did the notion of tradition get its potential to analyse temporal processes, to illuminate certain kinds of cultural change that took place over time? Assessing the position of folklore studies in the mid-1990s, Henry Glassie situates the discipline at the crossroads between anthropology and history. A key concept in his argument is tradition, which, accord-

ing to him, allows an approach that mediates between the systematic orientation of anthropologists and the historians' focus on change. This approach is the "secret weapon" of folklore studies, so to speak, and does not only supply our discipline with a unique take on the historical study of culture (or vice versa), but also represents a remedy for the alleged shortcomings in the two other. In Glassie's line of argument, the (anthropological) concept of culture comprises a "synchronic state of affairs. Overreacting to the excesses of evolutionism, anthropologists stripped culture of history and shaped it to fit the scientific fashion prevalent in the period from 1910 to 1960" (Glassie 1995: 399). Even the more recent perspectives developed by Geertz, Turner and others cannot be said to give cultural theory a more pronounced temporal dimension. History, on the other hand, not only is predominantly about change, but also tends to see change principally in terms of rupture and upheaval, to "segment time into trim periods" and to disregard "the massive fact of continuity" (ibid.: 396). Glassie's conclusion is that the notion of tradition unites the two perspectives, and gives each of them what they lack. He is emphatic that tradition is a historical way of thinking about culture, because tradition itself is a temporal concept: "Now define tradition as culture's dynamic, as the process by which culture exists, and it emerges as the swing term between culture and history, the missing piece necessary to the success of a cultural history that would bring anthropology and history, with folklore as the mediating agents, into productive alliance" (ibid.: 399).

Glassie's argument rests on an understanding of history and historical investigation that emerged during the latter half of the nineteenth century and that was fundamental to the shaping of history as a modern academic discipline. The same processes were highly significant to folklore studies and the notion of tradition. These two ways of conceptualising the past represent two different but closely entangled and truly modern ways of thinking about time. In historical writing, time (as chronology) had long been understood as the "location" where historical events had taken place. History itself was, nonetheless, not about understanding time or temporal processes, but rather about exemplary and memorable actions (cf. above). The new experience of temporality not only undermined the old and conventional ideas of identification with past persons and events, it also brought with it "the discovery of the uniqueness of historical processes and the possibility of progress" (Koselleck 1985: 32). History emerged as a collective singular.

In this new role as History, "historical narrative was expected to provide the unity found in the epic derived from the existence of Beginning and End," and each incident was expected to be part of a larger whole and illuminate "history in general." History could be understood as "the latent power of human events and suffering, a power that connected and motivated everything in accordance with a secret or evident plan to which one could feel oneself responsible, or in whose name one could believe to be acting" (Koselleck 1985: 29ff.). It was no longer the virtues and vices, cunning or foolishness of individual persons that represented history, these were merely the external expressions or representations of History as a driving force. Moreover, history was not the only concept to re-emerge as a collective singular in this period, according to Koselleck: "Freedom took the place of freedoms, Justice that of rights and servitudes, Progress that of progressions [...] and from the diversity of revolutions, 'The Revolution' emerged" (ibid.: 31). To this series of collective singulars, Tradition can be added.

For the modern discipline of history, the full effect of the transformation did not emerge until the nineteenth century. The Danish historian Bernard Eric Jensen contends that it was not until well after 1850 that the past itself became the historians' obvious field of study, and the discipline of history became the investigation of processual change over time (Jensen 2003: 123). Within its new frames, the modern historical discipline that took upon itself to investigate the processes of temporal change tended to be rather exclusive in its choice of issues and sources. The perspectives presented by both Koselleck and Jensen describe a process of purification and delimitation. The modern historical discipline was defined by its method and material – written documents that could be subjected to strict source criticism – and by its systematic study of change, understood as temporal and processual. A historian came to be a person who was trained to master the specific methods, and not (as had been the case before) one whose position in society allowed a close observation of the events that he or she wrote about (Pocock 1999). As Gianna Pomata has pointed out, the new role largely excluded women, not only because they often lacked formal education, but also because their contributions to historical writing had used to be family chronicles and conventual histories, in addition to letters and memoirs (Pomata 1993). These fields of knowledge and types of material now largely fell outside the realm of historical inquiry.

In the same manner as "popular antiquities", even folklore represented cultural expressions that fell outside the realm of the historical discipline. However, as historical writing and methodology changed, the reasons for exclusion also developed. Even if old, folklore could only with difficulty throw useful light on the ruptures, upheavals and processes of change that history now was about. Its weaknesses in this respect were numerous. Folklore could not be dated. It did not fit into the system of historical periods, each now reckoned to have their own specific "style" and expression. And perhaps most fundamentally: Folklore did not fare well under the light of historical source criticism. Compared with the historical "facts" produced by the new methods, it seemed vague, imprecise and unreliable. This did not mean that folklore was exempted from the new experience of temporality as transformation. Rather, folklore no longer was seen as merely old – vestiges from a past or from a "before" – but was conceptualised in itself as the expression of temporal, transformative processes. The transformations reflected in folklore were nonetheless different from the ruptures and changes observed in history and examined by historians. Folklore represented another kind of alteration, another type of temporal process.

As a collective singular, Tradition concluded the development that was started by the shift from the plural to the singular form of the word. It emerged as a category of its own, in possession of strong transformative powers and inviting specific types of narrative structures, motives and representations. In this new form, Tradition could subsume traditions, folklore and popular antiquities – all the terms that had been used to designate specific narratives, customs, beliefs and collectable "items" from popular culture, and order them into a new whole. As with History, all particular items that were parts of Tradition could now be seen as the elements of a larger unity, subjects of overarching processes and forces, and fundamentally shaped by them. According to Reidar Th. Christiansen, it was distinctive to Tradition that

> ... all the particulars, both in their shape and their content are no longer marked by their individual origins, but have acquired an attitude and a homogeneity which correspond to the fact that they are not the utterances of a single person, but of all those who have made this material their own, polished it in their minds and then passed it on. The voice of "the folk" is heard here, "it is told" or "people tell" are the true authority in this. The material will of course always be presented by individuals and in the guise of single cases, but its distinctive character is nonetheless the universal and common, and the contribution that might have been added by the individual is not of primary significance. (Christiansen 1926: 14, translated here)

This argument was presented in a guide for folklore collectors, published in 1926. Christiansen, who later was appointed professor in folklore studies, was at this time responsible for the Norwegian Folklore Archive. Kyrre Kverndokk has argued that Christiansen used this small guidebook to present the prospective collectors with an entire folkloristic taxonomy. This system served to discipline the collectors, stopping them from collecting material that fell outside the definitions and categories. It also purified folklore, instructing the collectors "in how to make some sort of order out of chaotic and unsystematic oral utterances" (Kverndokk, forthcoming). In this work, a distinction between the specific utterances – which would bear the stamp of their immediate contexts – and the more fundamental processes and forces, was highly useful. Christiansen was emphatic that a collector had to "draw a line between random folk narrative and real folk tradition," even if he also underscored that in actual fact, the collector would meet tradition in the shape of specific and concrete narratives (Christiansen 1926: 14). Thus folklore – the particular expressions – reflected Tradition.

As was the case with History, the narrative representations and recurring motives of Tradition as a collective singular reflected the specific temporal principles that underpinned the entire category. For tradition, however, the span between beginning and end that gave the narrative its structure, as well as its overall message, differed from that of history. The beginning, when it comes to tradition, was invariably remote, and even if the questions of origin (of customs, fairy tales and so on) were fundamental in nineteenth-century folklore studies, they did not represent a quest for specific years or dates. Instead, the issue of origins was partly about a rather mythic past, and partly about the early phases of conjectured evolutionary processes. The temporal structure was nonetheless important, not least because the end tended to be themed as one of corruption, dissolution – hopefully followed by salvation, thanks to diligent folklore collectors, and an eternal life in the haven of the folklore archives. Between the two poles, change and development followed other patterns than those of history. According to Christiansen, the processes imply that folklore has a groundwork "old as the hills, unyielding and conservative, complemented with some external influences coming from the shifting layers of culture and knowledge that is being added to the common base, a seepage that is incorporated, coloured and transformed by tradition" (Christiansen 1926: 16). Tradition is the force that works on the particulars and slowly changes them.

As "tradition bearers" the superstitious old peasants and talkative old women who told the fairy tales and legends, sung the ballads, knew the healing charms and used the old ways of speaking, were also transformed. They still represented a fragmented and decaying "past", and they were still ignorant and superstitious, but all the things they could tell were now both parts of tradition and fundamentally shaped by it. Consciously or not, tradition bearers acted on behalf of tradition and sometimes also in its name. Tradition had become an overarching framework that gave meaning to all the bits and pieces contained by it, and at the same time a powerful super-organic force that was shaping this content, more or less independent of human will. The singers, storytellers and so on were its representatives on earth, vehicles at its disposal. Tradition acquired an agency of its own. Christiansen argued that tradition

> ... continuously incorporates new elements, but it does so slowly and it chooses carefully what to include, making it apparent that the groundwork is so strong that it will colour all the new elements that tradition lays its eyes on. It is therefore possible to detect more or less distinct sedimentations from different periods, while it at the same time is obvious that the groundwork rests on another understanding of the world than that of the sciences and textbooks of our own time. (Christiansen 1926: 15)

Tradition became a power that, for example, allowed or disallowed certain changes or deviations from well-known forms. It could be living or dead, flourishing or perishing, rich or poor. It acted, it worked, and even if often presented as dying or dissolving, it nonetheless tended to exert considerable normative pressure on cultural development, for instance by judging, accepting or rejecting innovations, variations or new and foreign cultural forms.

Used as a collective singular, then, Tradition came to be a number of different things at once. In part, it meant traditions: actual cultural forms and larger complexes of them. As such, tradition could be itemised, collected, inventoried, archived and published. It could be investigated, interpreted and compared. In part, tradition also meant actual processes of communication – singing, storytelling and so on – leading to the distribution and the handing down of

traditions in the first sense. On this level, tradition usually also included a certain degree of normativity and evaluation, representing the *right* way of doing, singing, telling, speaking, as well as the responsibility to do so and the right to sanction those who did not. However, tradition could also refer more analytically to cultural processes tending towards stability and creating long-lasting patterns. And on top of it all, Tradition towered as a general cultural process. Tradition and History – in the meanings discussed here – both emerged from the modern experience of time, and the fundamental idea of temporality as an inherently transformative power is the vital principle of both. The modern study of history and tradition both aim at understanding processes that in some way relate to or stem from this power. However, the actual processes that are investigated are different and complimentary. The study of tradition focused on patterns of stability, processes of transmission and on slow modes of change.

Concluding Remarks

The aim of this article has been to add one more dimension to the comprehension of tradition as a concept fundamentally related to modernity – produced by it as well as contributing to its articulation. Emphasising its inherent temporality and its very close entanglement with history, I have sought to develop the understanding that tradition not only reflects the experience of the deep divide between the (traditional) past and the (modern) present, but also that in itself it is an integral part of this modern present. Tradition refers to temporal processes that are as significant to the modern experience of time as are those of history. Its transformation from a term designating collectable items from popular culture into a collective singular in possession of independent agency reflects this temporal experience.

As pointed out above and by a number of other scholars, tradition is a term with many layers of meaning, ranging from the empirical to the theoretical and from the descriptive to the normative. The present argument can be read as an addition to this profusion. However, its concern has been neither to present an exhaustive overview of how the term tradition has been used (cf. Ben-Amos 1984), nor to prescribe how it *should* be used (cf. Oring 2013). Rather, my aim has been to investigate some of the conditions of possibility of tradition as a theoretical concept and to explore the principles of its powers as an analytical tool. In this context it has been important to underscore its profound and defining relationship with a modern notion of history. Tradition as a core concept of modernity presupposes the position of its twin, history, and the understanding of the modern idea of tradition hinges on a corresponding understanding of this relationship. Moreover, the perspectives presented here will indicate that tradition – as a collective singular and a theoretical concept related to the modern experience of temporality – not only is a handy tool for folklorists, but represents a significant contribution to general cultural theory. This insight may serve well in preparation for the next turn of the screw: the contemporary transformation of tradition into cultural heritage, adding new dimensions to the old story.

Note

1 "Naar de kom til Gjæstebud, siges de først at have hilset hinanden med Haandtag, hvorpaa de bleve tildrukne med et Horn, derpaa satte de sig ned, og gik det da lystig til med at drikke. Naar de bleve fulde, begynte de at larme og klamres: *Inqve repentinos convivia versa tumultus / Assimilare freto possis, qvod svæva qvietum / Ventorum rabies motis exasperat undis.* Derpaa trak man Dolken, slukkede Lyset, og lod saa træffe hvem træffe kunde, hvorved stort Nederlag ofte skede saavel paa Venner som Uvenner."

References

Anttonen, Pertti 2005: *Tradition through Modernity: Post-Modernism and the Nation-State in Folklore Scholarship.* Helsinki: Finnish Literature Society.

Bauman, Richard & Charles L. Briggs 2003: *Voices of Modernity: Language Ideologies and the Politics of Inequality.* Cambridge: Cambridge University Press.

Ben-Amos, Dan 1984: The Seven Strands of Tradition: Varieties in Its Meaning in American Folklore Studies. *Journal of Folklore Research* 21:2/3, 97–131.

Bennett, Gillian 1994: Geologists and Folklorists: Cultural Evolution and 'The Science of Folklore'. *Folklore* 105, 25–37.

Blank, Trevor J. & Robert Glenn Howard (eds.) 2013: *Tradition in the Twenty-First Century: Locating the Role of the Past in the Present.* Boulder, CO: Utah State University Press.

Bringéus, Nils-Arvid 1962: Peter Wieselgren och folkminnena. *Rig* 45:1, 1–24.

Bronner, Simon J. 2000: The Meaning of Tradition: An Introduction. *Western Folklore* 59:2, 87–104.

Bukdahl, Else Marie 1995: Diderot entre le "modèle idéal" et le "sublime". In: E.M. Bukdahl, M. Delon & A. Lorenceau (eds.), *Diderot: Ruines et paysages, Salons de 1767.* Paris: Hermann, pp. 3–18.

Burke, Peter 1978: *Popular Culture in Early Modern Europe.* London: Temple Smith.

Burnett, Linda Andersson & Alan Burnett 2011: *Blind Ossian's Fingal: Fragments and Controversy.* Edinburgh: Luath Press.

Christiansen, Reidar Th. 1926: *Norske Folkeminne: En veiledning for samlere og interesserte* (NFL 12). Oslo: Norsk Folkeminnelag.

Damsholt, Tine 2000: Being moved. *Ethnologia Scandinavica*, pp. 24–48.

Dorson, Richard 1968: William John Thoms. In: R. Dorson, *Peasant Customs and Savage Myths: Selections from British Folklorists.* London: Routledge.

Dundes, Alan (ed.) 1999: *International Folkloristics: Classic Contributions by the Founders of Folklore.* New York & Oxford: Rowman & Littlefield.

Eriksen, Anne 1994: "Like before, just different": Modern Popular Understandings of the Concept of Tradition. *Arv* 50, 9–24.

Eriksen, Anne 2014a: *From Antiquities to Heritage: Transformations in Cultural Memory.* New York & Oxford: Berghahn Books.

Eriksen, Anne 2014b: Antikvarianisme på norsk: Iver Wiels beskrivelse over Ringerike og Hallingdalen. *Tidsskrift for kulturforskning* 13:1–2, 5–18.

Faye, Andreas 1833: *Norske Sagn.* Arendal.

Foucault, Michel 1975: *Surveiller et punir: Naissance de la prison.* Paris: Gallimard.

Geijer, Erik Gustaf & Arvid August Afzelius 1814–1817: *Svenska Folkvisor från forntiden.* Samlade och utg. af Er. Gust. Geijer och Arv. Aug. Afzelius. Stockholm.

Glassie, Henry 1995: Tradition. *The Journal of American Folklore* 108:430, 395–412.

Hobsbawm, Eric & Terence Ranger (eds.) 1983: *The Invention of Tradition.* Cambridge: Cambridge University Press.

Jensen, Bernard Eric 2003: *Historie: Livsverden og fag.* Copenhagen: Gyldendal.

Jensen, Bernard Eric 2009: Using a Past – 'Magistra Vitæ' Approaches to History. In: Anne Eriksen & Jon Vidar Sigurdsson (eds.), *Negotiating Pasts in the Nordic Countries.* Lund: Nordic Academic Press, pp. 205–238.

Koselleck, Reinhart 1985: *Futures Past: On the Semantics of Historical Time*, trans. K. Tribe. Cambridge, MA: MIT Press.

Krefting, Ellen 2003: Følsomhet og opplysning: Omkring sensibilitetsbegrepet i Encyclopedien. *Tidsskrift for kulturforskning* 2:4, 3–20.

Kverndokk, Kyrre (forthcoming): Disciplining the Polyphony of the Herbarium: The Order of Folklore in the Norwegian Folklore Archives.

Landstad, Magnus Brostrup (1853)1968: *Norske folkeviser.* Oslo: Norsk folkeminnelag, Universitetsforlaget.

MacPherson, James 1760: *Fragments of Ancient Poetry, Collected in the Highland of Scotland, and Translated from the Gaelic to Erse Language.* Edinburgh.

Makarius, Michel 2004: *Ruins.* Paris: Flammarion.

Mazo, Jeffrey Alan 1996: A Good Saxon Compound. *Folklore* 107, 107–108.

Miller, Peter N. (ed.) 2007: *Momigliano and Antiquarianism: Foundations of the Modern Cultural Sciences.* Toronto: University of California Press.

Moe, Jørgen 1852: Indledning. In: *Norske Folkeeventyr samlede og fortalte af P. Chr. Asbjørnsen og Jørgen Moe.* 2nd ed. Christiania: J.Dahl.

Moe, Moltke 1888: Det mythiske Tænkesæt. Lecture. Published in K.Liestøl (ed.), 1926 *Moltke Moes samlede skrifter,* vol. II, pp. 265–283. Oslo: Instituttet for sammenlignenede kulturforskning.

Moltke, Erik 1958: *Jon Skonvig og de andre runetegnere: Et bidrag til runologiens historie i Danmark og Norge,* bd. 1. Copenhagen: Munksgaard.

Momigliano, Arnaldo 1990: *The Classical Foundations of Modern Historiography.* Berkeley, California: University of California Press.

Mordhorst, Camilla 2009: *Genstandsfortællinger: Fra Museum Wormianum til de modene museer.* Copenhagen: Museum Tusculanum Press.

Noyes, Dorothy 2009: Tradition: Three Traditions. *Journal of Folklore Research* 46:3, 233–268.

Olrik, Axel 1908: Episke love i folkedigtningen. *Danske Studier* 5, 69–89.

Olrik, Jørgen 1923: Indledning. In: J. Olrik (ed.), *Erik Pontoppidan: Fejekost til at udfeje den gamle surdejg...* Copenhagen: Schønbergske forlag, pp. iii–xxxii.

Oring, Elliot 2013: Thinking through Tradition. In: Trevor J. Blank & Robert Glenn Howard: *Tradition in the Twenty-First Century: Locating the Past in the Present.* Boulder Colorado: Utah State University Press, pp. 22–48.

Percy, Thomas 1765: *Reliques of Ancient English Poetry, Consisting of Old Heroic Ballads, Songs, and Other Pieces of Our Earlier Poets, together with some few of later Date.* London.

Phillips, Mark Salber 2000: *Society and Sentiment: Genres of Historical Writing in Britain, 1740–1820.* Princeton, NJ: Princeton University Press.

Pocock, J.G.A. 1999: *Barbarism and Religion, vol. 1, The enlightenments of Edward Gibbon, 1737–1764.* Cambridge: Cambridge University Press.

Pomata, Gianna 1993: History, Particular and Universal: On Reading Some Recent Women's History Textbooks. *Feminist Studies* 19:1, 6–50.

Pontoppidan, Erik (1736)1923: *Fejekost til at udfeje den gamle surdejg...* , ed. by J. Olrik. Copenhagen: Schønbergske forlag.

Shils, Edward 1981: *Tradition.* Chicago: University of Chicago Press.

Svestad, Asgeir 1995: *Oldsakenes orden: Om tilkomsten av arkeologi.* Oslo: Universitetsforlaget.

Sweet, Rosemary 2004. *Antiquaries: The Discovery of the Past in Eighteenth-Century Britain.* London: Bloomsbury Academics.

Syv, Peder 1695: *Et hundrede udvalde Danske Viser om allehaande merkelige Krigs-Bedrivt, oc anden selsom Eventyr, som sig her udi Riget ved gamle Kæmper, navnkundige Konger oc ellers fornemme Personer begivet haver: Forøgede med det andet Hundrede Viser om Danske Konger ...* Copenhagen: Bockenhoffer.

Wergeland, Henrik 1849: *Folkeviser.* Christiania: Roshauw.

Wiel, Iver 2005: Beskrivelse over Ringerige og Hallingdahlens Fogderie: Hvor-udi findes anført dets Grændser, Situation, Størrelse, Vasdrag, Skoug, og Mark, Dyr, Fugle og Fiske, Mineralia, Naturalia og Antiqviteter med videre. In: K. Røgeberg (ed.), *Norge i 1743: Innberetninger som svar på 43 spørsmål fra Danske Kanselli,* vol. 3, 88–196. Oslo: Riksarkivet og Solum forlag.

Worm, Ole 1626: *Fasti Danici, universam computandi rationem antiquitus in Dania et vicinis regionibus observatam libris tribus exhibentes ...* Hafnia.

Worm, Ole 1643: *Danicorum Monumentorum Libri Sex.* Hafnia: Joachim Moltke.

Anne Eriksen is a professor of Cultural History at the University of Oslo. Among her research interests are collective memory, theories of tradition and history, and popular piety. A recent publication is *From Antiquities to Heritage* (Berghahn Books 2014).

(anne.eriksen@ikos.uio.no)

Seawomen of Iceland
Survival on the Edge

Margaret Willson

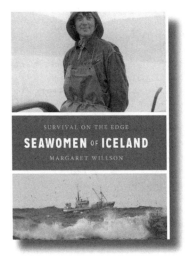

The plaque said this was the winter fishing hut of Thurídur Einarsdóttir, one of Iceland's greatest fishing captains, and that she lived from 1777 to 1863. "Wait," anthropologist and former seawoman Margaret Willson said. "She??"

So began a quest. Were there more Icelandic seawomen? Most Icelanders said no, and, after all, in most parts of the world, fishing is considered a male profession. What could she expect in Iceland? She found a surprise. This book is a glimpse into the lives of vibrant women who have braved the sea for centuries. Their accounts include the excitement, accidents, trials, and tribulations of fishing in Iceland from the historic times of small open rowboats to today's high-tech fisheries. Based on extensive historical and field research, *Seawomen of Iceland* allows the seawomen's voices to speak directly with strength, intelligence, and—above all—a knowledge of how to survive.

This engaging ethnographic narrative will intrigue both general and academic readers interested in maritime culture, the anthropology of work, Nordic life, and gender studies.

MARGARET WILLSON is affiliate associate professor of anthropology and Canadian studies at the University of Washington. She is the author of *Dance Lest We All Fall Down: Breaking Cycles of Poverty in Brazil and Beyond*.

"Seawomen of Iceland is a fabulous book, part memoir, part ethnography. Too often the presence of women at sea has been treated as an exception to be explained, but in this book the history and reality of seawomen is treated as fact and the stories follow from that. It's about time!"
—CHARLES MENZIES, UNIVERSITY OF BRITISH COLUMBIA

"This beautifully crafted saga about women at sea is framed as a mystery: not only why so many Icelandic women fished in the past and today, with clues found in harsh rural choices and wage equality at sea, but also why this story is not well known. Willson's findings are hugely important to both maritime and gender studies."
—BONNIE J. MCCAY, AUTHOR OF OYSTER WARS AND THE PUBLIC TRUST

2016 · xx + 274 pp. · HB w/dust wrapper · 16 × 23.5 cm

ISBN 978 87 635 4484 9 · DKK 298 · $ 45 · € 40

Between Magic and Rationality
On the Limits of Reason in the Modern World

Edited by Vibeke Steffen, Steffen Jöhncke and

Kirsten Marie Raahauge

In *Between Magic and Rationality*, Vibeke Steffen, Steffen Jöhncke and Kirsten Marie Raahauge bring together a diverse range of ethnographies that examine and explore the forms of reflection, action and interaction that govern the ways different contemporary societies create and challenge the limits of reason. The essays here visit an impressive array of settings, including international scientific laboratories, British spiritualist meetings, Chinese villages, Danish rehabilitation centers and Uzbeki homes, where they encounter a diverse assortment of people whose beliefs and concerns exhibit an unusual but central contemporary dichotomy: scientific reason versus spiritual/paranormal belief. Exploring the paradoxical way these modes of thought push against reason's boundaries, they offer a deep look at the complex ways they coexist, contest one another and are ultimately intertwined.

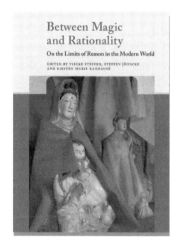

VIBEKE STEFFEN is associate professor in the Department of Anthropology at the University of Copenhagen, where STEFFEN JÖHNCKE is senior advisor. KIRSTEN MARIE RAAHAUGE is associate professor in the School of Design at the Royal Danish Academy of Fine Arts in Copenhagen.

380 pp. • Pb
ISBN 978 87 635 4213 5
Cultural Anthropology, vol. 4
April 2015
DKK 298 • $ 52 • € 40

Critical Anthropology

explores life on the margins of the modern world, and demonstrates the power of ethnography to provide new insights into the human condition.

GENERAL EDITORS: Michael Jackson (Harvard University), Richard Jenkins (University of Sheffield), Steffen Jensen (Roskilde University), Vibeke Steffen (University of Copenhagen), Henrik Vigh (University of Copenhagen)

MUSEUM TUSCULANUM PRESS
WWW.MTP.DK   UNIVERSITY OF COPENHAGEN   WWW.MTP.DK
BIRKETINGET 6 : : 2300 COPENHAGEN S

SIEF membership package

In December 2014 the membership of SIEF, the Société Internationale d'Ethnologie et de Folklore, voted in favour of making *Ethnologia Europaea* its official journal, after SIEF, the editors and the publisher of *Ethnologia Europaea,* Museum Tusculanum Press, had prepared the ground for a mutually agreeable association between organization and publication. SIEF was founded in 1964, *Ethnologia Europaea* in 1966, and as recent historiographic research makes quite evident, there was no love lost between the actors founding the two respective institutions. Some five decades later, it is safe to say that cooperation rather than particularization is the major coin of scholarship. Both partners share a profound interest in nurturing and promoting scientific research and communication within our field(s), in extending international collaboration among European ethnologists as well as in disseminating new ethnological knowledge to a wide readership.

Membership

SIEF gathers every two years for its international congress, where colleagues engage with one another's work and enjoy each other's company. The SIEF congress is an intellectual festival that showcases the state of the art in our fields and a ritual time in the academic calendar, crucial for building professional networks, a number of collaborative projects, finding inspiration, and cultivating friendships. Between congresses, SIEF's numerous working groups provide platforms for critical debate, networking, and exchange of information; they organize their own meetings and sponsor publications.

SIEF has two professional journals: *Ethnologia Europaea*, a printed subscription-based journal that all members receive by mail twice a year, and *Cultural Analysis*, an Open Access journal published online. In addition, SIEF communicates with members through its website and with two newsletters sent out every year.

The annual membership fee is € 35. Opting for a two-year membership in one go qualifies for a discounted price of € 67. Membership will support SIEF to grow as a strong professional organization, while allowing members to participate in the SIEF community and shape the future of the academic fields.

The membership package offers a great host of benefits, including a subscription to the lively and interdisciplinary, peer-reviewed journal *Ethnologia Europaea*. Members will receive printed copies of the biannual journal as well as electronic access to available backlist issues.

See more and apply for membership now at www.siefhome.org.

MUSEUM TUSCULANUM PRESS
WWW.MTP.DK   UNIVERSITY OF COPENHAGEN   WWW.MTP.DK
BIRKETINGET 6 : : 2300 COPENHAGEN S